BRIDGING

This book is dedicated to Fran Stott,
our beloved dean, the strongest supporter of the
Bridging project right from the start

BRIDGING

Assessment FOR Teaching AND Learning IN
Early Childhood Classrooms, PreK–3

Jie-Qi Chen

Gillian Dowley McNamee

FOREWORD BY

Samuel J. Meisels

CORWIN PRESS
A SAGE Publications Company
Thousand Oaks, CA 91320

For information:

Corwin Press
A Sage Publications Company
2455 Teller Road
Thousand Oaks, California 91320
www.corwinpress.com

Sage Publications Ltd.
1 Oliver's Yard
55 City Road
London EC1Y 1SP
United Kingdom

Sage Publications India Pvt. Ltd.
B 1/I 1 Mohan Cooperative Industrial Area
Mathura Road, New Delhi
India 110 044

Sage Publications Asia-Pacific Pte. Ltd.
33 Pekin Street #02-01
Far East Square
Singapore 048763

Printed in the United States of America

Library of Congress Cataloging-in-Publication Data

Chen, Jie-Qi.
Bridging: Assessment for teaching and learning in early childhood classrooms, PreK–3/Jie-Qi Chen, Gillian Dowley McNamee.
     p. cm.
Includes bibliographical references and index.
ISBN 978-1-4129-5009-1 (cloth)
ISBN 978-1-4129-5010-7 (pbk.)
    1. Early childhood education—United States. 2. Curriculum-based assessment—United States. 3. Curriculum planning—United States.
4. Performance in children. I. McNamee, Gillian Dowley, 1951- II. Title.

LB1139.25.C48 2007
372.126'4—dc22   2007004785

This book is printed on acid-free paper.

07 08 09 10 11 12 10 9 8 7 6 5 4 3 2 1

Acquisitions Editor:	Stacy Wagner
Editorial Assistant:	Joanna Coelho
Production Editor:	Denise Santoyo
Copy Editor:	Colleen B. Brennan
Typesetter:	C&M Digitals (P) Ltd.
Indexer:	Pam Onorato
Cover Designer:	Monique Hahn

Contents

List of Tables and Figures

Tables

Facilitator's Guide:

Figures

Appendices

Foreword

Good teaching is composed of many elements, including the teacher's ability to figure out what children are learning, how they are learning it, what might stand in the way of children's future learning, and how to use children's individual strengths to extend their knowledge, skills, or achievements. In short, good teachers are good diagnosticians: they are capable of insight about how children are learning and what might be done to help children more fully reach their potential. Work of this kind is very demanding, especially in today's classrooms, filled with children from a wide range of backgrounds, all of whom are expected to master increasingly challenging learning goals.

Bridging was created precisely for this kind of situation. It answers the question of how teachers can link what they know about a particular child's learning with what they should do next with that child in their classroom. Not a conventional assessment that provides a score, or grade, or normative ranking, Bridging is a performance assessment that helps teachers tailor their curricula to what children know and can do. In this book, Chen and McNamee describe an approach to instructional assessment that relies on systematic observations by teachers trained to observe, record, and evaluate children performing tasks that are part of their daily experience.

As an instructional assessment, Bridging focuses primarily on individual learning. It is not intended to be used for group reporting or to rank and compare children. Bridging is a tool for teachers, and its value is linked to its impact on instruction. Used well, Bridging clarifies what children are learning and have begun to master. It does this by relating everyday classroom materials and activities to carefully developed rubrics that provide information relevant to understanding individual children's learning profiles. Above all, Bridging guides instructional decision making so that teaching can be enhanced and learning improved.

Like teaching itself, Bridging is challenging. It challenges teachers to observe their children more carefully than they may have done previously. It calls on teachers to structure particular activities so they can learn about their students. And it assumes that teachers will be reflective about what they learn so that they can provide the best possible opportunities for children to grow and develop. Over time, and with experience, this approach becomes more and more intuitive for teachers because, in many ways, Bridging is primarily a carefully constructed account of what goes on in the mind of a good teacher.

Chen and McNamee have woven together sound child development theory, well-researched information about how children learn, and insights from the classrooms of outstanding teachers. They show how teachers can bring together what they know about individual children with what they need to do in order to become more effective instructionally. The examples provided here, along with the careful instructions and interpretive information, are a gold mine for practicing teachers. Bridging has the potential to help classrooms come alive for every child whose teacher uses this approach.

The word *assessment* comes from an old Latin derivation that means "to sit beside." In *Bridging: Assessment for Teaching and Learning in Early Childhood Classrooms, PreK–3*, teachers have the opportunity to sit beside two child development scholars who have set as their goal the improvement of practice in early childhood classrooms. Through this assessment, Chen and McNamee have made it possible for teachers to move even closer to their own students while those students are acquiring skills, mastering knowledge, and experiencing the wonder of a world that is becoming their own.

—Samuel J. Meisels
President, Erikson Institute

Preface

Russian psychologist Lev S. Vygotsky once compared the work of educators to that of farmers. Good farmers do not judge the plants under their care only on the basis of the harvest. They are aware of the stages that lead to the appearance of the fruit, monitor crops for signs of those milestones throughout the growing season, and make adjustments in their work of watering or fertilizing crops as needed to sustain growth. Similarly, effective teachers do not plan learning experiences based solely on what has already happened in the classroom; they observe the present with an eye toward the future. They can describe, at any moment in time, what concepts and skills the child is working on, why such development is important, where the child is likely to go in the near future, and what support is likely to further the child's growth.

Bridging: Assessment for Teaching and Learning in Early Childhood Classrooms, PreK–3 is an assessment and curriculum tool designed to help teachers do the work of good farmers. This includes helping teachers to:

- Make sense of the children's learning and development they notice on any one day;
- Understand where the children's developmental achievements have come from;
- Foresee where children's development is likely to go in upcoming weeks and months; and
- Recognize what they can do to create the conditions that will make development likely.

WHO IS THE AUDIENCE OF THIS BOOK?

Bridging is written for preservice and inservice teachers of children three to eight years of age, and for early childhood teacher educators. It assists new teachers preparing to enter the field, as well as those currently working in classrooms with young children, to understand the challenges and responsibilities behind having a good day in school with young children. It engages teachers in a classroom assessment process that helps them understand what children know and can do as well as how they learn. While doing so, it also helps teachers gain more in-depth understanding of the content knowledge present in the activities children are engaged in as well as further their insights into individual children in their class. Such careful observation provides the foundation for fine-tuning teaching to better serve the needs of diverse young children, insuring quality education in early childhood classrooms.

Is this a book about a new way to test young children?

No, this is not a book about testing; it is a book that supports teachers growing skilled in observing and analyzing children's learning while it is happening in familiar classroom activities. Take a look at Table 1.1 on page 7—Bridging Assessment and Curriculum Areas and Activities—and read through the description of the 15 activities. Reading books, acting out dictated stories, singing songs, and working with pattern blocks are old friends of most early childhood teachers. *Bridging* turns these familiar classroom activities into a tool that guides teachers in understanding and appreciating the significance in each small step of development in core curricular areas between the ages of three and eight. We call this process assessment, but the child is "assessed" in a playful, engaging classroom situation. Insights gained from the assessment process support teachers in providing the conditions for more effective teaching and learning in their classrooms.

Can this tool help early childhood teachers meet the demand of accountability?

Yes. Accountability is currently the most serious and pressing issue at all levels of the education system, from preschool through university. Teachers of young children are asked to show how well students are doing in relation to goals and standards. As an assessment system, *Bridging* goes a step further: it provides information on what young children know, but in a context and format that give teachers the ability to adjust their instructional approach to improve children's learning. Improved teaching and learning is the putative goal of all accountability efforts; *Bridging* is designed to ensure that early childhood teachers have a way to reach that goal.

How do early childhood teachers use *Bridging* to improve teaching and learning experiences in classrooms?

Teachers can use *Bridging* on their own, but it also holds great potential when used by teachers working together on an ongoing basis. The *Bridging* assessment activities provide an opportunity to discuss literacy, the arts, mathematics, and the various sciences and how knowledge develops in these subject areas in young children's lives. Integrating this knowledge with a careful analysis of children's learning enables teachers to provide solid curriculum appropriate to the needs of the children. Further, the insights gathered through the *Bridging* assessment process provide teachers with a language for articulating to professionals, colleagues, and parents what is happening in classrooms where there is joy, passion, commitment to learning, and intellectual challenge.

The work presented in this book is the result of seven years of research and fieldwork. We have been classroom teachers and teacher educators for most of our lives. We write this book as if we were in the classroom working with a group of children from diverse educational, family, and cultural backgrounds. The work of teaching young children is complex and challenging. The *Bridging* process models the thinking of skilled teachers who strive to understand children's learning needs and adjust learning opportunities to meet their needs. We hope that *Bridging* contributes to early childhood teachers' confidence in knowing how and why children are having a good day in school!

Acknowledgments

The work described in this book would not have been possible without generous funding from the Educational Foundation of America, Polk Bros. Foundation, McDougal Family Foundation, The Field Foundation of Illinois, Inc., Lloyd A. Fry Foundation, and Erikson Institute's Herr Research Center. We are grateful to these organizations for their support.

Many individuals have contributed in various ways to the development of Bridging. First, and most important, we would like to extend our heartfelt thanks and appreciation to many early childhood teachers in the Chicago Public Schools and at the University of Chicago Laboratory Schools. These teachers participated in year-long research and implementation of Bridging. They inspired us with their dedication to helping each and every child learn. They provided us with invaluable feedback in terms of effective uses of Bridging in their classrooms, and invited us into their classrooms to observe, document, and interact with children as we were piloting ideas for the project.

For their expertise and enthusiasm in helping us develop Bridging assessment activities, we would like to thank Lori Custodero, Patty Horsch, Mary Hynes-Berry, Dori Jacobson, Billy Kaplan, Gloria Oakes, Dan Scheinfeld, Tammy Steel, Bob Strang, and Heather Walters. For their helping in working with children and teachers, we are indebt to the assistance of Jackie Green, Megan Lynd, Lisa Sanchez, and Dianna Schacck. Kathy Richland also worked with us tirelessly in producing a videotape for teacher professional development.

Our sincerest thanks also go to Margaret Adams, Jane Curry, and Suzanne Wagner for their insightful comments and editorial expertise, to Stacy Wagner for her trust and belief in us as well as her wise counsel and patience in guiding this book to publication.

Finally, we want to express our gratitude to Samuel Meisels and Fran Stott who have given us their wisdom, guidance, and expertise without any hesitation since the inception of the project. Indeed, the name of this assessment tool, "Bridging" came from Sam. The steadfast support from Fran and Sam has been indispensable to the development of the Bridging idea, and to the completion of this book.

Corwin Press wishes to thank the following peer reviewers for their editorial insight and guidance:

Patricia A. Barto, Executive Director of Early Childhood Education
Cleveland Municipal School District, Cleveland, OH

Vicki Hawley, Early Childhood Trainer and Professional Development Consultant
University of Minnesota Center for Early Education and Development
Minneapolis, MN

Rebecca Huss-Keeler, Associate Professor and Program Coordinator of Early
   Childhood Education
University of Houston–Clear Lake, Houston, TX

Taddie (Katherine) Kelly, Reading Interventionist/Reading First Grant,
   Waco I.S.D., Waco, TX

Jan Jewett, Program Coordinator/Human Development Faculty
   Child Development Program/Department of Human Development
Washington State University Vancouver

Lisa A. McCabe, Extension Associate and Associate Director
Cornell Early Childhood Program (Applied Research and Outreach), Ithaca, NY

Deborah Nuzzi, Principal
Robert Frost Elementary School, Bourbonnais, IL

L. Kathryn Sharp, Instructor in the Early Childhood Department
Instruction and Curriculum Leadership, University of Memphis, TN

About the Authors

 **Jie-Qi Chen** is Professor of Child Development and Early Education at Erikson Institute in Chicago. As an applied child development specialist, Dr. Chen focuses her work on cognitive development, multiple intelligences theory, classroom assessment, and school-based intervention. A teacher first, she has taught young children in early childhood classrooms in China as well as the United States, and is also experienced in teaching elementary and college students. Dr. Chen has contributed to teacher professional development efforts in Boston and Chicago Public Schools for more than 20 years. She applies her extensive background in assessment and curriculum development to Head Start program enrichment and to teacher professional development in a variety of early childhood settings. She is a Fulbright Senior Specialist. She is coauthor of *Building on Children's Strengths* (1998) and *Effective Partnering for School Change: Improving Early Childhood Education in Urban Classrooms* (2004), editor of *Early Learning Activities* (1998), and contributor to the Multiple Intelligences entry for *The Encyclopedia of Education* (2nd ed., 2002).

 **Gillian Dowley McNamee** is Professor of Child Development and Director of Teacher Education at Erikson Institute in Chicago. She works closely with early childhood candidates during their preparation for teaching as well as working long term with teachers in schools, particularly those in challenging social and economic situations. She studies the process of educating young children from diverse cultural and economic circumstances nationally and internationally, and most recently, in China. Dr. McNamee's expertise is in language and literacy development in home, school, and community contexts, and is coauthor of the book *Early Literacy* (1990). She has been a Spencer Fellow with the National Academy of Education, and received a Sunny Days Award from Children's Television Workshop/Sesame Street Parents in 1998 for her work in developing an innovative early childhood teacher preparation program.

SECTION I

A Guide for Teachers

Jie-Qi Chen and Gillian Dowley McNamee

Introduction to the Process of Bridging

Bridging: *Assessment for Teaching and Learning in Early Childhood Classrooms, PreK–3* presents a performance-based, curriculum-embedded assessment tool (hereafter referred to as Bridging) designed for early childhood teachers. Using familiar curricular activities, the Bridging assessment process provides a practical approach for understanding individual children's learning within daily classroom activities. It helps teachers determine each child's progress in relation to developmental changes in different curricular areas between the ages of three and eight. With a

—— Curriculum-embedded assessment ——

Teachers observe, document, and analyze children engaging in classroom activities from different curricular areas that serve as a window for gauging their developmental progress.

fresh, individualized perspective, teachers adapt ongoing curriculum planning to further children's learning in areas of strength as well as those where they will benefit from experience, intervention, and practice. The result is improved learning and teaching.

ASSESSMENT AND TEACHING

One of the most difficult and most important tasks in becoming a teacher is learning how to accurately assess individual children and use the results to inform curriculum planning and teaching. James Popham, an educational psychologist at the University of California at Los Angeles says, "Teachers who can test well will be better teachers" (2005, p. 1). By this he means that when teachers are careful observers, they know what children can do, what children are working on, and when and how to introduce new challenges to support children's learning. Appropriate assessments, including careful listening and observing, help teachers monitor students' progress, clarify their instructional intentions, and determine the effectiveness of instructional practice. Understanding assessment and knowing how to use it appropriately are crucial to effective teaching.

Early childhood teachers, however, for the most part, dislike assessment and testing, and in many ways, for good reasons. Traditional assessments take time away from children's play and their engagement in sustained projects and activities. Numbers do not tell the whole story of a child's development, particularly because young children do not reliably perform well on standardized testing formats. Furthermore, one-time testing cannot accurately measure young children's learning because their skills are in flux and development can be sporadic. In terms of performance-based assessment, classroom observation is useful, but connecting it to curriculum and methods of teaching can be challenging. Some teachers find it difficult to know what kinds of materials to collect for portfolios and what criteria to use to evaluate them. These concerns and criticisms are legitimate. Overall, the assessments currently available to early childhood teachers have not fulfilled the promise of integration with learning and teaching processes.

——————— Assessment ———————

A global term for gathering information for the purpose of decision making. For classroom teachers, assessment is the process of listening, observing, and gathering evidence to evaluate the learning and developmental status of children in the classroom context.

If the purpose of assessment is to improve classroom learning by informing teachers about each student's progress in relation to learning standards, assessment cannot be an add-on task that takes place occasionally throughout the year. It must become part of daily learning activities. By the same token, assessment results cannot require outside experts to interpret them. To be useful, the results must be transparent to teachers and immediately useful in curriculum planning and teaching. Bridging addresses these teacher concerns. Teachers document their observations of children in core curricular activities in a way that provides feedback on each child's progress, while simultaneously informing a teacher's planning for furthering the learning of individuals as well as the whole group.

BRIDGING IN CLASSROOMS

Mrs. Rogers and her colleague, Ms. Williams, in the classroom next door each have 24 kindergartners in their classrooms. They meet once a week to discuss their children's learning progress and needs, and to plan the curriculum. Since the opening days of school, several activities have been staples in their school day. An estimation activity is one of them.

Mrs. Rogers is at the door greeting her kindergartners as they arrive in the classroom on a chilly October morning. "Good morning, Edward! Hi, Sam! Hang up your coats and come see what you find in the counting bowl!" The first 8 to 10 minutes of the morning are a bustle of activity as children put backpacks and lunch boxes away and then visit the display table, which holds a clear glass bowl with approximately two dozen dominos in it. By the glass bowl is a clipboard with the children's names listed and a space for each to enter their response to the question, "About how many?" printed at the top of the page.

Later in the morning, when the children gather for morning meeting, one of the activities includes reviewing children's estimates and discussing strategies they used to make their estimates. Mrs. Rogers then has the children assist in counting the number of objects in the bowl, represent the total number in several ways, and then compare their various estimates to the actual number.

This estimation activity reflects a deliberate choice by the teachers; it organizes and focuses children's entry to the classroom at the beginning of the school day, and it meets learning goals for mathematics. The activity is also good assessment in that it provides the teachers with a daily record of their children's learning that can guide teaching. These goals are accomplished in an environment and context that meet children's social and emotional learning needs: these teachers greet each child by name, welcome them to the classroom in conversational exchanges, and guide the children into a learning activity that is developmentally appropriate and responsive to the level of challenge for which the children are ready.

In Mrs. Rogers's kindergarten, and in the early childhood division for her district including preschool through third grade, curriculum goals are set for literacy, math, sciences, the arts, and health and physical development. Learning is conceptualized as a dynamic of children interacting with peers and materials under the teacher's guidance to accomplish learning goals that have meaning, purpose, and challenge for children. Assessment completes the curriculum equation informing teachers' next steps. It provides the evidence teachers use to gauge on a daily basis how learning is going for the children. It also guides teachers in seeing where adjustments need to be made within the classroom setting in order to facilitate further learning for individual children as well as the class at large.

The children's responses to the estimation activity are assessment data that Bridging makes available to these teachers. Every day these teachers gather information on their children's emerging understanding of how to estimate number quantity through the process of learning to account for the size of the objects in the bowl and the amount of space they occupy, while at the same time considering information from previous counts of estimated objects. Critical to a teacher's ongoing work with this activity is (1) knowing the challenges and goals the activity holds for children; (2) having a clear understanding of the developmental continuum for estimation skills and concepts represented in this task; (3) organizing the school day to include regular opportunities for children to practice these emerging skills; (4) paying close attention to children's work and recording observations of what each child does as well as how each child engages in the task; and (5) intervening to coach and guide children's efforts based on this ongoing careful review of their efforts in the activity.

These kinds of activities and the record of progress that can be seen by the children, teacher, parents, and administrators are at the heart of the Bridging approach to assessment and curriculum. Bridging activities are good curricular activities that provide a window into a child's developmental progress on a continuum of learning that spans not just weeks or months but several years.

OVERVIEW OF BRIDGING

Bridging is a performance-based and curriculum-embedded assessment tool designed to help teachers identify intellectual strengths and construct learning profiles of individual children between the ages of three and eight. It uses teachers' observation of children engaged in activities in their classrooms. Bridging's 15 classroom activities represent diverse curricular areas, including language arts and literacy, visual arts, mathematics, sciences, and performing arts (see Table 1.1). It provides early childhood teachers, both preservice and inservice, with a means of gathering, organizing, and interpreting observations to inform curriculum planning and teaching.

—— Curriculum planning and teaching ——

Within each subject area, teachers have a planned sequence of activities guided by a theory of what and how children master concepts, knowledge, and skills.

Curriculum planning is the process by which teachers monitor the needs of the students in relation to the path of learning in the content area they are pursuing.

Because no one task samples all of the concepts and skills in an area, *Bridging* includes three activities in each of the five curricular areas. The three activities in each area are carefully chosen to complement one another. They represent varied aspects of learning in a subject area. Together, they use a variety of materials for the expression of ideas in that curricular area. For example, a child's narrative skills and knowledge in language arts and literacy are assessed in the child's reading of a book, story dictation, and dramatization of narratives. The child's ability to create visual images is assessed through the use of different media, such as pattern blocks, pencil, and crayons. Each material offers distinctive representational qualities that children use to convey a range of artistic expressions and understandings. The design of multiple activities using a variety of materials helps to ensure that the Bridging assessment process more accurately portrays a child's current level of development.

As an assessment instrument, Bridging produces a profile of a child's learning from two perspectives:

The *content* of the child's learning—that is, their understanding of key concepts and their mastery of particular skills in a subject area;

The *process* of the child's learning—that is, their working approach or how they engage in tasks, including such qualities as goal orientation, pace of work, and sense of humor.

Thus, Bridging guides teachers in determining both **what** a child has learned and **how** the child goes about learning. In so doing, teachers identify the child's strengths as well as areas where specific instruction, intervention, and practice will help further their learning.

Table 1.1 Bridging Assessment Areas and Activities

Areas	*Activities*
Language Arts and Literacy	**Reading a Book (Child's Choice** and **Teacher's Choice)**—Each child reads two books to the teacher: his or her "favorite" book in the classroom followed by one that the teacher chooses appropriate to the child's level. While the child reads, the teacher keeps a running record of the child's reading behavior. **Dictating a Story**—The teacher invites a child to tell a story, writes the story down, and then reads it back to the child. **Acting Out a Story**—Children act out stories composed by individual children during the story dictation time.
Visual Arts	**Experimenting With Crayon Techniques**—Children use crayons to experiment with varied artistic effects and then use these techniques to create pictures. **Drawing a Self-Portrait**—Children use a pencil to create a self-portrait showing themselves in a setting, such as home or school. **Making Pattern Block Pictures**—Children use pattern blocks to construct representational pictures on black construction paper.
Mathematics	**Creating Pattern Block Pinwheels**—Children view and discuss examples of "pattern block pinwheels" showing radial symmetry and then construct their own pinwheels using pattern blocks. **Solving Pattern Block Puzzles**—Children arrange pattern blocks on preprinted puzzle sheets and work to cover successively more difficult puzzle forms. **Exploring Number Concepts (Counting, Subtracting, Fair Share, Estimating)**—Children participate in a story where bears are on a picnic eating cookies, and within the story, they solve a series of math problems related to number concept.
Sciences	**Exploring Shadows and Light**—Children explore making shadows with a flashlight using different objects and materials that are opaque, transparent, and translucent. **Assembling a Nature Display**—Children classify a variety of objects collected through nature walks. **Building a Model Car**—Children build small model cars using a variety of recycled materials.
Performing Arts	**Moving to Music**—Children listen to recorded music with a definite beat in various styles and then improvise movement to the music. **Playing an Instrument**—Children explore and use a variety of classroom musical instruments and then create an instrumental accompaniment to recorded music. **Singing a Song**—Using a plastic microphone, children take turns singing a song they know.

The goal of Bridging is for teachers to use children's learning profiles to inform their instructional decision making in the classroom. Because the assessment activities sample from a range of curricular areas, teachers can use assessment results to set appropriate levels of challenge in daily planning. Teachers can also use results to guide selection of materials that children prefer. Referring to children's learning profiles, teachers make informed decisions about what is most likely to engage and support each child's participation in classroom activities. In this way, assessment findings inform teaching and learning, making both continuously more effective.

──────── Rubrics ────────

Behavioral indicators that describe different levels of performance in a range of curricular activities. Each level of performance marks a developmental step toward mastery of specific skills or concepts.

Bridging assessment is a process. It begins with the teacher observing children while they engage in activities in varied curricular areas. Teacher observation is guided by specific rubrics that detail the developmental trajectories of children's learning and understanding in different subject areas. The teacher continues the process by planning and implementing curriculum that is based on the newly acquired knowledge of children and their status in the content areas assessed. Of particular importance in Bridging is the direct connection between assessment results and classroom practice, a process that guides continuous refinements in teaching (see Figure 1.1). Thus, Bridging spans the often-wide chasm between assessment and curriculum by directly connecting assessment to the daily activities teachers carry out with children.

Figure 1.1   Overview of Bridging Assessment Process

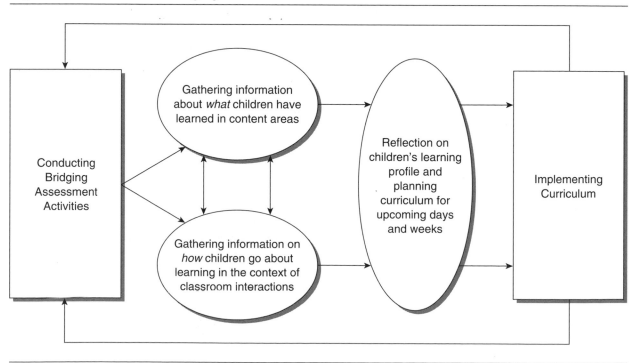

DISTINCTIVE FEATURES OF BRIDGING

There are five ways that the Bridging assessment process helps teachers become more proficient in their daily work with children. Bridging helps teachers to:

1. **Identify a child's developmental progress** in relation to key concepts, knowledge, and skills in five broad areas of school curriculum;

2. **Describe a child's working approach,** including the child's attentiveness throughout the task, preferred social interaction patterns, experience with different materials, and expression of individual characteristics when engaging in activities;

3. **Construct a child's learning profile,** a visual map portraying a child's current level of development across a range of areas, as well as the child's disposition toward learning in each curricular domain;

4. **Select curricular activities and teaching methods** that match the learning needs of individual children as well as the classroom as a whole; and

5. **Study and reflect on key concepts and skills** in various curriculum areas and how they develop over time during the early childhood years.

As an assessment tool, Bridging supports teachers achieving these goals by means of five unique characteristics: scope, focus, method, approach to assessment, and curriculum connection (see Table 1.2). The interrelationships among these characteristics make Bridging effective for both assessment and for improving teaching and learning over time.

Table 1.2   Distinctive Features of Bridging

Features	What Bridging Is
Scope	It identifies a child's developmental progress in relation to key concepts, knowledge, and skills in five broad areas of school curriculum.
Focus	It assesses how children learn (process) as well as what they learn (content).
Method	It uses classroom activities as a structured means for observing and documenting children's learning.
Approach	It engages in an ongoing process that is authentic to daily classroom learning.
End goal	It integrates assessment with curriculum planning to continuously improve teaching and learning.

Scope—Attending to Broad Curricular Areas and a Wide Age Range

Bridging is designed to identify young children's strengths and approaches to learning in five broad curriculum areas: language arts and literacy, visual arts, mathematics, sciences, and performing arts. Within each of the five curricular areas represented, Bridging assessment activities reflect essential key concepts outlined by national standards for the early childhood period. Instead of focusing primarily on children's language and mathematical abilities as most traditional school-based tests do, Bridging equips teachers to observe and document each child's engagement in a wide range of learning areas. Attending to the breadth of curriculum areas, Bridging makes it possible to detect the many ways a child can be "competent," "skilled," and "capable."

Bridging activities are appropriate for children ages three to eight in preschool, kindergarten, and primary classrooms. In addressing this five-year span, Bridging activities make it possible to locate each child on a developmental continuum, thereby recognizing the wide variability in levels of achievement that are inevitable in any group of young children at any moment in time. This span also helps teachers recognize continuities from one point in development to another.

--- **Developmental continuum** ---

A developmental continuum describes changes in skills and concepts in an area of development (for example, learning to read) over a span of years. A developmental continuum characterizes the qualitative and quantitative shifts that mark the growth and changes in a content area.

Focus—Looking at the Content and Process of Learning

As an assessment tool, Bridging is unique in that it examines two aspects of children's learning: what they learn (content) and how they learn (process). The content aspect of learning focuses on children's mastery of key concepts, knowledge, and skills in different subject areas. The process aspect of learning includes a detailed examination of individual children's working approaches. Assessment of both the content and process of learning is sensitive to the influence of several additional factors on children's performance, for example, whether the child understands the goal of specific tasks and is open to help from peers and teachers when needed.

In the field of child assessment, what children learn and how they learn are rarely examined together. However, understanding a child's working approach can provide important insights when interpreting a child's performance level. Working approaches help pinpoint the circumstances under which a child shows strengths or vulnerabilities. Classroom teachers know that the social arrangement of an activity—whether smaller groups or large group—is an important variable in the performance of some children. For other children, however, the same variable matters little. Recognizing varied working approaches helps teachers create the conditions under which each child will thrive as a learner.

--- **Working approach** ---

A process dimension of children's learning that describes how a child interacts with materials and responds to the demands of a task in a specific subject area.

Method—Using Curricular Activities

Bridging provides a structure that elicits children's knowledge and skills while supporting teacher observation and documentation of performance. This structure is a set of 15 specially selected curricular activities. Using such activities represents a significant departure from the methods of most existing assessment instruments. Teachers assess children in the context of classroom learning, not separate from it. They examine the social interactions that elicit, encourage, and mediate children's performance and progress in school. Attending to children's work and behavior in one activity at a time, teachers' observations are organized, purposeful, and content specific. Bridging helps teachers learn how to assess while teaching, and how to look for evidence of developing key concepts and skills in children's performance.

Approach—Providing Multiple Ways to Demonstrate Mastery

In Bridging, children have opportunities to demonstrate their mastery of concepts and skills in a variety of ways both within a curricular area and across curricular domains. For example, a child's development of mathematical knowledge and problem solving is viewed through a series of activities focused on number concepts and geometry. A child's performing arts skills may be seen through dramatization of stories, singing, and moving to music.

Bridging activities can be carried out in a variety of ways. Some activities can be implemented in a large group, providing an efficient way to engage the entire class in an activity while focusing on a few children for assessment purposes. Most activities can also be carried out in small groups or in dyads to allow for a more detailed view of children's thinking. As such, Bridging uses social situations that mirror the classroom's learning environment and that can be responsive to the children's developmental needs. Teachers can make choices that fit a particular moment in time for their children.

Goal—Integrating Assessment With Curriculum Development and Teaching

Bridging informs and supports curriculum development in several ways. First, it covers five subject areas commonly featured in early childhood classrooms. The alignment with school curricular areas enables teachers to more readily translate Bridging assessment results into curriculum plans. Second, Bridging activities are based on curriculum activities familiar to most early childhood teachers. Use of these activities helps teachers integrate assessment results with curriculum planning and instruction. Assessment and curriculum are two sides of the same coin. Each is more effective when they are integrated to form a continuous teaching–learning process.

Additionally, Bridging can be used as a tool for curriculum analysis. It identifies key concepts to be taught, learned, and evaluated in preschool through third grade. With an in-depth understanding of key concepts and skills, teachers become more confident using them to plan learning experiences. Further, Bridging's rubrics specify indicators of children's learning and mastery in varied content areas. Using performance rubrics, teachers can pinpoint the skills a child currently possesses as well as those the child is currently developing in various curriculum areas. The child's zone of proximal development—that is,

——— Zone of proximal development ———

Introduced by L. S. Vygotsky, this term describes a child's development in relation to the skills and concepts that are already mature and mastered as well as those that are in the process of unfolding, developing, and on the way to maturity.

those skills and knowledge currently undergoing change in specific content areas—is revealed in the assessment process.

Finally, to support linking assessment to curriculum, each Bridging assessment activity includes guidelines for further promoting children's development in that subject area during the school year. Teachers can tailor curricular experiences by using assessment results to support and challenge children's learning at particular levels in diverse areas.

BRIDGING FOR PRESERVICE AND INSERVICE TEACHERS

The research and development process for Bridging extended over seven years. Experts in different subject areas—math, literacy, the arts and sciences—contributed to the process, and hundreds of early childhood preservice and inservice teachers have field-tested the system, both in the United States and in China. With preservice teachers, Bridging can be integrated into coursework and student teaching experiences. In the teacher education program at Erikson Institute in Chicago, we introduce Bridging to teacher candidates in assessment, curriculum, and methods courses. They implement Bridging activities, document children's behavior, and interpret results to guide their ongoing work with children in classroom learning.

During student teaching, each teacher candidate selects several children to focus on for assessing while carrying out all 15 Bridging activities. At the end of the student teaching period, teacher candidates write a reflection paper describing their experience using Bridging to learn about individual children, changes in their content knowledge in different curricular areas, and how they used insights from the assessment process to inform their teaching.

For use in inservice teacher professional development, we have developed two models. One is to invite teachers from different schools to a central location for professional development. Using this model, we have provided yearlong seminars to approximately 300 early childhood teachers, preparing them to use the Bridging assessment process in their classrooms. We meet with participating teachers (25 in a seminar) once a month. Between seminar sessions, teachers implement Bridging activities in their classrooms, focusing on detailed documentation of two to four children. During seminar sessions, we study and analyze Bridging activities, examine the implementation process, and discuss the experiences of children in each activity as well as the pattern of experience for individuals across the full range of activities. Finally, teachers discuss how their views of children and views of their own teaching are changing as a result of the Bridging implementation process.

The second model of professional development is to engage all of the teachers within a single school that serves PreK–3 in carrying out the Bridging assessment process over the school year. To date, we have field-tested this approach with two schools in the Chicago Public Schools System. In contrast to the first model, where teachers come to us for a professional development class, in the second model we carry out all work with teachers in their classrooms merging the use of Bridging into the different school cultures. In this model, the Bridging assessment process is adapted to meet the specific needs of the school. Teachers within each of the schools work together, reviewing their teacher professional development and school improvement plans in light of what they are learning about children's development and their teaching needs.

The teachers we have worked with are diverse in many ways—they work with children in PreK–3 classrooms; they represent varied ethnic groups and have different educational backgrounds; and they serve highly diverse student populations—diverse in cultures, languages, and special needs. Teacher feedback helped us to refine Bridging and to confirm its usefulness, particularly in guiding teachers to systematically learn about children who are unfamiliar or inexperienced with typical school tasks and activities.

In the chapters that follow, we include anecdotes from these classrooms to highlight teachers' thinking while using the Bridging assessment process. In addition to working with preservice and inservice teachers, we have collected Bridging assessment data from 156 children in PreK–3 classrooms. The analysis of data from these children is also introduced in several chapters to illustrate the type of outcomes and insights possible when using the Bridging assessment process.

OVERVIEW OF THE *BRIDGING* HANDBOOK

Section I: A Guide for Teachers

The *Bridging* handbook includes Section I: A Guide for Teachers, and Section II: Implementation of Assessment Activities. Section I provides an overview of the Bridging assessment system, its theoretical underpinnings, and different components of this assessment tool and process. Chapter 2 focuses on how Bridging assesses the content of children's learning. Drawing from Howard Gardner's theory of multiple intelligences, the chapter establishes the basis for sampling a wide range of curricular areas referencing key concepts and skills identified for each. The chapter includes a detailed description of how

> ——— Learning profile ———
>
> A visual map portraying a child's current level of development across a range of areas, as well as the child's working approaches while engaging in tasks.

Bridging's performance rubrics assess the content of children's learning and how to construct a child's learning profile. The chapter concludes by discussing why it is critical to view the content of children's learning as a continuous process from the past, to the present, and to the future through curriculum planning and teaching.

While in Chapter 2 we look at ways to assess what children learn, in Chapter 3 we focus on how children learn. We introduce a new idea to guide teacher observations of the process of children's learning—the concept of working approach. The chapter defines the concept and then elaborates it by describing two kinds of working approaches: evaluative approaches and descriptive approaches. The former refers to a child's way of approaching tasks that enhances or hinders learning, whereas the latter describes a child's working approach that specifies salient individual differences. We present assessment results from our work with children that demonstrate the fact that working approach is not a stable trait located within an individual child. Rather, a child's working approach is a profile of tendencies describing the interaction of children within specific activities. The discussion also helps illustrate the impact of a child's working approach on children's performance scores.

Chapter 4 highlights a central premise of the Bridging assessment process—observing the development of a child while that child is engaged in a meaningful activity, a notion proposed by Russian psychologists L. Vygotsky and A. Leont'ev. In this conceptual framework, children are not taken outside of the learning context to have their performance and abilities observed and analyzed in isolation. Instead, children are observed in activities where their learning and development take place, that is, through interactions with adults, peers, tasks, and materials. This chapter also describes the criteria we used to develop and select Bridging assessment activities, and how the dynamic relationship between teachers and children that emerges when engaging in an activity becomes the unit of analysis in the assessment process.

Chapter 5 provides a more detailed account of task parameters in the Bridging assessment process, including (1) the goal of the task, the stated outcome for the task as presented to the child; (2) the key concepts and skills, indicating the organizing ideas from the curriculum area that are embodied in the activity; (3) materials involved in carrying out the activity; (4) the structure of the activity on a continuum from teacher-directed to open-ended; and (5) social arrangements or grouping for activities such as large and small groups as well as one-to-one interactions. We take a close look at each of these task parameters for how they might influence children's performance. We discuss how teachers can arrange and adjust many of these task parameters to create optimal conditions to support children's learning.

―――――― **Key concepts and skills** ――――――

Ideas, principles, procedures, or strategies that are central to a child's eventual proficiency in various content areas.

Chapter 6 focuses on the teacher's role in the Bridging assessment process. We delineate five salient roles: decision maker, participant, observer, interpreter, and translator. In traditional assessment practice, teachers have little flexibility in carrying out assessment tasks, constructing expected performance levels of their children, and adjusting task parameters to meet children's learning needs. In the Bridging assessment process, teachers play an active role that draws on their experience and requires expertise in each of these areas. Bridging relies on teachers to know how to elicit a child's best efforts and how to use the assessment information to guide teaching and learning experiences in subsequent days and weeks. Bridging guides teachers in the challenge of integrating assessment, curriculum, and teaching practice. In doing so, teachers grow in their confidence and skills as teachers.

Section II: Implementation of Assessment Activities

This section includes one "how to" chapter, five activity chapters, and a Facilitator's Guide. Chapter 7 provides a step-by-step guide to what the teacher is doing with children in the classroom when implementing Bridging assessment activities. It details the logistics to be considered when planning to use Bridging in an early childhood classroom. It offers suggestions for how to interpret the assessment results and connect them to teaching. Whenever necessary, we describe the implementation process separately for preservice teachers and inservice teachers, taking into account their different teaching situations, requirements, and constraints.

Following Chapter 7 is a description of the 15 Bridging assessment activities with detailed protocols for implementing each. Activities are grouped according to the five subject areas addressed in most school curricula: language arts and literacy, visual arts, mathematics, sciences, and performing arts. We introduce each curriculum area by answering three questions: What do we know about development in this area? What does Bridging provide classroom teachers to assess this development? Why were these three particular activities chosen? Each introduction offers teachers a brief but essential understanding of the subject area as well as rationale for the specific Bridging activities selected.

Following the introduction to each subject area, we include a table of national early childhood learning standards for the curricular area and how the Bridging activities relate to them. The table reinforces the importance of national learning standards for teaching, learning, and assessing content knowledge as it develops in the lives of young children. It makes it clear that the design of Bridging is in alignment with standards set by various professional organizations.

Teachers should use Section II during the assessment process as a guide to implementing each activity and to assist with subsequent curriculum planning. Procedures for implementing each activity within the school day are presented. The Bridge to Curriculum describes follow-up activities for teachers when using assessment findings to differentiate and fine-tune learning experiences to individual children's needs.

Following the five activity chapters is a Facilitator's Guide describing ways Bridging can be used in preservice and inservice teacher professional development programs. It presents guidelines for the use of Bridging in specific courses and time frames and provides foci for discussion and study as teachers use Bridging to understand their children and strengthen the effectiveness of their teaching.

2

Assessing the Content of Children's Learning

*B*ridging: *Assessment for Teaching and Learning in Early Childhood Classrooms* focuses on uncovering the developmental progress of young children in relation to key concepts and skills in a range of curricular areas. A child's performance on the full range of Bridging activities reflects the child's current level of development using a variety of symbol systems and materials for solving problems in different school content areas. It also points to the new skills and concepts that a child is working on and will be learning and developing in the upcoming weeks and months.

DIVERSITY AND INDIVIDUAL DIFFERENCES

Diversity is a basic characteristic of the human species. No two fingerprints are identical, nor do any two minds work in the same way. Some children show a great interest in numbers and computation problems from an early age, whereas others have the potential for astonishing grace and expressiveness in movement. Some children express themselves through language, while others prefer to think in pictures or images, easily visualizing changes in spatial orientation. Some children spend hours watching bugs, naming each of them and describing their features and characteristics. Other children frequently gravitate toward problems of a mechanical nature, such as fixing a pencil sharpener or repairing an unstable chair. These children are in our classrooms; their individual differences present both opportunities and challenges to our teaching.

Respecting individual differences and supporting the diverse learning potentials of young children are basic tenets in the developmentally appropriate practice advocated by the National Association for the Education of Young Children. The accountability movement has challenged this practice with its strong focus on academic achievement. Consider the likelihood of young children's diverse interests, talents, and potential being recognized if school assessments focus only on academic subjects such as reading and mathematics. Consider also the number of children who are labeled as low achievers because their strengths in performing arts, scientific exploration, or drawing go unrecognized. Consider further how the lack of appreciation and support for children's diverse interests and talents contributes to the loss of inventors, singers, dancers, architects, archeologists, and engineers for our society. Unfortunately, limited recognition of diverse talents is a reality in our schools today.

Recognizing and nurturing diverse talents is especially important in the early childhood years. The talents of young children most often do not find full expression and development until a much later age. Teachers of young children have to assume that any one child might someday make important contributions to medicine, literature, business, science, or the arts. Since children's futures are unknown, it is our responsibility to expose children to all of these areas of potential expertise. Bridging equips early childhood teachers for assessment and teaching across this full range of potential.

The more teachers value the diverse strengths of young children and provide environments to support them, the earlier children enjoy school life and the more likely they are to experience school success. This success contributes to the development of children's positive self-image and high self-esteem. In addition, the more children engage in a wide range of curricular activities, the more pathways teachers have to reach each child, and the less likely it becomes that young children fall through the cracks and experience school failure at an early age. It is with these convictions that Bridging focuses on studying young children's development across a range of curricular areas, namely, language arts and literacy, visual arts, mathematics, sciences, and performing arts.

DIVERSE CURRICULAR AREAS

Bridging assessment of diverse curricular areas is based, in part, on Howard Gardner's (2004) multiple intelligences theory (hereafter referred to as MI theory). Gardner's theory contends that human beings develop and use several distinct, relatively autonomous intelligences over the course of a lifetime. Challenging the traditional conception of intelligence as one general factor called IQ, Gardner proposes that there are at least eight different intelligences: linguistic, logical-mathematical, musical, spatial, bodily-kinesthetic, naturalist, interpersonal, and intrapersonal. Though linguistic and logical-mathematical intelligences have been emphasized in traditional psychological testing and in school settings, Gardner maintains that the eight intelligences ought to have equal claims to priority. Each can be seen as valid and important in terms of opening pathways for individuals to achieve their human potential and contribute to society.

By assessing performance in a range of curricular areas, Bridging activities uncover children's diverse strengths and interests. The range of content areas assessed is deliberate in that findings consistently portray uneven developmental profiles as the rule rather than the exception in describing young children's learning. By sampling work in a wide range of curriculum areas, Bridging captures individual differences in development across curricular areas that reflect the diversity of learners in every classroom. The breadth of its coverage enables teachers to see children from multiple perspectives rather than through a narrow academic window. By recognizing and valuing the diversity of intellectual talents and potential, teachers can support children's learning and development based on information about their strengths, interests, and approaches to learning.

The uncovering of children's strengths and interests in the Bridging assessment process are reflected in the following observations of Mrs. Gates and her student teacher, Ms. Brown, in their first-grade classroom in early October. There are 28 children in the class, 6 of whom are still learning English as a second language. Mrs. Gates has been focusing on large group activities during the opening weeks of school to establish classroom expectations and routines.

Six-year-old Luisa has been among the quietest children in the classroom, responding to questions only when I am persistent in both waiting for her to respond and coaxing some verbal remark out of her. While both her kindergarten teacher and her mother report that Luisa has well-developed speaking skills in English, so far in first grade Luisa appears anxious, moving her mouth without saying any words at times, and shifting back and forth in her seat. Her participation in class activities has been minimal; we have had little sense of her skills in any subject area.

This week Ms. Brown and I worked with Luisa one-on-one and then in a small group with three other children to carry out Bridging activities. To our surprise, she began to open up like a flower! She started talking and using skills we had not seen before in the classroom. She was creative when drawing pictures and made a garden with pattern blocks creating symmetrical pinwheels or "flowers" as she called them. She discussed a book I had read to the class a few days before and then dictated the following story that she enjoyed letting her classmates act out during our group meeting while she preferred to watch:

The mouse got stuck in the trap and the cat got stuck. And the cat gave the mouse a present. And the cat and the mouse was [sic] friends. The mouse helped the cat get out. They lived happily ever after again.

Ms. Brown and I could finally see Luisa's verbal and visual representation skills start to emerge when she was in the company of just a few other children. Now we have a starting point to begin working with her and helping her to benefit from classroom activities.

The starting points for Luisa's teachers come from insights gathered across a wide range of school tasks. The varying materials as well as formats for participation help guide Mrs. Gates and Ms. Brown in understanding how Luisa can become more at home learning in school.

The content areas in Bridging assessments are grounded in curricular areas practiced in schools rather than the intelligences identified by Gardner since school subject areas reflect configurations of intellectual abilities valued in this society. Though not a one-to-one correspondence, Bridging activities do assess knowledge and skills derived from the multiple intelligences proposed by Howard Gardner (see Table 2.1). Using school curriculum areas makes the assessment process more meaningful and more directly relevant to school settings. Also, aligning assessment areas with subject areas studied in school facilitates teachers' integration of Bridging activities into ongoing curriculum planning. This relationship helps teachers connect their daily practice to the development of children's overall intellectual abilities.

Table 2.1 Multiple Intelligences and Bridging's Assessment and Curriculum Activities

Intelligences Identified by Gardner	Bridging's Assessment Activities
Linguistic	• Reading a Book • Dictating a Story
Logical-Mathematical	• Exploring Number Concepts • Exploring Shadows and Light • Solving Pattern Block Puzzles • Creating Pattern Block Pinwheels
Musical	• Singing a Song • Moving to Music • Playing an Instrument
Spatial	• Solving Pattern Block Puzzles • Creating Pattern Block Pinwheels • Building a Model Car • Making Pattern Block Pictures • Drawing a Self-Portrait
Bodily-Kinesthetic	• Acting Out a Story • Experimenting With Crayon Techniques • Moving to Music
Naturalistic	• Assembling a Nature Display
Interpersonal and Intrapersonal	• Documented through observation of child's working approaches and responses to social structure of activities across Bridging assessment areas

PROMOTING UNDERLYING CONCEPT DEVELOPMENT

Through carefully selected diverse curricular activities, Bridging offers a lens to view the underlying developmental progress that children are making in thinking processes that will take years to fully master. In the meantime, the very activity being used to assess development is also the means to encourage and sustain it. This principle of supporting development while being able to observe progress is evident in the storytelling and story acting activities that Mrs. Gates began to carry out with her children several days each week.

Mrs. Gates recognizes that her first graders have very rudimentary skills in writing words, but she also has seen that she can harness their lively imaginations into short stories that they dictate to her, Ms. Brown, or even a parent volunteer. Mrs. Gates read several books by teacher Vivian Paley who made this activity, along with its extension of acting out the narratives in impromptu dramatizations, central to her classroom. Through Paley's modeling in the videotape, *Storytelling and Story Acting With Vivian Gussin Paley* (2002), Mrs. Gates introduces this activity to children by inviting a child to tell her a short story (three to five sentences) while she writes down the words. At a group time before lunch, Mrs. Gates gathers the children in an open area of the classroom where they listen to a storybook being read, and now also, the child's story that was dictated earlier that morning.

Mrs. Gates has the children sit pretzel style on the edge of the rug while the story is read. Afterward, the author and classmates enact the scene using nothing other than gestures and body movements. The children are given two reminders: (1) no touching anyone or anything and (2) no leaving the story circle. Mrs. Gates gives the author the choice of which part she wants to play, and then offers children around the edge of the group, one by one, a chance to play the additional characters in the narrative. The story enactment takes two to three minutes. The children are attentive throughout and then eager to have their own narrative written down. Mrs. Gates assures them that she will make time for a few stories each day.

When Mrs. Gates writes down the dictated stories of her first graders, she provides them with a critical early writing experience comparable to the experience of reading to young children. She invites them to participate in the process good writers develop: learning to envision a scene where there are characters, a plot, and a resolution. In this activity, she is not concerned with the children's mechanics of writing, that is, their handwriting and knowledge of punctuation. Their awareness of, and practice with, these conventions are the focus of instruction in separate activities. For now, she wants them to grow in their experience developing their thinking in language that grows clearer, more concise, and more elaborated when written down and shared with others through dramatization. From reading Mrs. Paley's books, *Wally's Stories* (1981) and *The Boy Who Would Be a Helicopter* (1990), Mrs. Gates recognizes that dramatization of their stories is the children's way of connecting a new area of development (writing) to an earlier form of symbolic activity (pretend play).

The work of Vivian Paley over the past 25 years has demonstrated the power of storytelling and story acting activities for young children in early childhood classrooms. These curricular activities (in *Bridging,* we put Acting Out a Story in the Language Arts area) provide a powerful entry point for young children to master many of the key concepts and skills identified by national standards for language arts and literacy, including learning about language (oral and written) as a means for communication, a rule-governed symbol system, and learning intimately about the connections between speech and text. Cultivating the development of narrative skills in oral language is the precursor to doing so in written language. Narrative skills are at the root of understanding and using written language for the huge variety of purposes that we put it to work in school and society.

Arthur Applebee's research uncovered a series of stages in narrative development that are evident in stories children tell. When looking at the development of children's narratives between the ages of three and eight, he looks at the logic children use to connect story events. With Luisa's mouse and cat story, Mrs. Gates recognizes that today's narrative is a primitive narrative as Applebee (1978) describes (also see p. 124). Structurally, the story has two characters that encounter a problem that gets resolved. The narrative is a skeleton for the action that the children happily expand on during its dramatization.

The works of Applebee and other researchers describe narrative development and its conceptual underpinnings taking years, not weeks or months, to develop. Over the months and years that narrative skills are developing in increasingly complex ways, children's thinking is shaped and nurtured by the oral and written language experiences of daily life. Experiences such as extended conversations and storytelling encounters with adults and peers—family members, friends, teachers and schoolmates of all ages—constitute the healthy diet supporting its continued growth. All of daily development matters! This is the reason storytelling and acting are included in Bridging's assessment: it is an important curricular experience supporting the thinking and speaking skills of young children, *and* a child's narrative provides a snapshot as to where the child is in this area of development between the ages of three and eight.

When Mrs. Gates carries out the storytelling and story acting activities in her classroom, she illustrates the connection between two Bridging activities and key concepts and skills in the area of language arts and literacy development. The principle of promoting underlying conceptual development that sustains growth in the core areas of curriculum in school holds true for all Bridging activities. Research demonstrates that concepts in mathematics, the sciences, the arts, as well as in language and literacy, do not emerge in fully developed form in weeks or months, or even in the units of a school year, an academic calendar. Likewise, development of the concepts that are the focus of schooling are not age-dependent but rather are subject to experience and guidance over a period of years. Bridging activities present concepts and skills in the form of activities that can be carried out, following a consistent procedure, with children three to eight years of age. This makes it possible to observe changes over time in the children's development while holding the task constant.

KEY CONCEPTS AND SKILLS

Within each curricular area, Bridging activities facilitate assessing key concepts and skills rather than a wide array of factual knowledge or isolated skills. The key concepts and skills are ones identified in national standards set for early childhood education. Standards reviewed during the development of Bridging activities include those issued by the National Council of Teachers of English, International Reading Association, Consortium of National Arts Education Associations, National Council of Teachers of Mathematics, National Science Academy, and various early learning standards and content standards.

In Bridging activities, key concepts are defined as ideas or principles that are central to mastery in a curriculum area. For example, in the area of mathematics for young children, some of the key concepts for number sense include one-to-one correspondence (there are equivalent numbers of objects in two sets), cardinality (the last number named signals the total number of objects in a group), and order irrelevance (a group of objects can be counted in any order). While essential to a curriculum area, key concepts may also be relevant to other areas. For example, recognizing spatial relationships, symmetry, and matching shapes are key concepts relevant to the visual arts, performing arts, and some science activities. As concepts, they can be discussed and explained through formal as well as informal teaching.

Key skills in Bridging activities refer to procedures or strategies, generally associated with a related, observable behavior. They are essential to performance of the Bridging activity, but not necessarily to competency in the entire curricular area. In terms of Bridging's counting activity, for example, key skills include naming number words and naming them in order, tracking the objects that have been counted, using different counting strategies (for example, counting on, skip counting), and representing numbers visually via drawing, tally marks, or Arabic numerals. Key skills can be taught, and may become more automatic and effective with practice.

A child's performance in each Bridging activity is examined against a developmental continuum of key concepts and skills for that content area. Bridging activities remind teachers of the key concepts and skills in each activity and model how teachers can monitor a child's emerging development related to them. To extend children's learning, the "Bridge to Curriculum," at the end of each assessment area, offers teachers ways to support and further children's learning of key concepts within and across different subject areas, making learning and teaching for child and teacher meaningful and sustained.

PERFORMANCE RUBRICS

For each Bridging activity, the continuum of development in each content area is measured through a 10-level, criterion-referenced rubric. Research in child development and in content areas provides the basis for each rubric. For example, for the book reading activity, the rubric is based on the stages of pretend reading developed by Elizabeth Sulzby (1985) as well as on work in guided reading by Irene Fountas and Gay Su Pinnell (1996) (see Figure 2.1). Validity of the rubrics was further established through consultation with content area experts and classroom teachers.

——— Criterion-referenced rubric ———

Rubrics that reflect the developmental trajectory of knowledge and skills within a content area to describe children's performance levels.

Bridging performance rubrics allow teachers to assess a child's developmental level in a specific activity by locating the child's performance on a continuum that measures key concepts and skills. Each developmental level has both a name and specific performance indicators to assist the teacher in appropriate scoring. Level 0, for example, indicates that the child declines to participate in the activity while Level 10 reflects a child's rich and complex understanding of the key concepts and skills while participating in the activity. The child's performance score on each activity is the same as the rubric level.

——— Face validity ———

The face validity of Bridging rubrics describes the extent to which each performance level reasonably reflects possible behaviors among children. They are established through consultation with experts, clinical experience, and review of relevant professional literature.

In the following example, we see a first-grade teacher, Mrs. Atwood, engage one of her students in reading one of his favorite books, a language arts Bridging activity. We see how the rubric helps the teacher recognize the significance of

Figure 2.1 Sample Performance Rubric

Reading Books: Child's Choice

Level	Name	Performance Indicators
0	No participation	• Child declines to participate in activity.
1	Attending to pictures, not forming stories	• Child looks at picture but does not say anything.
		• Child "reads" by looking at the storybook pictures; conversation is about the picture in view. Comments about what is in the pictures are not necessarily related to each other.
		• "Reading" consists of labeling and commenting on discrete story pictures (for example, pointing out a ball, naming animals).
2	Attending to pictures, forming oral stories	
3	Attending to pictures, forming written language-like stories	
4	Reading verbatim-like stories	
5	Initial attending to print	See Language Arts and Literacy Section for complete rubric
6	Attending to print, strategies imbalanced	
7	Attending to print	
8	Attending to print, strategies balanced	
9	Attending to print, beginning fluency	
10	Independent reader	

Adapted and modified from Sulzby (1985) and Fountas & Pinnell (1996).

his developmental achievements to date as he reads, as well as what developmental changes will follow in upcoming months.

> Mrs. Atwood invites Curtis to read her one of his favorite books. He picks a class favorite, *The Three Billy Goats Gruff*, written by Paul Galdone. She notes that Curtis is at Level 4 according to the rubric, "reading" the story while looking at the pictures and reconstructing the text from memory. His eager and expressive retelling reflects a rich knowledge of book language and the nature of written narratives. When he gets to "Trip trap, trip trap trip trap. . . ." for each billy goat, he points to the print (which grows larger and larger along with the size of the goat)! He reads these lines in an increasingly louder voice.
>
> The next level on the rubric is "initial attending to print"—that is, the child shows awareness of letters in words, as well as an initial understanding that reading means decoding the print on the page. Mrs. Atwood understands that the development of reading does not proceed in a linear fashion and that children function on a number of levels at any given time. The Bridging rubric gives her specific information about where Curtis is with this story and the nature of the learning that will follow. She can see the importance of continuing to reread texts the children enjoy. She also is conscious of selecting books where the text presents clear opportunities to notice print conventions, opening the way for the new set of skills Curtis will be ready for in the near future.

Mrs. Atwood does not see the assessment results as a tool to control Curtis's learning, insisting that he learn specific information on a specific day. Rather, with the assessment information she has about his development as a reader, she is prepared to support and further his awareness in learning as it unfolds in front of both of them. The information she derives from the assessment adds to her expertise in knowing what to expect at this point in time in his book reading and what content is appropriate to be ready to nurture and draw attention to.

The Role of Teachers' Experience and Expertise

It is important to note that although Bridging rubric levels are criterion-referenced, they are not intended to be age-specific. Classroom teachers know that a younger child, depending on the child's proclivities and experience with any particular activity, can obtain a relatively high score. Likewise, an older child who has not had extensive experience in a curriculum area or with the materials used in the activity can reflect a low score. Bridging does not provide age norms for interpreting assessment results for this very important reason.

Instead, Bridging asks teachers to identify expected performance levels for a given grade or age at particular points in the school year, usually October and May (see Figure 2.2). Teachers then assess children in their classroom in relation to this expected level of performance. Multiple strategies are necessary to determine the expected levels for students; these strategies may include studying State standards for each grade level, considering the characteristics of the student population served by one's school district, conversing with parents, observing classrooms, and consulting with colleagues.

Elliot Eisner (1977) is one of the first educational researchers who emphasized the importance of teachers' content knowledge expertise and experience in assessing students' work in the teaching process. This practice is now recognized by many leading teacher educators and educational researchers, including Linda Darling-Hammond and John Bransford (2005). To set appropriate expected levels or learning goals for the class of children, teachers need to study the performance rubrics carefully. In the process, their knowledge of key concepts and children's developmental progressions in varied subject areas increases. Because Bridging asks teachers to set performance standards for children, the learning goals are no longer determined by an unknown source. Because they set the expected levels, teachers are more likely to internalize the learning goals and to monitor their teaching interventions in relation to the children's efforts toward achieving them.

The challenges that teachers can face at different points in their teaching career, as they compare expectations for the content children ought to be working on with what the children are actually ready to learn, are reflected in the comments of two professionals (see boxes).

────── Expected performance levels ──────

Expected performance levels are levels of development reflected in the rubrics that teachers specify as goals for learning in that school year for the children in their classrooms in relation to their understanding of children's background knowledge and experience.

────── Performance standards ──────

Developed by state boards of education and professional organizations in the various content areas, performance standards are a comprehensive description of the knowledge and skills students are expected to achieve at different grade levels.

Figure 2.2   Expected Performance Levels

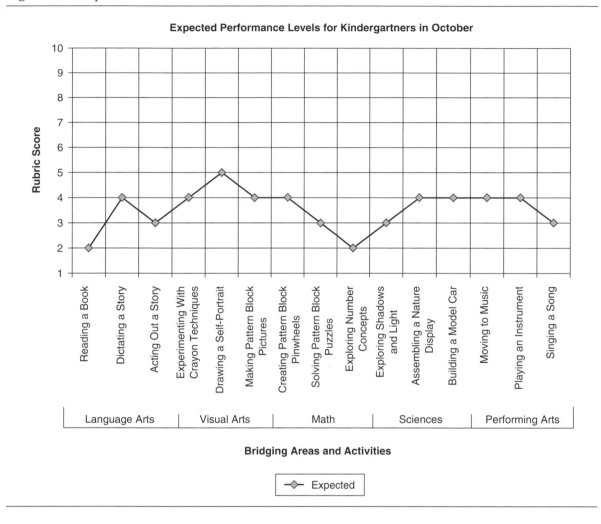

For both teachers, their gauging of children's learning needed fine tuning through close observation of the children and careful study of subject area knowledge. Such practice of setting expected levels helps teachers further develop their abilities to observe students and to think critically about what they can do to help children take the next step in learning. By attending to teachers' expertise and experience in evaluating students' work, Bridging grants a central place to the teacher as a professional who first understands and then makes decisions about what children do, how they do it, and why.

LEARNING PROFILES

Bridging uses a learning profile, rather than a single score, to describe a child's performance. This profile, including a diagram and a summary table, specifies the child's performance on all Bridging activities (see Figures 2.3 and 2.4). Learning profiles typically reveal uneven levels of performance across activities and curricular areas, which we call jagged profiles. Profiles also enable teachers to understand a child's development and move beyond expectations based on characteristics such as family economic circumstances, ethnic group, and gender. In studying profiles, teachers see that it can be misleading and inaccurate to assess a child either by looking at performance in only two or three areas, or by limiting the range of their abilities to an average score.

——————— Jagged profiles ———————

In reviewing children's learning profiles, we describe them as "jagged" when referring to the uneven points of development that children have achieved at any moment in time when observed across a wide range of tasks.

Figure 2.4 presents a teacher's charting of profiles for three children who each earned a mean score of .60 for the 15 Bridging assessment activities. Because this score was an average, one would expect to find some variation in each child's performance levels. The observed variability, both within a child's set of scores and across children's profiles, is striking. Reviewing these profiles, the message is clear that an average score or a limited sampling of curriculum areas can obscure the actual range in children's performance levels.

As another example of how constructing children's profiles can contribute to teacher insights, consider a teacher who created two profiles for one child based on Bridging assessments she did in October and May (see Figure 2.5). Both profiles were jagged, indicating the child had strengths and weaknesses in different activity areas. However, the patterns of unevenness shifted. In May, some areas were stronger than in October, whereas others had not kept pace. Further, areas that were emphasized in the school curriculum (for example, reading) showed the greatest change. The profile reveals that performance at one point in time does not necessarily accurately describe a child's future developmental course and that school learning experiences contribute to advances in a child's performance levels.

The purpose of constructing learning profiles is both to help teachers understand each child as completely as possible and to give teachers the specific information they need to help every child meet educational goals. The use of profiles makes it impossible to reduce the differences among children to simplistic rank ordering, with one child ranked higher than another. Rather, profiles reveal the complex nature of each

Figure 2.3   A Child's Learning Profile Summary

Child: Age: Gender:	• Language Arts			• Visual Arts			• Math			• Sciences			• Performing Arts		
	Reading a Book	Dictating a Story	Acting Out a Story	Crayon Techniques	Self-Portrait	PB Pictures	PB Pinwheels	PB Puzzles	Number Concepts	Shadows & Light	Nature Display	Model Car	Moving to Music	Music Instrument	Singing a Song
Date															
Social Structure															
Rubric Score															
Evaluative — Initial engagement															
Focus and attention															
Planfulness															
Goal orientation															
Resourcefulness															
Cooperation															
Descriptive — Chattiness															
Pace of work															
Sense of humor															
Social referencing															

Note: PB = Pattern Block

child's status as a learner in terms of that child's interests, strengths, proclivities, and vulnerabilities.

The learning profile reflects our understanding that all children are capable of participating in learning experiences and developing their intellectual potential through activities that draw on concepts and skills from multiple disciplines. For both hereditary and environmental reasons, children are distinguished by their particular profile of abilities and strengths. A child's learning profile represents that child's particular configuration of relatively stronger and weaker areas of knowledge and skill across the full range of curricular areas at a moment in time.

The practice of creating learning profiles is supported by Gardner's MI theory. From an MI perspective, individuals differ from one another in personality and in their particular array of intelligences. While we all possess some potential in all of the intelligences, no two persons, not even identical twins, exhibit them in precisely the same configuration. Moreover, the strengths of various intelligences and relationships

Figure 2.4   Learning Profiles of Three Children

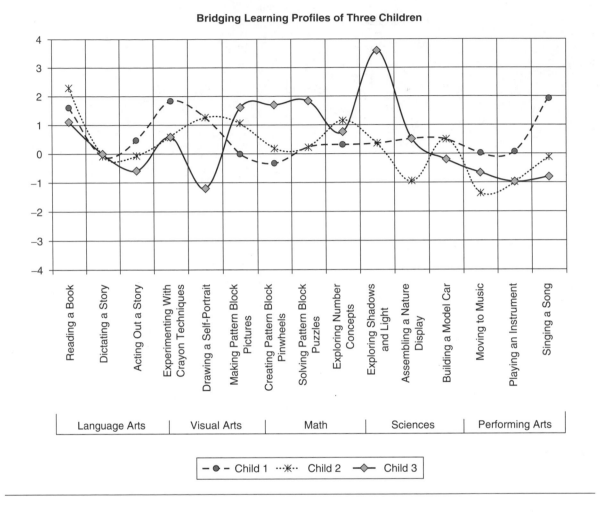

among them will shift over time in response to an individual's experiences as well as societal values.

ACTUAL AND POTENTIAL DEVELOPMENT

By design, Bridging activities provide opportunities to assess the present and future of a child's development of key concepts and skills in a particular subject area. This practice is rooted in Lev Vygotsky's (1978) unique contribution to developmental psychology, summarized in his concept of the "zone of proximal development." Vygotsky recognized that in order to adequately describe a particular child's development, an educator needs to account for both what a child has achieved *and* what the child is likely to be able to do in the near future. He proposed a way for educators to understand this continuum of what has matured in development and what is still in the process of developing. The key is to monitor a child's activity to determine what she can do alone (indicating those processes that are fully matured) and what

Figure 2.5   A Child's Mid-Year and End-of-Year Learning Profile

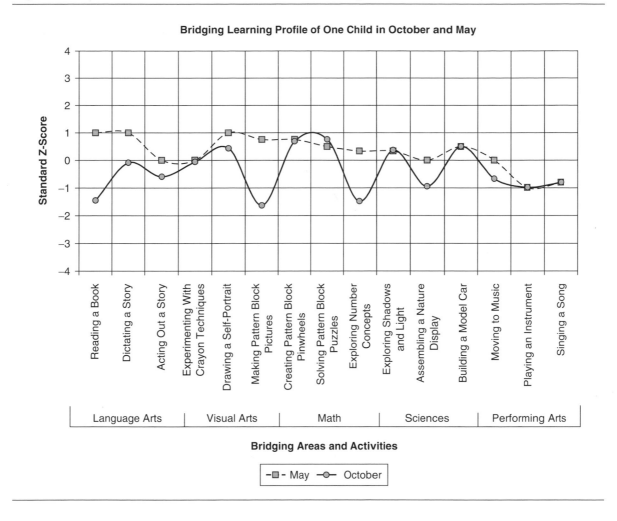

she can do with the help of adults or more capable peers (indicating what is still in the process of developing).

An analogy from Vygotsky (1978), comparing the work of educators to that of farmers, further illustrates the point:

> A child's mental development is a process that is no less simple than the growth of peas or beans in a garden; and well before the fruit appears, the gardener can discern the stages that lead to the appearance of the fruit. It would be a poor gardener who would judge the plants under his care only on the basis of the harvest, and equally deficient is the educator who is able to determine nothing more than what has already happened developmentally, that is, nothing more than a retrospective developmental summary.

Bridging provides a tool for teachers to carry out this professional responsibility. With Bridging activities, they can look at the child in the present, recognize the developmental achievements of the past, and see indicators of what the child will be working on in upcoming days, weeks, and months. Each assessment activity has a rubric describing 10 levels of change that characterize children's development between the ages of three and eight. This allows teachers to recognize the progress a child has made in a subject area, document what she is working on at present, and anticipate areas of development where the child shows signs of readiness for growth. In the Bridging assessment process, the number assigned to a child's performance is not an isolated or absolute score; rather, it indicates a point on a developmental continuum. Knowing what a child is ready to learn enables teachers to link Bridging assessment to curriculum planning.

While recognizing the heuristic potential of the zone of proximal development to increase our understanding of past and future learning, we also recognize that neither Vygotsky's theory nor Bridging assessment activities tell the whole story of a child's development. The substance of what is learned, the meaning that it holds for a child, and how the child will make use of what is learned in the future are not explained. The critical point here is to recognize that educators can discern patterns of thinking and behavior in a child's present that illuminate the outlines of concept and skill development that lie ahead.

Assessing the Process of Children's Learning

Teachers readily recognize that children in their classrooms differ in not only what they know but also how they learn. Children vary enormously in how they approach learning tasks in terms of their pace of work, level of engagement, and degree of focus. Factors defining how children learn are as important in accounting for school success as what children are learning. In Bridging assessments, this process dimension of children's learning is called "working approaches." This chapter provides an introduction to assessing children's working approaches and explains how assessing these approaches offers teachers a more complete understanding of the kinds of support each child needs to maximize her potential for learning in school.

APPROACHES TO LEARNING

What contributes to children's success in school? Although people's responses to this question vary considerably, there is a general consensus with regard to the following four dimensions: health and physical development, emotional well-being and social competence, communication skills, and cognition and general knowledge. In *Reconsidering Children's Early Development and Learning: Toward Common Views and Vocabulary*, a document developed by the National Education Goals Panel, Sharon Lynn Kagan, Evelyn Moore, and Sue Bredekamp (1995) included approaches to learning as a fifth area of development that is critical for school success. Approaches to learning include a range of attitudes, habits, and ways of participating in activities.

Every teacher recognizes that children differ not only in levels of achievement or what they learn, but also in how they acquire school knowledge and skills. In a typical classroom, a teacher can point out many examples of distinct approaches to learning among her students. Tasha is eager and impulsive in her work. Nataki is usually deliberate and slower to take on new challenges. Anthony loves to talk with his friends regardless of the task at hand. Katrina tends to be quiet and observant when working with peers. Lee knows how to get help whenever she needs it. Kiah often looks helpless when she initially encounters a new problem or challenge.

Understanding children's approaches to learning is an inherent part of effective teaching. It helps teachers recognize factors in addition to content knowledge that influence children's learning as individuals and as a group. When teachers can identify behaviors that regulate children's learning experiences, they are in a stronger position to select strategies that support children's engagement in daily classroom activities. Mrs. Scott, a second-grade teacher, describes her experience noticing a child's approaches to learning.

> Sarah is a playful child but she daydreams a lot during class time. To help her become more focused, I placed her desk in the front of the room so that I can have more eye-to-eye contact with her. Being closer to me, and being able to see my introductions to lessons and materials, has helped her to concentrate. I have become more concise and careful in my instructions as I anticipate Sarah's needs.
>
> I also give the children a chance to write in their journals or read a book when they are done with tasks throughout the day so that Sarah and others like her can let their minds wander in productive ways after attending to my goals for a period of time. The quality of Sarah's work and my teaching are both improving tremendously!

As Mrs. Scott notes, the benefits to child and teacher are enormous when teachers study how to align their teaching strategies with children's needs. Like Sarah, children who start school as engaged and successful learners are more likely to persevere and succeed in school through the later years.

DEFINING APPROACHES TO LEARNING

Though deemed a key dimension of children's learning by the National Education Goals Panel, approaches to learning have received limited attention in the practice of early education. One reason for this is the difficulty defining this construct. Beginning in the 1960s and continuing today, numerous researchers have studied the "how" of children's learning by describing their style of working. Learning styles can reflect several aspects of a child's effort. Some researchers focus on how people take in information, whether they favor auditory, visual, and/or kinesthetic modalities. Others characterize learning styles as an individual's habitual way of behaving, such as attending to detail or hesitating to take initiative. Still others describe styles in terms of how the brain processes information, connecting variability in styles to mental functions such as attention and memory.

Research on learning styles fell out of favor among researchers and educators during the 1980s. In addition to the lack of a clear definition, using sensory modalities to describe learning styles makes the relevance of the construct unclear for those who have no strong preference or style. If a conceptualization of approaches to learning is to be useful to educators, it must provide a way to see the unique aspects of every individual, not just those who have a strong tendency in a particular area.

In recent years, two additional lines of research have increased our understanding of individual difference in approaches to learning. One is the literature on executive functioning, which attempts to describe how the human mind organizes itself to solve problems and what influences the development of such mental functioning. Another line of research describes the importance of self-regulation, which refers to a set of behaviors that a person uses flexibly to guide, monitor, and direct the success of one's performance in an activity. Despite these recent advancements in the research literature, no general consensus about the essential elements of approaches to learning has been reached. Lacking agreement about how to describe and measure children's processes of learning, advances in our understanding of this area of child development have been limited. Little can be done to develop comprehensive educational applications of the construct for classroom practice.

Based on our review of the literature and our years of experience working with young children, including children with learning challenges, we have reconceptualized the construct of children's learning process to make it more applicable to classroom situations and more useful for teachers. In the Bridging assessment process, we call children's way of engaging in an activity their "working approach." Working approaches describe how a child interacts with materials and responds to the demands of a task in a specific subject area. "Working" indicates that the construct refers to a child's observable behaviors while the child is engaged in an activity rather than the child's internal mental states or processes. Working approaches pertain specifically to a child's behavior in schoolwork rather than to broader life situations. "Approach" establishes that the child is an active agent, engaging in or responding to a task, rather than passively "having" a style.

RUBRICS TO MEASURE WORKING APPROACHES

For Bridging assessment, two criteria guided our selection of working approach variables. First, we reviewed studies of affect, motivation, disposition, temperament, gender, personality, self-regulation, perceptual preference, learning styles, and executive functions. Through this review, we identified a large number of variables relevant to studies of the process of learning. We then sorted variables that are more biologically constrained and relatively stable over time (for example, chattiness and sense of humor) from those that are more malleable and affected by socialization processes (for example, focus and attention during a task and resourcefulness). From this review of the research literature, we developed two sets of working approach variables: evaluative and descriptive. Evaluative approaches affect a child's performance. Descriptive approaches capture salient individual differences.

The second criterion we used to identify the working approach variables was their potential relevance and use by classroom teachers. All working approaches had to be observable in regular classroom settings. They each had to be applicable to all children, not just to a few who showed extremes of the approach. Each variable had to be described in terms that are meaningful to teachers. The number of approaches had to be manageable to record. Applying these two criteria in the selection process, Bridging assesses a total of 10 working approaches: six evaluative and four descriptive. These approaches are observed across all 15 assessment activities.

Evaluative Approaches

Expected to either promote or hinder a child's performance, Bridging assesses six evaluative approaches: initial engagement in an activity, goal orientation, planfulness, focus and attention throughout a task, resourcefulness, and cooperation. Table 3.1 provides a definition of each evaluative working approach variable. All children use

Table 3.1 Definition of Evaluative Working Approach Variables

Variable	Definition
Initial engagement	• The child's response and demeanor when first introduced to the activity, evidenced by words, body language, and gestures.
Focus and attention	• The degree to which the child is on-task throughout the activity, evidenced by attentiveness and persistent work.
Goal orientation	• The degree to which the child works toward the activity's goal described by the teacher, evidenced by words and use of materials.
Planfulness	• The extent to which the child uses strategies to complete the task, evidenced by words, use of materials, and sequencing of activity.
Resourcefulness	• The extent to which the child seeks help to solve problems when needed.
Cooperation	• The extent to which the child works with peers willingly and competently toward task accomplishment, evidenced by taking turns, sharing materials, and problem solving with others.

these approaches; the difference among children is a matter of degree. Evaluative approaches are assessed using a rating scale from 1 to 5, with higher scores indicating that a child's approach is more adaptive, more goal-oriented, and more organized, and thus more conducive to successful participation in the classroom learning activity. Table 3.2 presents the behavioral indicators used in the rating scale for each evaluative approach.

When implementing Bridging activities across a wide range of early childhood classrooms, we found a positive correlation between children's evaluative working approach scores and their performance scores. On average, a child who earns higher evaluative working approach scores is also likely to earn higher rubric scores. In addition, some evaluative working approach variables seem to have a greater impact on children's performance than others. In our research, we found goal orientation, planfulness, and focus were more highly related to rubric scores than the other three approaches were. This is consistent with research reporting that goal orientation and planfulness are among the central components of executive functions in higher mental processes. When teachers become aware of the importance of such behaviors for mental functioning, they are in a much stronger position to help children develop these approaches that pave the way to successful learning.

Descriptive Approaches

A total of four descriptive approaches are observed in the Bridging assessment process. They are chattiness, pace of work, social referencing, and playfulness. The definition of each approach is provided in Table 3.3. Like evaluative approaches, descriptive approaches are measured through a five-point scale (see Table 3.4). Unlike evaluative approaches, higher scores do not indicate more effective working approaches. Instead, they indicate simply that a child shows a greater degree of those behaviors and a stronger use of that approach in a specific task.

Descriptive approaches do not appear to impede or enhance performance. Rather, they provide another perspective from which to view how a child approaches tasks. As an example, consider pace of work. A child whose pace is slow may be either careful and thorough or indifferent and passive. By the same token, a child who gets work done quickly may be careless and impulsive or experienced and skillful. Through systematic observation and documentation, a teacher can determine how speed affects a child's work and whether her pace is the same in all curriculum areas.

Descriptive approaches may affect a child's performance indirectly by influencing the teacher's perception of the child. Children who score very high or very low on these approaches exhibit behaviors that may appear problematic for the child's school learning from the teacher's point of view. For example, a child who is very chatty may seem inattentive and disruptive. A child who is quiet may appear disengaged and withdrawn. A child who is serious may seem to lack enthusiasm and interest. To the extent that a teacher sees these as approaches, rather than problematic traits, she gains an opportunity to consider what these behaviors mean. As approaches, the teacher can look at when, how, and why the child uses them. The teacher may also find activities where the child's use of these approaches is adaptive.

Take the example of a child who scores high on chattiness during a task. Through observation, the teacher may learn that the child is very chatty only during tasks she works on independently. Being chatty appears to help the child relax and focus. Thus, what initially appeared to be a disruptive behavior may be a strategy the child uses to

Table 3.2   Rating Scale for Evaluative Working Approach Variables

---

Initial Engagement: How does the child initially respond to the activity?

Hesitant _____ Eager

1	2	3	4	5

very hesitant or unwilling to begin activity

becomes involved on his or her own

eager to begin activity

Focus, Attention: How on-task is the child throughout the activity?

Distractable _____ Attentive

1	2	3	4	5

very easily distracted by other children, events, or materials

attentive some of the time

sustained, absorbed attention to activity

Goal Orientation: To what extent is the child working toward the activity's goal?

Personal goal _____ Activity goal

1	2	3	4	5

works on personal goal rather than activity goal

vacillates between personal goal and activity goal

works efficiently toward activity goal

Planfulness: To what extent is the child organized in working toward task completion?

Haphazard _____ Organized

1	2	3	4	5

random or impulsive; no evidence of organization of materials or approach

organized some of the time

well-organized, methodical in approach or with materials

Resourcefulness: What does the child do when stuck?

Helpless _____ Resourceful

1	2	3	4	5

does not ask for help; unable to use help when offered

moves forward a step when help is given

seeks help and makes good use of it to figure out challenges

Cooperation: How does the child work with peers to accomplish the task?

Difficulty working with others _____ Helpful to others

1	2	3	4	5

has difficulty sharing materials or attention, taking turns, supporting the efforts of others

gets along with other children

helps other children with activity, materials, or as a mediator; models ideas for others

Table 3.3   Definition of Descriptive Working Approach Variables

Variable	Definition
Chattiness	• The amount of talking about matters unrelated to the activity (for example, personal concerns, events outside of school, or fantasies the child engages in)
Pace of work	• The speed of child's work in comparison to others in the group
Social referencing	• The extent to which the child is aware of others and checks with others during the activity
Playfulness	• The degree to which the child shows a sense of humor during the activity

Table 3.4   Rating Scale for Descriptive Working Approach Variables

Chattiness: How much of the child's talk is unrelated to the activity?

Very quiet _____ Very chatty

1	2	3	4	5
little conversation and self-talk throughout the activity		talks from time to time		constantly talks about unrelated topics

Pace of Work: What is the child's pace of work?

Slow _____ Fast

1	2	3	4	5
slow to start and carry out the activity		moderate pace throughout the activity		quick start and quick finish

Social Referencing: How often does the child check with teachers or peers?

Little interaction _____ Constant checking

1	2	3	4	5
focuses on own work		pays attention to others' work and checks with others about own work occasionally		frequently asks teacher or peer if own work is on track

Playfulness: How animated, lively, or happy is the child during the activity?

Serious _____ Playful

1	2	3	4	5
mood/demeanor is serious and cheerless		business-like with activity		cheerful and sense of humor related to activity

achieve learning goals. If the teacher curbs the child's chattiness, the child may find it more difficult to concentrate. Through observation of children's descriptive approaches, a teacher gathers information about how to design learning environments that accommodate approaches different children use and benefit from.

SOURCES OF VARIABILITY IN WORKING APPROACHES

As shown in Chapter 2, children tend to have distinctive performance profiles when they engage in activities from a wide range of curricular areas. Likewise, children's efforts vary on every measurable working approach characteristic. Each child tends to have different constellations of working approaches depending on the activity. Susan's approach to drawing a picture differs from Molly's, who diverges from David's. How Susan approaches a math problem might readily differ from her approach to drawing. Both approaches may differ from how peers in her class learn. How children approach tasks—including their focus, resourcefulness, and playfulness—is as diverse as what they learn.

Differences in children's working approaches can be traced to multiple sources. Each contributes to our understanding when we interpret working approach data. Among the major contributing sources to variability observed through the Bridging assessment process are biological givens (gender and temperament), cultural patterns and values, characteristics of the activity, and the child's age and socialization to school. Here we describe the possible role that each source plays in the child's use of working approaches, and we discuss how awareness of these sources might inform the interpretation of working approach data.

Gender

Numerous research studies indicate that, although gender is not a determining factor of development in the long run, boys and girls do differ in their maturation or developmental rates. Girls are frequently found to have language advantages at early ages, whereas boys generally perform better in spatially oriented tasks. Though it is impossible to separate individual differences due to innate characteristics from those that emerge through socialization processes, gender is an important influence on children's predispositions toward learning. For example, girls may tend to be chattier and more conversational than boys when engaged in activities. Boys, on the other hand, may be eager and more planful when moving about in space and involved with building materials because they may be more biologically attuned to understanding spatial reasoning.

Temperament

Characteristics such as being shy, calm, or quick-tempered are predispositions that may be present at birth and may set the stage for how children approach learning. Jerome Kagan of Harvard University describes temperament as "any moderately stable, differentiating emotional or behavioral quality whose appearance in childhood is influenced by an inherited biology, including difference in brain neurochemistry"

(Kagan, 1994, p. xvi). Temperament influences children's approaches to learning because it helps set the patterns of their reactions to stimuli, organizes their responses to a variety of experiences, and influences the manner in which they exhibit competencies and understanding. In short, temperament can affect the way children perceive, judge, comprehend, and solve problems. Although biologically attuned, temperament, like gender, is moderated by cultural and contextual influences. A shy child, for example, can become more outgoing in an environment where the teacher encourages and supports her interaction with peers.

In the Bridging assessment process, descriptive working approaches—pace of work, chattiness, social referencing, and playfulness—have been found to be more stable across tasks and are hypothesized to be more reflective of children's temperaments. A child's evaluative working approaches, on the other hand, appear to vary by activity and by age. If a child's planfulness or resourcefulness is influenced by temperament, the effect appears to be more indirect than it is for descriptive working approaches.

Cultural Patterns and Values

For many years, researchers who studied the process dimension of children's learning focused only on individual differences. Cultural patterns and values were not considered when examining variations in children's approaches to learning. However, as American society has become more culturally diverse, more studies have begun to investigate the impact of acculturation on how children learn (Gutierrez & Rogoff, 2003a, 2003b; Zhang & Sternberg, 2006). For example, in some cultures children are encouraged to engage in dialogue with their parents, to raise questions and express their opinions. In other cultures, children listen and follow their parents' directions, trusting their guidance and respecting their parents' wisdom. Cultural variations may affect a child's approach to initial engagement in an activity and her comfort level while working in groups. Some cultural groups encourage children to learn by observing first and then becoming more actively engaged over time.

Understanding a child's distinctive cultural heritage contributes to a more complete understanding of her particular approaches to learning. When considering the cultural roots of working approaches, it is critical to avoid stereotyping of cultural patterns and values. Stereotypes suggest that all individuals who share a cultural heritage think and act in similar ways. Stereotypes are not accurate representations of behavior. Cultures are not homogeneous; they are multifaceted and diverse. Further, individuals are affected by cultural values and practices in different ways. They have distinctive life histories and unique points of view. All individuals use a variety of approaches, regardless of their cultural background.

Variations in working approach that result from different acculturation processes must first be understood from the perspective of the child's home culture. Through observation in the classroom and discussion with the child's parents, a teacher can determine which approaches derive from the child's home environment and community settings. Understanding, respect, and a nonjudgmental mind-set are the most important starting points in following the story of a child's behavior. While different, approaches are never deficient. In some cases, children may benefit from developing a working approach that differs from the approach they use at home. Recognizing cultural variation in the use of different working approaches and helping children select the most effective approaches for school will help children succeed in school and grow up respecting the integrity of their cultural values.

Characteristics of the Activity

Much of the literature on approaches to learning contends that children's learning styles show stability across tasks (Dunn, Beaudry, & Klavas, 1989; Hanson, 1989; Riding, 1997). Our studies indicate the opposite: that children's working approaches, both descriptive and evaluative, vary by activity. Close observation suggests that because activities present different learning opportunities and exert distinctive performance demands, children use particular working approaches for specific tasks. Both our study data and classroom observation suggest that a child's working approach may be affected by (1) whether or not she understands and subscribes to the activity's goal, and (2) whether or not she is familiar with the materials and the task.

As an example of familiarity effects, consider children's participation in two Bridging Number Concept activities: Estimation and Counting (see pages 203 and 205 for these activities). In both activities, children use miniature figures of bears and button-like objects to solve a series of math problems. In the Estimation activity, children are shown two plastic jars containing bears. The teacher tells the children there are 23 bears in the first jar and then asks the children to estimate the number of bears in the second jar (the actual number is 50). The teacher also asks the children to describe how they figured out their answer. We found that, in their approach to this specific math problem, children were least likely to be planful and most likely to rush through the activity. Having little or no experience with estimation activities, children had not developed an organized approach to the task. Without a plan, they merely guessed a number and finished the activity quickly.

In the Counting activity, the teacher presents the child with a set of plastic bears and asks the child how many bears there are. Unlike in the Estimation activity, a majority of the children were planful and they were least likely to finish quickly. Being familiar with counting activities, children more readily knew how to organize themselves and their materials. They understood the importance of being careful and methodical, and they proceeded at a relatively slower pace of work.

Familiarity with materials, understanding the activity, and pursuing the activity's goal are dimensions of the learning experience that moderate the child's choice of working approaches. These dimensions appear to be interrelated. Working approaches become visible in interactions between the child and the activity, neither belonging to the child nor reflecting inherent properties of the activity. Further classroom observation and empirical work are needed to describe the workings of these relationships.

Age and Socialization to Schooling

Examining the working approaches of children from preschool through the primary grades, we find that some approaches remain relatively constant across the early childhood period while others change as young children advance in school. For example, older children's goal orientation scores tend to be higher than those of younger children. Other differences, like the amount a child talks, appear to be less related to age and may be relatively stable in children over time.

While looking for patterns in working approach data, we found that older children are more likely than younger children to show higher levels of evaluative working approaches. We think this trend reflects, in addition to maturation, another important influence: the process of becoming socialized to school and its unique way of organizing large groups of children to work and talk. Children do not come to school knowing what is expected of them, knowing what kind of behavior and activity is valued and rewarded. They have to learn how to learn in school!

Beginning in the early grades, teachers send a strong message to children that school tasks require goal orientation, focused attention, and being organized. These are the evaluative working approaches measured in Bridging. Children seem to respond to this message by developing those types of working approach behaviors over time. As children continue in school, they are more likely to adapt to teacher expectations for how to approach learning tasks. Awareness of this socialization to schooling offers teachers another means of helping children succeed in school. Working approaches are observable as well as teachable. Teachers can have a strong effect on children's performance by modeling and explicitly describing effective working approaches.

WORKING APPROACH IN THE BRIDGING PROCESS

In the Bridging assessment process, teachers use information about a child's working approaches and their content knowledge to plan curriculum and instruction. Bridging's working approach scales guide teachers in documenting their observations of how children approach and complete each of the 15 assessment activities. Integrating information about content knowledge and working approach helps teachers determine more specifically what help a child needs and what a child is ready to learn.

Constructing Working Approach Profiles

Children's working approaches are not fixed traits that remain stable across activities. Rather, they constitute a profile of tendencies that vary depending on the nature of the activity the child is engaged in. In addition, approaches may change over time. To integrate information about a child's working approaches into planning, a teacher examines a child's assessment activity sheets and looks for patterns in approaches the child uses. With 10 working approaches for each of the 15 activities, the child's profile of approaches is more complex than her profile of content knowledge (see Table 3.5). Teachers will want to respect this complexity and give themselves time to observe and document this aspect of children's experience. The process will bring the teacher continuously closer to the information and thinking at the heart of effective teaching.

Looking at all of a child's working approaches across 15 activities is overwhelming. Instead, teachers will want to construct and think about working approach profiles in stages. Teachers can begin by studying individual activities, examining the approaches a child used, and reviewing her performance rubric score. Questions teachers might raise include the following: What was surprising, unusual, or noteworthy about the child's working approach? In what ways might the child's approach have influenced her performance?

Table 3.5 Working Approaches Profile

Child:

Age:

Gender:

Observation Date:

	Language Arts and Literacy				Visual Arts					Mathematics				Sciences			Performing Arts		
	Reading Books		Dictating Stories	Acting out a Story	Crayon Technique	Self-Portrait	PB Pictures	PB Pinwheels	PB Puzzles	Number Concepts				Shadows and Light	Nature Display	Building a Model Car	Moving to Music	Music Instrument	Singing a Song
	Child's Choice	Teacher's Choice								Counting	Subtraction	Division	Estimation						
Evaluative Initial engagement																			
Focus and attention																			
Goal orientation																			
Planfulness																			
Resourcefulness																			
Cooperation																			
Descriptive Chattiness																			
Pace of work																			
Sense of humor																			
Social referencing																			

Note: PB = Pattern Block

Next a teacher can consider the approaches a child used in one particular curricular area. What kind of variability characterizes the child's working approaches in this area? Does the child tend to use the same or different approaches for the Bridging activities within the area of mathematics? Within visual arts? To the extent that approaches vary, are reasons for the variability apparent? When considering multiple activities, a teacher may begin to see strengths and weaknesses in the working approaches that a child uses.

Table 3.6 illustrates a teacher's detection of patterns. The teacher sees that Jason tends to be highly focused and planful in all of the science activities. Both of these approaches promote higher levels of performance. The teacher also sees that Jason has a relatively fast pace of work in one of the language arts activities. He quickly finishes dictating a story. Although pace of work does not uniformly promote or hinder a child's performance, it may influence performance in this instance. Jason does not give himself time to develop a plot or describe characters. Further, because he finishes quickly, the teacher does not have the opportunity to support and expand Jason's storytelling through questioning and discussion.

Examining Jason's working approaches in the area of language and literacy more closely, the teacher realizes that a fast pace appears in only one of these activities. Based on other Bridging activities, Jason does not appear to lack knowledge about what a story is or to lack enjoyment of stories. He reads stories and acts them out with zeal. The teacher's further probes might include: Is fast pace in the story dictation activity related to the assessment situation? For example, is there something else more attractive going on in the classroom at the same time? Could Jason have been influenced by Mike, his best friend, who came to the table for the activity first and finished the story dictation as soon as Jason arrived? The close examination of a child's working approaches in classroom context provides information that draws teachers' attention and reflection beyond superficial or simplistic judgments about a child's approach to learning.

In constructing and reviewing working approach profiles, the teacher may next compare a child's approaches in two curricular areas. This level of comparison may indicate the extent to which a child's approaches are influenced by content. Mrs. York, a kindergarten teacher, noticed that Mei Mei was goal-oriented, planful, and focused in mathematics activities. In the area of performing arts, however, this same child was hesitant and easily distracted. Looking at these approaches in relation to performance, Mrs. York saw that Mei Mei's scores for performing arts activities were lower than her scores for mathematics. Mrs. York wondered what might be making her uncomfortable when singing and moving to music. She found time to talk with Mei Mei about joining in with the class during these group activities. Mei Mei said she couldn't because she is not good at these activities but her sister is. In talking with Mei Mei's mother, Mrs. York learned that her older sister is a talented dancer and singer. She hears family members talk of her sister's skills often. With this background, Mei Mei's mother and teacher began to think of ways to encourage Mei Mei to join her classmates in exploring and expressing herself in creative movement and singing. Mrs. York understood what was likely inhibiting her and therefore was in a better position to explore ways to open new avenues of participation for her.

Following a review of individual activities, activities within curricular areas, and comparisons between curricular areas, the teacher may look at a child's profile of working approaches across all 15 activities. The complete profile consists of a complex array of numbers that needs to be considered carefully for the story it holds. Reviewing the

Table 3.6 Jason's Working Approaches Profile

Child: Jason
Age: 4.2
Gender: M
Observation Date: 6/16

| | Language Arts and Literacy | | | | Visual Arts | | | | | Mathematics | | | | Sciences | | | Performing Arts | | |
| | Reading Books | | Dictating Stories | Acting out a Story | Crayon Technique | Self-Portrait | PB Pictures | PB Pinwheels | PB Puzzles | Number Concepts | | | | Shadows and Light | Nature Display | Building a Model Car | Moving to Music | Music Instrument | Singing a Song |
	Child's Choice	Teacher's Choice								Counting	Subtraction	Division	Estimation						
Evaluative																			
Initial engagement	4	4	4	5										5	4	5			
Focus and attention	5	4	4	4										5	4	5			
Goal orientation	5	5	4	4										5	5	5			
Planfulness	4	4	2	3										5	5	5			
Resourcefulness	3	4	1	4										5	5	5			
Cooperation	NA	NA	NA	4										3	5	5			
Descriptive																			
Chattiness	2	2	2	2										3	3	4			
Pace of work	2	2	5	3										3	3	3			
Sense of humor	1	1	1	1										3	3	3			
Social referencing	2	2	1	2										3	3	3			

Note: PB = Pattern Block

profile from different angles may reveal additional patterns that inform the teaching-learning process. Looking across all activities, a teacher may see that a child varies in her degree of focus and planfulness. Recognizing this, the teacher can build on the child's use of these approaches in selecting activities and encourage her to apply these same approaches in other activities. In looking at the complete profile, a teacher will consider again the extent to which the social grouping for activities (large group versus small group), the use of certain kinds of materials (paper and pencil as opposed to manipulatives), or the goal of the task (using pencils to draw as opposed to writing) affected the child's approach and the outcomes of the activity.

Setting Learning Objectives and Selecting Instructional Strategies

The purpose of assessing children's working approaches is the same as the purpose for assessing their content knowledge—to systematically observe, document, and set objectives that target children's learning processes as well as their content knowledge. To help young children develop effective evaluative working approaches, teachers need to be clear about their goals when planning curriculum activities. They also need to make these goals clear and meaningful to children. Goal orientation and planfulness are not inborn traits. Rather, children develop these approaches through interactions with adults and teachers who help them understand the goal of an activity and help them make plans to achieve it.

In terms of instructional strategies, a child's approach may indicate an optimal point of intervention. For example, a child who engages quickly, but does not organize materials or develop strategies, will benefit from teacher attention as the activity begins. At the beginning, before the child encounters problems, the teacher can work with the child while verbalizing the importance of being planful and explaining the steps one takes to get organized. A child who becomes more planful is likely to improve performance in a range of activities.

A child's working approach may also prompt a teacher to encourage the child to interact more with others during activities. For example, based on reviewing her profile, the teacher may realize that a child tends to score lower in some activities on initial engagement and focus, and higher on social referencing. Reflecting on this pattern, the teacher might wonder if the child is unsure of her own ideas or needs input from others to formulate her own ideas. The child's higher score on social referencing in these activities may reflect her effort to observe others, to gather ideas to bounce her own thinking off of, or even to copy the actions of others as she formulates her own thinking. In this situation, the teacher may talk with the child about what she sees in the thinking of others. By recognizing her strategy and encouraging her to talk with others, the teacher might help build the child's confidence in how she learns. This may also lead to increased focus during activities.

Structuring Learning Activities

In addition to planning curriculum and instruction, children's working approaches may have implications for how activities are structured. Considering children's working approaches will help teachers create optimal learning situations. A child might find it easier to slow her pace of work in a small group than in an independent activity. A child who shows little interest in the number activity with bears may find a different kind of manipulative more appealing. A teacher may also structure activities to build on children's preferred approaches. For example, a child who is chatty may prefer to work in small groups rather than work alone.

In conclusion, studying working approaches are an integral element of the Bridging assessment process. They contribute to a more complete understanding of the child's strengths, weaknesses, and preferences as well as their learning needs. Gathering and integrating information about approaches helps a teacher to make decisions about how to teach. Teaching decisions that include thinking about these variables result in making more flexible accommodations to young children's needs and interests while they are in school. These accommodations build bridges that lead to children's experience of success in school.

4

Activity as the Unit of Analysis in Bridging Assessment

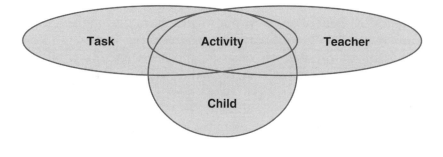

I n this chapter, we introduce a new concept: activity as the unit of analysis in child assessment. Fundamental to many current assessment practices is the assumption that the child is the unit of analysis. In this tradition, the individual child is the focus, with assessment results describing the child's behavior or abilities. In contrast, Bridging places activity at the center of the assessment process. From this perspective, the people involved in the activity and the characteristics of the task are seen as integral to the child's performance outcome. Assessment parameters include the child's understanding of the goal of the task, characteristics of the materials involved, the social dynamics surrounding the child and task (for example, small or large group setting), and the structure of the task (for example, open-ended versus more teacher-directed). Rather than attribute learning difficulties, or achievements, to a child alone, Bridging yields information teachers can use to set activity parameters where children learn and perform at their best.

UNIT OF ANALYSIS IN CHILD ASSESSMENT

The practice of assessing children's learning and development began with French psychologist Alfred Binet. In 1904, in response to a request from the French Ministry of Public Instruction, Binet devised a set of tests to identify children who required special education due to learning difficulties. More than a century has passed since Binet's first tests for children. Although the content and the structure of child assessment have been significantly diversified and improved, one feature remains essentially unchanged—the individual child continues to be the sole focus of, or the basic unit of analysis in, the assessment process.

A variety of assessments and tests are currently used in schools. These include screening tests that are used to identify children who may be developmentally delayed; diagnostic tests that identify a child's strengths and weaknesses to qualify them for special or gifted education programs; readiness tests that indicate whether a child is prepared to benefit from formal instruction; and achievement tests that assess how much children have learned through school instruction. Despite their varied purposes, all of these tests focus on measurement of what is within the child—what the child can or cannot do, the child's mastery or lack of skills, and the child's strengths or weaknesses.

If the context is considered, it is frequently placed in the background rather than the foreground for interpreting the assessment results. Contextual information, such as the influence of peers and task familiarity, is often regarded as "noise," details that are not relevant to the "true" measure of the child. These interferences are controlled for as much as possible in the assessment process. Measuring the performance of the child, with external factors standardized or restrained, is the goal of assessment.

When assessment focuses solely on the child's performance, it ignores the fact that children are fundamentally social beings. They learn through interactions with peers, parents, and teachers. As they learn and develop, they make sense of the world by interpreting societal and cultural expectations, using cultural tools such as books and computers, and actively participating in informal and formal learning experiences. Ironically, despite increasing recognition of the central importance of such relationships to the child's development in the fields of developmental psychology and early education, the influence of social factors typically falls outside the parameters of assessment.

When children are seen as the source and the cause of their own performance, their difficulties will be seen as their own individual shortcomings. Performance is not understood to be the product of interactions between individual children and factors in the learning environment. Locating problems within the child, we may hear educators describe low-performing children as "slow learners" or as children who "can't concentrate." Seeing difficulties only in terms of the child prevents teachers from closely examining factors that influence children's learning and performance. In reality, teachers can alter many of these factors, for example, by making the goal of a task clear to a child or by arranging the groupings in which children carry out school tasks. If an assessment eliminates these sorts of contextual factors from analysis of the results, teachers lose information that can be used to elicit children's best performance. The factors that affect children's learning are the very ones that can support the development of their knowledge, skills, and abilities.

The field of child assessment may resist moving beyond the practice of viewing the child as the unit of analysis for several reasons. Conceptually, this practice is rooted in the Western psychometric tradition that defines learning and development in terms that can be measured by isolating individuals. Individuals can be examined, analyzed, and described in a standardized situation with standardized stimuli. Individual differences reflect internal abilities that are self-contained.

Related to conceptualizing the child as the unit of analysis is the issue of meeting methodological challenges in assessment. When the unit of analysis goes beyond an individual to include, for example, other people with whom the child is interacting, or materials that the child is using, we are left without tools or statistical techniques to examine the effects of these irregular interrelationships on a child's performance. In statistical analyses, we often define the child's behavior as a dependent variable and intervention factors, such as teacher's instruction and stimulation, as independent variables. However, educators readily recognize that the child's behavior can significantly alter the teacher's behavior. Recognizing these possibilities makes it unclear who is the independent variable and who is the dependent variable, teacher or child. The lack of complex analytical tools makes it more difficult to examine the social interactive aspects of children's learning and development (Rogoff, 1998).

ACTIVITY AS THE UNIT OF ANALYSIS IN BRIDGING ASSESSMENT

In a significant departure from instruments designed to look only at the child's performance, Bridging places activity at the center of assessment, documentation, and analysis of children's learning. Bridging's focus on the child in the context of classroom activities is guided by the work of Alexei Leont'ev (1978, 1981). Leont'ev recognized that children come to know the world through participation in activities where they interact with others in their family, school, and community, and with materials that are involved in the tasks of daily life.

A child's life, when looked at closely, is a chain of activities. Dressing in the morning is an activity, so too are brushing teeth, eating breakfast, and walking to school. As soon as children enter the classroom, they start participating in one activity after another, from reading a book to listening to a story, from joining circle time to working on a group project, from drawing a picture to getting involved in a science experiment. Some of these school activities are carefully planned by teachers; others are initiated by children, given the appropriate materials and environment. In both cases, learning takes place. Activity is the most basic element of a child's life, in and out of school. Bridging assessment activities use familiar curricular activities to take snapshots of children's learning and development in the context of ongoing classroom settings and common daily routines.

As the basic element of a child's life, activities provide the most ready and authentic windows to reveal children's mental abilities. To understand children's learning, we need to know how they function mentally. Mental processes are not observable, however. Activities make it possible to study a child's internal world of interests, approaches, and proclivities through observable behaviors, such as the choice of activity, the degree of engagement, the level of productivity, and the quality of products. When the teacher assesses a child who engages in a Bridging activity using the activity and working approaches rubrics, the teacher observes and documents the child's mental abilities—where the child is at the moment and where he or she is heading in the near future.

Each activity not only provides a means to study children's mental functioning, but it also reflects the demands and support from a child's external world of home, school, and society. Each of these contexts and their participants hold expectations for children to learn information and symbol systems important to the culture they live in. In the case of Bridging assessments, each activity reflects a set of learning standards outlined by the field as an expectation for young children to meet. For each Bridging activity, teachers are asked to provide necessary materials and appropriate social arrangements to support the child's involvement with the activity. By analyzing children's performance in activities that involve interacting with different kinds of materials in different social circumstances, Bridging assessments provide teachers with tools to examine how children function as mental and as social beings; that is, how they internalize external demands, interact with the environment, and use support as they work toward expected outcomes.

With activity as the unit of analysis in the Bridging assessment process, understanding individual differences includes understanding the context of performance. When an assessment is designed and analyzed based on the child as the unit of analysis, individual differences are attributed largely to the child's internal mental status and biological givens. From Bridging's perspective, an activity connects a child's internal mental work with the external circumstances of a context. Individual differences in activity participation and outcome are a blend of both children's unique intellectual resources and their response to the specific external factors defining the classroom learning environment.

A final reason for using activity as the unit of analysis is its relationship to development. As children grow older, their way of approaching activities, as well as their activity performance, changes dramatically and rapidly. Bridging assessment activities focus on the child's engagement in the same 15 activities over time to provide teachers with opportunities to observe changes in the development of children's skills, problem-solving processes, understanding of concepts, and ways of interacting with peers. Focusing on activity as the unit of analysis, Bridging maintains that children's performance over time reflects their change and growth as a function of the interaction between what they as individuals bring to the task and what the teacher and the classroom environment have contributed to their development.

It is important to point out that making activity the unit of analysis for assessing learning is not only a methodological issue; it also reflects the theoretical foundation for our conceptions of learning and development. In Bridging, thinking and learning are regarded as inextricably intertwined with people and objects; they are impossible to understand without also considering how a child's mind interacts with materials, peers, and teachers. In this conceptual framework, an individual does not think and learn in a vacuum and, therefore, should not be assessed in one. The Bridging process of assessing recognizes the influences of the teacher, peers, and task. Assessment results are understood by looking at interactions among the child, teacher, and task. To attempt to exclude any of these influences from the assessment process is to miss opportunities for understanding the child's behavior.

CONCEPTUAL FRAMEWORK OF BRIDGING

In the Bridging assessment process, which uses activity as the primary unit of analysis, factors in addition to the child's internal state are included in the analysis of performance and learning. Although a child's learning profile, describing both performance levels and working approaches, is the outcome measure of Bridging assessment, profiles are not examined in isolation. Rather, they are analyzed and interpreted in the context of the goals, materials, structure, and social setting that define the assessment activities. Figure 4.1 is a graphic representation of the conceptual framework of Bridging, showing activity as the primary unit of analysis. A child's performance in Bridging assessment activities is understood by examining the interactions among task characteristics, teacher influences, and the child's participation. When analyzing and interpreting assessment results, each of the variables related to the child, task, and teacher's decision making is a potential source of insight in understanding the child's effort.

Figure 4.1 Conceptual Framework of Bridging

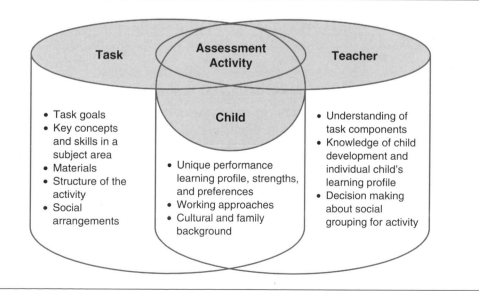

Task

The tasks in Bridging's assessment process reflect best practices in early childhood curriculum and research on promoting and assessing children's learning in various subject areas. Each task can be described in terms of familiar components such as stated goals, key concepts and skills the task embodies and requires for participation, materials used to carry out the activity, and the structure of the activity: how open-ended as opposed to how teacher-directed the task is.

Task characteristics are external to the child but significantly influence the child's behavior. In the case of goals, each Bridging activity is introduced with a specific direction and purpose. The goal of the Acting Out a Story activity is to use body movements, facial expressions, and voice to portray story characters through interaction with classmates. The goal of the Experimenting With Crayon Techniques activity is to use crayons to create different effects and then use these different techniques to create representational and nonrepresentational pictures. Goals guide children's efforts, orient their strategies, and signal completion when some approximation of the goals is achieved. Whether the child understands and subscribes to the goal of the activity is a determining factor of the child's performance level.

Other task components are integral elements of children's performance as well. Of fundamental importance to children's learning in a particular content area is their understanding of key concepts and mastery of key skills. As such, each Bridging activity embodies concepts and skills that are necessary for achieving the goals of the activity. In terms of task materials, a child's knowledge and skills are revealed in what the child does with materials provided for performing the task. From viewing a child's work, a teacher may find that a child's performance was affected by preference for a different material or by limited familiarity with the material available. In terms of effects of the task structure, it is largely determined by the goal of the activity. The Exploring Number Concepts activity, for example, is a set of teacher-directed tasks that call for one answer—a number. In contrast, the Making Pattern Block Pictures activity is open-ended in nature and gives the child plenty of room to decide what to portray. Although there is a developmental progression in children's creation of pattern block pictures over time, there is no single prototypical picture expected of a child. In this sense, the structure of the task affects children's performance by constraining and organizing their behavior in response to the task goals.

Teacher

Teachers are also central in the Bridging conceptual framework. They play a vital role in the assessment process. In many of the assessment instruments used in schools today, teachers are viewed as passive participants. They administer a test and receive results from a central administrative office. They are expected to link the results to curriculum planning. Very few teachers see a clear path from one to the other as the assessment is often imposed, rather than an integral part of the existing curriculum. In addition, results are often delivered at a time far removed from the time of the assessment.

In the Bridging assessment process, teachers are active participants. They observe but also think, reflect, make decisions, and take actions before, during, and after the assessment. Table 4.1 details the activities that a teacher engages in during different phases of the Bridging assessment process. As active agents, teachers in the Bridging assessment process mediate the child's experience in activities and create environments that elicit the child's best performance. In this process, the teacher is sensitive to the child's abilities, skills, and strategies and observes the child's performance in relation to task components that the teacher can change. Through these actions, the teacher helps to shape the assessment process and begins to build bridges from assessment to curriculum.

The concept of activity as the unit of analysis in the Bridging assessment process has profound and exciting implications for classroom teachers. It means that teachers can systematically study, control, and vary components of the classroom environment that contribute to children's learning. Teachers can learn to design experiences that create optimal support for children's learning—both as individual children and as a group.

Child

Now we are ready to discuss the child's place in Bridging's conceptual framework. Shifting attention from tasks and the teacher to the child is not a matter of shifting the focus of assessment from what is outside the child to what is inside. Rather, our focus on the child reflects a process of understanding that requires moving back and forth between the individual and the assessment context.

The child comes to any assessment task at a particular age and with a particular background. Each activity presents a distinct and unique lens from which to view the child. By viewing the child in relation to the simultaneous influences of the subject matter, the objects or materials used, and the host of decisions the teacher has made, Bridging creates a unique and dynamic assessment portrait rather than a static assessment "result."

Table 4.1   Teacher as an Active Agent in the Bridging Assessment Process

Assessment Process	Teacher's Activity
Before the Assessment	• Studying the rubric of Bridging activities • Determining the expected level of performance for students • Preparing task materials • Selecting an appropriate social arrangement for the activity
During the Assessment	• Explaining the goal of the task to children • Engaging the children in the process of completing the task • Recording their performance and working approaches in relation to task components
After the Assessment	• Creating learning profiles based on each child's scores on performance and process rubrics • Examining the patterns in each child's profile • Interpreting the pattern in relation to the child's interests, abilities, experience, as well as in relation to task components • Planning the curriculum for the next day and month based on information gained through the Bridging assessment process

Focusing on activity in Bridging assessments does not mean disregarding the child's uniqueness—the child's interests, skills, knowledge, and personal approaches to tasks. On the contrary, the child's distinctiveness is illuminated in relation to the goals of the activity, the use of cultural tools, and interactions with others. The focus of the assessment is not the performance outcome per se but the outcome as it is revealed in the interaction among child, task, and teacher. This focus provides teachers with three kinds of information: (1) the child's performance profile or learning outcomes in a range of curriculum areas; (2) working approaches and external factors that influence the child's performance; and (3) links from assessment performance and process to curriculum planning that will facilitate learning and development. Bridging's focus orients assessment toward the future rather than the past. It is prospective in that assessment leads to teaching, learning, and development in the upcoming days and months.

In sum, the conceptual framework of Bridging is a relational and interactive framework. It attends to the dynamic relationship of the child, the task, and the teacher. In the Bridging perspective, a child's performance must be examined in relation to task parameters and teacher's efforts. Glossing over interactions among child, task, and teacher, we lose opportunities to link assessment to teaching and learning processes.

BRIDGING ACTIVITIES AS BASIC ACTIVITIES

Bridging assessment activities are typical classroom activities in the sense that they can be adapted or extended based on the needs of a teacher in a particular classroom context. It is important to note, however, that the development and selection of Bridging activities was a carefully organized process. Each activity selected or developed had to meet the following criteria:

Be appropriate for children three to eight years of age following the same procedures and using the same materials;

Be strong exemplars of concepts and skills in one of the five curricular areas;

Be readily implemented in a wide variety of early childhood classrooms serving children three to eight years of age;

Use simple and inexpensive materials that could be found in early childhood classrooms; and last,

Promote learning in both the assessment context and in ongoing early childhood classroom settings.

These criteria are derived from the concept of "basic activities" developed by Cole and Griffin (1986). According to Cole and Griffin, a basic activity includes the three characteristics described in Leont'ev's theory about activity. It has goals to be achieved, tools for achieving goals, and social circumstances surrounding and supporting the activity. A basic activity speaks to the educational dilemma: How do educators promote the development of basic skills necessary for literacy and numeracy while achieving the goal of learning and teaching for meaning and understanding?

Cole and Griffin propose the concept of basic activities as a means to integrate these seemingly disparate goals for learning. Below we list how Bridging activities meet the criteria for a basic activity:

- A basic activity has a purpose and meaning that children understand. Each Bridging activity presents a task with a clear goal that is developmentally appropriate for children three to eight years old.

- A basic activity capitalizes on the active and social nature of children's learning processes and their interest in play. Bridging activities involve a wide variety of engaging materials that children use in playful yet challenging situations. By using a variety of social arrangements, Bridging activities are more likely to accommodate a child's preference and provide the type of social support they need to put forth their best effort, demonstrating fully what they know and can do.

- A basic activity allows children at different levels of skill and understanding to participate alongside one another. Each Bridging activity provides opportunities for a child to work alone or with peers so that a child can learn from and with others. Further, the same materials are used by children at differing levels of knowledge, allowing ample opportunity for peer exchange and elaboration.

- A basic activity introduces children to the basic skills that are necessary for completion and mastery of the task. Embedded in each Bridging activity are key concepts and skills derived from national standards set for each subject area. Children get exposure to and practice with basic skills in the context of meaningful activities.

- A basic activity invites children's participation long before they are able to carry out the task independently and makes it possible for them to get help from others to carry it through to completion in the initial stages. The 10 developmental levels described in the performance rubric for each Bridging activity make it clear that mastery of key concepts and skills requires time, involvement, effort, teaching, continuous practice, and different forms of help over a period of years.

- A basic activity proceeds from the child's need for help with decision making and strategies for carrying out steps to complete a task, to the child's having an understanding of the task and its goals, making plans to complete the task, and doing so. Each Bridging activity includes procedures for teachers to observe *how* children approach tasks, and in particular, their awareness of and willingness to get help from others. This information becomes as important as what a child is learning for the purpose of improving classroom teaching.

Bridging activities are basic activities. Placing such activities at the center of the assessment process highlights the nature of developmentally appropriate learning and teaching—intentional, social, challenging, meaningful, as well as engaging. As basic activities, Bridging makes it possible to articulate the common ground between assessment and curriculum. It provides a lens for analyzing a child's current development as well as promoting learning and growth into the future. It respects the integrity of children's unique proclivities and experience alongside the expectations from the society.

BRIDGING ACTIVITIES AND PLAY

Play is the most basic activity in young children's lives. Although play is culturally specific in content and structure, children in all cultures have some form of play. Play presents the original and quintessential form of abstract thinking. Young children are "naturals" at it. Vygotsky's (1978) theory proposes that the capacity for play in children creates the zone of proximal development. By this he meant that in play, children organize, bring meaning to, and transform how they approach the future with the new insights they gain from reworking their past. Children exercise, practice, and develop representational skills and symbol-using abilities as they create imaginary worlds. When play is included in the school day, children experiment with, negotiate, and expand on ideas with peers inside a community that makes room for the development of individuals.

During the development of Bridging assessment activities, we debated and experimented with the possibility of assessing children's play. This proved difficult for a number of reasons. First, types of children's play vary enormously. Children play with objects (for example, blocks and other small objects), they create pretend characters and imaginary scenarios involving them, and they play games with rules, such as checkers. Types of play change as children grow older. It was not possible to take only one form of play and follow its developmental trajectory in children from three to eight years of age.

Second, key to children's play is its imaginative, innovative, and creative nature. Children's play does not progress in a linear fashion. It was impossible to develop a rubric that would say with any certainty what 10 levels of play look like from three to eight years of age in any one type of play. Finally, in attempting to assess children's play, we encountered a methodological challenge as well. When inviting children to play, the teacher cannot and should not set up a goal for the activity. Although the teacher can provide materials to engage children in certain kinds of play, for example, dramatic play, it is up to children to take the lead to play a school scenario or a family event, to play alone or with peers. When children play, there is no way to structure their response for assessment and it would be unthinkable to do so.

In our attempt to assess children's play activities, we also frequently found children playing when working with the materials set out for Bridging activities and even creating pretend scenarios when, for example, they constructed a pattern block picture or explored shadows and light. We ensure that Bridging assessment activities presuppose a playful attitude in the setup and introduction of each activity to young children. Bridging does not assess play as an independent activity. Rather it embraces play throughout the assessment process. Bridging activities are basic and playful activities. In recognizing the importance of play as central to the organization of curriculum for the early childhood years, Bridging assessment activities are fulfilling the goals of assessing key concepts across subject areas as well as encouraging the highest level of children's thinking and actions.

5

Task Parameters in Bridging Assessment

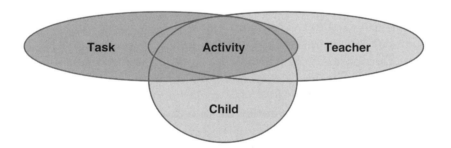

Using activity as the unit of analysis, Bridging focuses attention on the dynamic interactions among child, task, and teacher in the assessment, teaching, and learning processes. While uncovering diverse characteristics of children and their development, the assessment process also provides insights about how particulars of the tasks and teacher involvement influence what a child achieves at any moment in time. In this chapter, we take a close look at parameters of the tasks presented to children in Bridging assessment activities. What are the characteristics of the tasks, and why are they important to attend to when assessing children and analyzing the assessment results? How can teachers change these task parameters to support individual children's learning and performance?

TASK PARAMETERS IN BRIDGING ASSESSMENT

In the Bridging assessment process, tasks are defined by the physical and structural components of the activity. We view the task as separate from the social aspects of the activity defined by what the teacher and children bring to the task. Each Bridging task has five parameters that are relevant to the assessment situation. They are (1) a specific goal, that is, an expected outcome that the child is asked to work toward; (2) key concepts and skills indicating the organizing ideas from the curriculum area that are embodied in the task; (3) materials that are presented for carrying out the task; (4) a structure that is located along a continuum from teacher-directed to open-ended; and (5) social arrangements or groupings including large and small groups as well as one-to-one interactions. Each of these task components is discussed below in relation to Bridging assessment experiences and findings gathered from early childhood classrooms.

Each of the five task parameters can potentially influence a child's performance. Recognizing this allows us to see the effect that each particular parameter, and teacher adjustments of that parameter, can have on a child's performance. Each source of influence is only a possibility; it may or may not be relevant in the analysis of any given child's performance. In order to appreciate the significance of each task parameter, each one is described separately. In practice, they are integrally related and affect children's performance to varying degrees.

TASK GOALS

Each Bridging task has a goal that the teacher expects a child to accomplish when engaging in the activity. In early childhood classrooms, the emphasis is often on creating rich learning environments with a variety of materials for children to explore. This is necessary and desirable. In addition, research now indicates the importance of intentional teaching for children's learning. Intentional teaching refers to the teacher's recognition of goals for engaging children in an activity. A teacher's goal could be to expose children to new materials, to give children a chance to experiment with various ways of using them, or to engage children in rich conversation. Effective teaching depends upon a purposeful environment where materials and activity choice support teaching and guide children's efforts to discover, experiment, learn, and grow.

A critical role for teachers in relation to children's learning on a daily basis is to communicate the goal for each activity in ways that children understand. In order for children to work with school materials to reach activity goals, the teacher has to be mindful of articulating them throughout the school day in clear and explicit ways.

Hearing goal statements reinforces the efforts of children who are developing strategies to complete activities and encourages children who are developing qualities such as attentiveness and persistence in the face of challenges. The child's success in the activity depends in part on the teacher's clear communication of the activity's goal.

Each of the 15 Bridging activities starts with a clearly stated goal. For example, in the Reading a Book activity where the child chooses the book, the goal of the activity is for the child to demonstrate her knowledge of books and apply her reading skills to a familiar and favorite book. This goal is explained to the child and guides the teacher's observation, documentation, and analysis of the child's behavior.

To further support teachers' understanding of Bridging's activity goals, the activity procedures specify how the teacher explains the goal to the children. For example, in the Reading a Book activity it is very important that the teacher says clearly to the child, "Read me your favorite book" in the case where the child chooses the book, and "I have a new book that I want you to read to me" in the case where the teacher chooses the book. The child's behavior following this request is evidence of the child's current reading development. If the teacher asks the child, "Tell me about your book," the child is likely to do just that—talk about the book as opposed to reading it. While the possible settings and times of day for carrying out the Bridging activities are broad and flexible, the specific goal is delineated and precise within each Bridging activity.

Several factors may be at work if a child does not attempt to move toward a goal that the teacher has carefully explained. The child may not be ready for the experience. If so, the teacher might decide to create more opportunities for the child to experience the activity alongside others and explore its materials. Alternately, the child may not be interested in the activity at this time. Or, the child may be interested but may have other ideas about how to carry out the activity. For example, a child may want to build an airplane or a garage for a friend's car rather than build his or her own model car. In each case, the teacher gathers important information about the child, including level of readiness for a new concept or skill, personal interest or preference for a particular type of activity, or persistence in carrying out the activity to the end.

KEY CONCEPTS AND SKILLS

As described in Chapter 2, key concepts in Bridging assessment are defined as ideas or principles that are central to mastery in a subject area. Key skills refer to procedures or strategies that are essential to performance in the Bridging activity. The developmental progression of mastering key concepts and skills in each curriculum area is captured in the levels defined in Bridging's performance rubrics. By emphasizing key concepts and skills, Bridging focuses teacher attention on helping children develop and understand the fundamentals of knowledge in each subject area.

While the goal defines learning and behavioral objectives that guide a child's actions and strategies toward completion of an activity, key concepts and skills are embedded in the content of that activity. A child's performance on the activity is the lens we have for gaining insight into the nature of the child's current understanding and proficiency with the concepts and skills involved. Because key concepts and skills go beyond factual knowledge, a child's performance or response is not deemed "right" or "wrong"; rather, it is viewed in terms of the child's level of development in relation to these key concepts and skills.

For example, in the Counting activity, one of the Exploring Number Concepts activities in the Bridging assessment, a three-year-old diligently counts a set of seven small objects saying: one, two, three, five, eight, nine, ten. When asked to count again, the child points to each object carefully while reciting the same number sequence. In this example, the teacher observes that the child has not yet mastered the conventional labels for the number sequence from one to seven but does understand one-to-one correspondence as indicated by giving each object one, and only one, number label. The teacher notes that this child will benefit from songs, poems, and counting opportunities that provide practice with the sequence of number labels.

Of critical importance in supporting children's mastery and continued development of key concepts and skills is teachers' deep understanding of these concepts and skills—what they are in different curricular areas, what their development looks like at varying ages, and how they connect and influence one another. Only by mastering these key concepts and skills can a teacher consistently differentiate the fundamental from the peripheral when observing children in assessment as well as in teaching. When teachers recognize the developmental trajectory of each key concept and skill, they see what children are currently learning and what they are ready to learn. Through the identification of key concepts and skills, Bridging helps teachers further their understanding of children's development within each curriculum area. With this knowledge, teachers' use of assessment findings becomes more effective as they are better equipped to support the development of key concepts and skills in their students.

MATERIALS

Young minds often rely on concrete objects for mental operations. Although they do not automatically lead to meaningful learning, materials that are carefully selected for learning activities invite children's questions, stimulate their curiosity, facilitate discoveries, promote communication, and encourage the use of imagination. Several criteria were used to select materials for the Bridging assessment activities. All materials are engaging and meaningful to children, are economical and accessible, and, in most cases, are familiar to children. Each criterion is briefly described below.

Engaging and Meaningful to Children

The materials used in Bridging were chosen because of their appeal to children and their potential for creating optimal conditions for children to display their thinking. For example, Bridging takes advantage of children's fascination with games and miniature figures to assess understanding of number concepts. A child plays with toy bears and pretend cookies in a series of game-like scenarios while the teacher assesses an array of mathematical skills: one-to-one correspondence, counting, estimation, and mental representation of numbers and math operations. In another example, Bridging's science activities use materials that children love to work with, including recycled materials to construct a model car, making shadows with a flashlight, and creating a nature display using found objects, such as shells, leaves, rocks, pebbles, and seeds. Children are easily attracted to these materials because they are inviting and stimulating. The appeal of materials is a prerequisite for assessment with young children. Only when children are actively engaged with materials can assessment provide an accurate reading of their skills and abilities.

Familiar to Children

Because prior experience with materials directly affects a child's performance on tasks, Bridging emphasizes using familiar classroom materials. Paper, pencils, crayons, picture books, pattern blocks, musical instruments, audiotapes, and other items easily obtained from a home, school, or the natural environment are the types of familiar materials used to elicit a child's optimal participation. Thus the materials themselves contribute to the authenticity of the Bridging assessment process in a school setting.

Economical and Accessible

Bridging also takes into consideration the realities of school budgets and teacher preparation time. All materials are commonly available in classrooms, are recyclables, or are easily and inexpensively obtained. To be economical, Bridging also uses the same materials for a number of activities. For example, pattern blocks are used in three activities to assess different aspects of spatial relationship in the areas of visual arts and mathematics. Plastic counting bears and button-like counting chips are used in all four Exploring Number Concepts activities.

Effect of Materials on Performance

Materials affect children's task performance in a number of ways. Children's work is influenced by their familiarity with the material, its novelty, the type of end products the material yields, the symbol systems associated with the material, the thinking skills inherent in the use of the material, and the fine or gross motor skills involved. Table 5.1 illustrates how materials in Bridging activities can have differing effects on children's performance.

As shown in Table 5.1, children evidence different rubric scores for drawing a self-portrait and making a pattern block picture. Although both tasks represent the same subject area, visual arts, and the goal for both is creating a representational picture, the tasks involve the use of very different art media. The self-portrait is drawn with paper and pencil. To create a pattern block picture, such as a person or a house, children use pattern blocks. Looking at each child's scores on the two tasks, materials appear to

Table 5.1   Variability in Visual Arts Task Scores by Materials

		Visual Arts	
Child	*Age*	*Self-Portrait*	*Pattern Block Pictures*
Sara	4.0	4	2
Darren	4.4	5	2
Melanie	4.8	6	4
Oscar	5.2	3	8
Ashley	5.4	4	2
Michael	5.5	3	4

play a noticeable role in performance. For Darren and Oscar, the difference in scores is particularly striking.

When looking for the possible effects of materials on a child's performance, teachers can observe the extent to which the child's performance is hindered by difficulties encountered using the material. They can also determine whether a child might benefit from additional opportunities to explore the material, become more familiar with it, and perhaps become more skilled in its use. Looking at how children's performance is affected by materials may suggest additional resources the teacher can introduce to support the child's development of key concepts and skills.

STRUCTURE OF TASKS

How a task is structured can affect a child's performance and thus the results of assessment. Some children are more apt to work well in a tightly structured task while others feel more comfortable with those that are open-ended, allowing for more choice and self-expression. Also, children's preference for a particular type of structure may reflect classroom practices. If a classroom is full of opportunities to explore and create, children may enjoy and do well in open-ended activities. On the other hand, if the dominant mode of the curriculum is teacher-directed lessons, children may be more comfortable with tasks that have a clear path to follow.

Continuum of the Bridging Task Structure

Bridging uses both types of tasks: those that are structured and those that are more open-ended. When familiar with Bridging tasks, teachers will find that the 15 tasks are not simply one or the other. Rather, they reflect a continuum of open-endedness where, from time to time, teachers will be more directive (see Figure 5.1). For example, when dramatizing a story, there are clear parameters that children need to follow to make the activity safe and productive. Inside those parameters, there is a great deal of room for children's improvisations with movement.

On the left side of the continuum illustrated in Figure 5.1 are structured tasks; they are teacher-directed with clearly defined procedures and goals. In the Bridging assessment, tasks in language arts and mathematics tend to be more concentrated along this side of the continuum. In these tasks, the teacher leads the activity and the child follows instructions. An answer is required in each step; flexibility in using materials or altering the task objective is minimal.

Tasks on the right side of the continuum are more open-ended. All five curricular areas in the Bridging assessment have one or more open-ended tasks, but they are most often found in the areas of visual arts, performing arts, and science. Like directed tasks, open-ended ones have a clearly defined goal. Unlike directed tasks, children have some choice in how they approach and complete the task. The teacher gives a brief introduction, and then the child decides how to use materials to reach the task goal. For example, in Building a Model Car, the goal is clear—using recycled materials to construct a car that rolls—but children have great flexibility in what kind of car they create with the materials at hand.

Effect of Task Structure on Performance

When studying Bridging assessment findings, teachers will want to examine children's performance in relation to the structure of the activity. As Figure 5.2 shows,

Figure 5.1   A Continuum of Bridging Task Structure

Reading a Book (Language Arts and Literacy)

Exploring Number Concepts (Mathematics)

Solving Pattern Block Puzzles (Mathematics)

Acting Out a Story (Language Arts and Literacy)

Creating Pattern Block Pinwheels (Mathematics)

Dictating a Story (Language Arts and Literacy)

Experimenting With Crayon Techniques (Visual Arts)

Making Pattern Block Pictures (Visual Arts)

Drawing a Self-Portrait (Visual Arts)

Exploring Shadows and Light (Science)

Assembling a Nature Display (Science)

Building a Model Car (Science)

Playing an Instrument (Performing Arts)

Moving to Music (Performing Arts)

Singing a Song (Performing Arts)

Structured   Open-Ended

structure can contribute to striking contrasts in a young child's performance. The scores presented in Figure 5.2 are those of a five-year-old boy on the three Bridging assessment activities that involve the use of pattern blocks. All of the activities were carried out in a small group setting. Note how the child's performance is influenced by the activity structure. When the activity is neither too structured nor too open-ended, the child performs at his highest level. The child is least successful when the activity is completely open-ended.

Like other task parameters, such as the goal of the activity and materials involved in carrying out the activity, activity structure in and of itself is not likely to provide the whole story in explaining a child's learning. However, it can suggest possibilities for teachers to consider when planning future learning and assessment experiences. Any factor that might affect children's learning and performance can help teachers respond to the diversity that characterizes young children's learning. When a factor can be altered or adjusted, the teacher has discovered another means of contributing to a child's developmental progress.

SOCIAL ARRANGEMENTS

Bridging allows a variety of social arrangements or groupings to be used during the assessment process. Teachers select the social conditions that are likely to contribute to a child's optimal performance and learning. Bridging focuses on three types of arrangements: large group, small group, and one-to-one interactions with a child. By attending to possible effects of these different social arrangements, Bridging acknowledges that thinking and learning are social processes. Decisions about social

Figure 5.2 Variability in Child's Performance by Task Structure

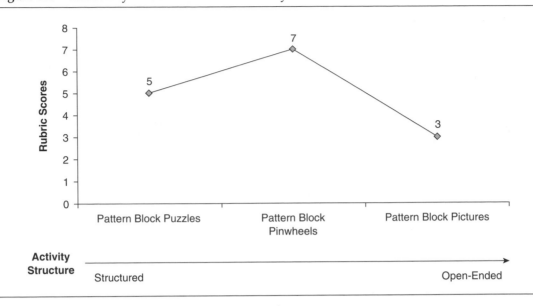

arrangements are an integral component of planning for learning in any activity system, including classrooms.

In early childhood classrooms, teachers shape the dynamics of how children learn. With their understanding of the assessment activities and the children, teachers are best qualified to determine the most appropriate social arrangements for a particular activity and the individual children in their classes. The Bridging assessment process helps teachers gather information about how a particular child learns from and with others in a given activity as well as how various social arrangements affect a child's performance.

When looking at the effects that social arrangements have on children's learning and performance, it can be helpful to compare scores across activities that offer a striking contrast. Table 5.2 presents such an example—a five-year-old boy's rubric scores on six assessment activities that used different social groupings. When this child's teacher looked at this configuration of scores, she immediately recognized that large group activities are not suitable for this child at this point in the school year. To do his best work, the child needs one-on-one attention from the teacher for now.

Every child needs to learn how to interact with other children in a group and to be a member of a learning community. Children develop these skills at different rates. For the child whose variability is documented in Table 5.2, the teacher believes that giving him the social supports he needs to participate in learning is as important as helping him learn to get along with peers in the larger group. Teachers recognize that they need to work gradually toward goals. In this case, the teacher prioritizes: she decides to support the child's learning in small group or one-on-one interactions while giving the child the option to observe or participate when a large group is carrying out music activities. She will continue to observe and look for opportunities for the child to successfully join in large group activities. Having clarified this child's need, she is confident that she can find opportunities for this child to progress in this area of learning.

Table 5.2 Variability in Child's Performance by Social Arrangement

Child: Harold Age: 5.1 Gender: M		
Activity	*Social Arrangement*	*Rubric Score*
Counting	One-on-one	7
Subtracting	One-on-one	3
Fair Share	One-on-one	2
Pattern Block Pinwheels	One-on-one	3
Pattern Block Pinwheels	Small group	1
Moving to Music	Small group	3
Moving to Music	Large group	0
Playing an Instrument	Large group	0

By emphasizing social arrangements, Bridging opens another way to view the dynamics of classroom teaching and learning. Bridging asks teachers to attend to the social dimension of learning when planning an activity. Bridging encourages teachers to experiment with varied social arrangements to identify the conditions that best meet the needs of individual children in the classroom.

SUMMARY

In summary, task goals, key concepts and skills, materials, task structure, and social arrangements are features of Bridging tasks that can influence the outcomes of assessment and teaching processes. By focusing on activity as the unit of analysis in assessment, the Bridging assessment process brings these situational factors to teachers' attention. This makes it possible for teachers to specify and plan features of teaching and learning processes that go beyond exclusive attention to the ability of individual children. Teachers have a way to systematically study, control, and vary classroom dynamics that can make a difference in learning. It is in this sense that Bridging assessment is a teaching and intervention process. Teachers assess children at the same time they seek ways to support their learning and development. Bridging illuminates how each child's learning is affected by multiple factors. It also looks at how each child's learning is affected by the teacher, attending to interactions of the child in relation to the various dimensions of the teacher's role. It is this last variable in the assessment process, the teacher's role, that we turn to in the next chapter.

Teacher Roles in Bridging Assessment

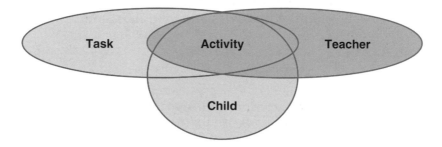

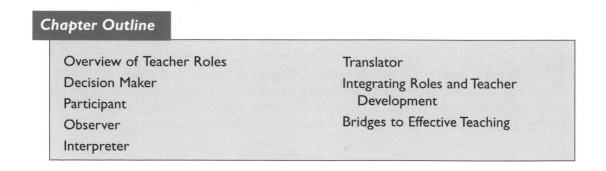

The roles that a teacher plays in Bridging assessment differ from what is required of a teacher in more traditional forms of assessment. Specific teacher roles in Bridging include decision maker, participant, observer, interpreter, and translator. In this chapter, we discuss these roles to illustrate how teachers carry out Bridging activities in the course of daily classroom teaching. Our goal is to highlight the unique and specific responsibilities of teachers as they strive toward the goal of effective teaching through careful assessment of children's learning. In this process, we also engage teachers in analyzing and reflecting on their own practice, helping them locate areas of strength in their work as well as areas where they will want to marshal help and resources while working with colleagues to better understand and support children's learning needs.

OVERVIEW OF TEACHER ROLES

In Chapters 2 and 3, we focused on the child in the Bridging assessment process: the child's content knowledge and working approaches. In Chapter 4, we presented a new conceptual framework for thinking about classroom assessment that we derived from activity theory. Adopting this framework, *Bridging: Assessment for Learning and Teaching in Early Childhood Classrooms, PreK–3* invites teachers to look closely at what the child brings to the learning situation, what an assessment task entails and requires of the child, and what the teacher contributes to the assessment process. Chapter 5 provided an up-close view of the components of each task and how they influence children's assessment performance. Completing the conceptual model based on activity as the unit of analysis, we now consider the teacher's role in assessment, teaching, and learning.

In traditional assessment, teachers follow instructions to assess children, compute their scores, and then read a test guide's interpretation of what scores mean. Settings and procedures are standardized. There is little flexibility in carrying out assessment protocols. Many assessment instruments have a specific function. There is a right and a wrong way to use it. For teachers, Bridging is a very different sort of tool and process. It is not a scripted assessment instrument. There are many right ways to use Bridging. It is flexible to enable teachers to gather the information they need about children in order to plan for the children's learning in the coming days and weeks.

In Bridging assessments, teachers play an active role in making decisions about how to use Bridging that draws on their experience and requires their expertise. They participate in setting the stage for assessment activities, embedding them in the curriculum, and integrating them with daily activities. Teachers understand what Bridging assesses and what scores mean. They observe children's performance on tasks and interpret the meaning of assessment findings. Moving seamlessly from assessment to curriculum, they translate assessment results into plans for future curricular activities, instruction, and ongoing observation.

In Chapter 4, we described what teachers do before, during, and after the assessment (see Table 4.1). In this chapter, we provide more detailed description of the varying roles that a teacher plays in the Bridging assessment process and how these roles can be further extended to curriculum and teaching practice (see Table 6.1). For the sake of clarity, we describe teacher roles in a sequential order—what teachers do

Table 6.1 Overview of Teacher Roles in the Bridging Assessment Process

Teacher Roles	Bridging Assessment	Follow-up Curriculum Planning
Decision Maker: How do I want to use Bridging?	• Determine scope of assessment, including how many children to assess and which activities to use. • Locate assessment in daily routine, considering when and where to make activities available. • Set expected performance levels for children.	• Make decisions about specific ongoing curriculum to be implemented. • Examine curriculum activities in relation to individual profiles to create an integrated learning environment for this class of children.
Participant: What do I do to facilitate Bridging?	• Review understanding of key concepts and skills in the various activities and their developmental progression. • Organize materials for assessment activities. • Select methods for assessment activities that make implementation seamless with daily curriculum.	• Support children's participation in activities through coaching and guiding.
Observer: What are children doing? What concepts, skills, and approaches are they learning and developing?	• Score children's performance on assessment activities. • Indicate each child's response to specific components of activities (for example, materials, grouping). • Record children's working approaches to activities.	• Note additional aspects of children's engagement in activities that are striking or may be relevant to planning curriculum. • Reinterpret assessment results based on further observation. • Adjust curricular plans to children's needs and preferences given ongoing observations.
Interpreter: What do results mean?	• Detect patterns and relationships as well as strengths and areas in need of further experience in individual profiles. • Locate zones of proximal development in different content areas.	• Continue to study children's engagement with Bridging activities that are an ongoing part of the curriculum. • Monitor children's learning and performance through daily classroom activities in relation to their profiles.
Translator: How do I use results to further children's learning and development?	• Use results to inform setting curriculum goals, selecting materials, and designing learning activities. • Identify points of entry for individual children in particular areas of the curriculum.	• Use children's engagement with curriculum activities to inform further planning for the group.

before, during, and after the Bridging assessment. In reality, teacher roles are fluid—they vary as a function of the assessment activity and in response to individual children. Often a teacher is carrying out several roles simultaneously in any phase of the Bridging assessment process. The purpose of describing these roles is not to prescribe or limit what teachers do. Rather, our goal is to highlight what is unique and unusual about the roles of teachers in the Bridging assessment process.

DECISION MAKER

Teachers are decision makers in the Bridging assessment process. This role is particularly apparent before conducting the Bridging assessment. During the preparation phase, the teacher makes decisions about the scope of assessment, including how many children to assess, who to focus on for detailed documentation, and which activities to use. The teacher also makes decisions about how to embed the assessment in the daily routine, considering when and where activities will be available. Additionally, the teacher needs to identify the expected level of performance for each child. In making decisions, the teacher draws on knowledge of individual children in the classroom as well as level of children's participation in related curriculum activities. The teacher also considers curricular goals in terms of subject areas and activities to assess.

Decision-making responsibility is both exciting and challenging for teachers. The excitement comes from being trusted and valued as a professional. The challenges come from concerns of being held accountable for decisions. Unlike many traditional assessments that tell teachers what to do and how to do it, Bridging believes that teachers know what is best for their classroom and their children. Bridging invites teachers to fully utilize their experience and expertise in the decision-making process. Bridging encourages teachers to study the learning goals and activity rubrics to make decisions conducive to learning and realistic for implementation.

As the leader of the classroom group, teachers are used to decision making. In any typical school day, teachers are making many decisions in the moment as to whether to extend an activity for a longer time frame, reschedule an activity for a later day, discontinue an activity that is not working, or change the order of activities to fit with how the day is going. From Bridging's perspective, such flexibility or "reading" the children is the cornerstone of teacher involvement in authentic assessment. Bridging asks teachers to draw on the same decision-making skills they use in classroom teaching when they make decisions about the assessment process.

Being flexible in using Bridging's assessment processes is not equivalent to having loose standards. Chapter 7 will clearly outline the appropriate assessment practices and the "bottom line" procedures teachers need to consider when making decisions. Bridging gives teachers authority and trusts them to follow best practice principles to guide their thinking and behavior. Bridging also assures teachers that they are not stuck with the decisions they make. As with many aspects of daily activity in the classroom, if something is not working, the teacher makes another decision. Tracking these decisions helps uncover the steps that make teaching and learning more effective.

PARTICIPANT

As with the role of decision maker, the teacher's role as active participant in the Bridging assessment process begins before the assessment starts. One form of teacher participation is preparing materials for Bridging activities. For example, three science activities require special sets of materials. For the Shadows and Lights activity, the teacher needs to purchase several flashlights if the classroom does not have them. In addition, the activity requires opaque, transparent, and translucent materials. In the case of the Nature Display activity, the teacher is encouraged to take children for a nature walk and collect a variety of natural objects for the activity. To engage children in the Building a Model Car activity, the teacher needs to amass recycled materials for construction.

Another form of teacher participation before conducting Bridging assessment is becoming familiar with key concepts and skills in each of the five subject areas and advancing their understanding of how these key concepts and skills develop. As a teacher's understanding of these developmental progressions grows, the teacher will feel more confident in making decisions to set expected performance levels for the children. As well, the teacher's readiness to assume other roles in the Bridging assessment process (that is, decision maker, observer, interpreter, and translator) increases.

During the Bridging assessment, the teacher's role as a participant expands. As a participant, the first and the foremost task for the teacher in this phase is to introduce the assessment activity to children. How will I explain the goal of the activity to children? How will I describe the activity procedures to children? How will I demonstrate particular concepts or techniques? These and many other "how to" questions demand teachers' action, action that engages children in the activity and action that is based on thoughtful decision making.

Consider the events in a kindergarten classroom as described below. Ms. Williams is working with two children in Bridging's Dictating a Story activity.

Ms. Williams starts her kindergarten day by asking children to choose an activity from the many available in the classroom. While children engage in activities, Ms. Williams first moves around the room to observe the children's choices. Then she sits at the drawing-writing table and invites children who are ready to dictate a story to her that she will write down for them. Today Marcus and Anthony are first at the table. Marcus dictates the following story as Anthony listens intently.

"Once upon a time a little girl, she ride on the pony. Then she flew with the eagles. And she went home and got dressed for school. Then she ride on a helicopter and ride on a ghost."

When he's done, Ms. Williams says, "Marcus, great story! I think the group will really like the idea of flying with the eagles when we act this out at group time." Ms. Williams then asks Anthony if he wants to tell a story and he responds eagerly with "Yes!" This time, Marcus listens.

In this scenario, Ms. Williams is a participant in recording the children's story and in offering comments about its dramatization. The teacher, not an outside testing specialist, administers Bridging assessment. Both its integration and its administration involve the teacher as an active participant. Further, as seen in Ms. Williams' room, Bridging is embedded in the curriculum and becomes an integral feature of the classroom context. This sets it apart from traditional assessments that remove the child from the flow of daily activity.

OBSERVER

As observer, the teacher watches and captures what children do when engaged in the Bridging assessment activities. Guided by the key concepts and skills for children in a curricular area, the teacher observes children's interaction with materials and performance on each activity. Based on these observations, the teacher scores each child's performance, notes the child's reaction to task components such as social grouping, and records the child's working approaches. The teacher may note additional information such as comments the child makes or unexpected uses of materials.

The teacher's role as observer prepares that teacher to link assessment to curriculum. When a teacher is given a set of assessment scores, having had no input in decisions related to the assessment and no recognized role in children's participation in assessment tasks, it is difficult for the teacher to make use of the results in relation to daily activities in the classroom. In the Bridging assessment process, teachers observe, record, and score children's participation in assessment activities. Teachers' understanding of key concepts and skills as well as various working approaches leads them to see children's activity in greater detail, understanding it in terms of a developmental progression and scoring it with greater confidence. Through this process, the teacher gains a deep understanding and appreciation of the performance of individual children as well as the group as a whole.

In addition to observing children, the teacher also observes the progress of the assessment process and curriculum implementation. The teacher notes what is working well in terms of logistics with this particular class of children and what needs to be changed or adjusted. Location of assessment activities, grouping children, and the setup for materials are among the implementation decisions the teacher may want to modify.

Observation skills are one of the most critical characteristics of an effective teacher. An effective teacher sees everything and knows what is going on at all times in the classroom. Bridging holds that being a good observer—gathering information about children as individuals and as a group—is not a role that is reserved for moments of assessment per se. What a teacher learns about a child from the way the child walks into the room and engages with peers is as important as noticing how the child picks up a pattern block piece during the Bridging assessment. Likewise, what a teacher learns about the children from last week's potluck supper with families is also critical to the kinds of insights the teacher will bring to bear on the analysis of Bridging assessment results. Bridging assessments depend on teachers gathering information at all times and being able to keep it in mind when interpreting a child's performance.

INTERPRETER

As interpreters, teachers make sense of the various kinds of information they gather. In the Bridging assessment process, teachers review each child's profiles of performance scores and working approaches. They look for patterns and relationships as well as identify each child's strengths and areas of inexperience or weakness. In Bridging, the child's activity is understood in a context that considers characteristics of the task and qualities of the teacher as well as the status of the child. Teachers consider how different dimensions of the assessment activity interact, rather than attribute a child's performance to the effects of a single dimension.

Cultural psychologists Michel Cole and Sylvia Scribner (1974) once urged the field to see assessment data as possibilities. By possibilities, they meant that assessment information can and should be regarded as "hypothesis generators," interpreted from a number of points of view and used "as an opportunity to reexamine what good performance entails" (p. 198). Bridging asks teachers to look at assessment results in terms of not only what a child does or does not know but also what the child's performance *means*. The meaning they hold and the story that they tell come from looking at the findings from various points of view given knowledge of individual children, the chemistry of how children learn together in this particular class, and the possible influences of task structure, materials, social arrangements, and the content area on a child's performance. Instead of attributing children's performance effects to a single dimension, Bridging invites teachers to constantly consider how different dimensions of the assessment process interact. In the Playing an Instrument activity, for example, a child's uninspired playing of an instrument could reflect the child's lack of interest in the instrument or inexperience with it. A child's reluctance in joining the Moving to Music activity could result from the child feeling shy or inhibited in a group setting rather than the child disliking the activity.

The meaning of Bridging assessment results cannot be laid out and described in this book. Results are particular to individual children. Their meaning is relative to a specific educational context and is influenced by a child's family background. When interpreting the assessment results, teachers will benefit enormously if they can work with colleagues, a topic we address later in this chapter. Interpreting data takes patience and willingness to consider various possible explanations.

TRANSLATOR

The teacher often assumes the role of translator after the assessment activities have been carried out. In the Bridging assessment process, being a translator involves interpreting the results and putting them into terms that guide curriculum plans for short- and longer-term goals. The translation begins when teachers are encouraged to ask themselves questions, such as what are the priorities for learning and teaching among the many assessment findings? What will I focus on tomorrow and in the upcoming weeks? How can I align instructional methods with what I learned from the assessment process?

Translating assessment results into planning for activities and instruction also includes identifying starting points for individual children and the group as a whole. In the following reflection by Ms. Goldsmith, a preschool teacher, she recounts her uncertainty about how to launch the story dictation activity and her need to find a moment that was ripe for opening it up to the children as a new way of learning and self-expression.

> The story dictation was new to me. I did not know how I was going to implement this. From group time, I knew they enjoyed listening to stories. I decided to build on that interest. I didn't want to assign children to telling a story. How could I get them excited? I thought about inviting children to tell stories about pictures they drew.
>
> The next day I just said to a group of children, "I'm looking for some people who want to dictate a story." The children sat there and nobody wanted to do it. So a little later, I approached one child who hadn't made a choice yet of what to do during playtime. At group time earlier that day, I had read a book to the children called *It's Ok*. I had that book with me and we were looking at it. I asked this child to tell me his own story about what it is okay to do. He thought of all kinds of things like, "It's okay to run. It's okay to build with blocks!" Now I was excited. He did it! He dictated a story. When we came back together as a group, I read his story and we acted it out. Then other children said things like, "I didn't get to do my story! I want to do one!" So now the fire is lit. They all want to tell stories!

Ms. Goldsmith sees that her initial stories are mostly one and two sentences long and they mimic each other. She recognizes that this is a starting point for these children as they help each other learn to be a community of story tellers. The dictated stories also provide Ms. Goldsmith solid evidence of what she can do to enhance the children's language and literacy skills, including plans for organizing the school day to extend opportunities for children to practice emerging narrative skills. Most important, it is through this starting point that Ms. Goldsmith turns the story dictation into an ongoing activity for all children.

As translators, teachers further look for points of entry for the child to reach new goals. For example, how might the child use a strength to enter an area where improvement is needed? How can a child's interests become an entry point for a curriculum area the child has little experience in? Teachers can also involve the child in the translation process. A teacher may want to ask the child which of the assessment tasks the child thought were easier and which were harder. The teacher might engage the child in a conversation about the child's strengths, areas where the child has difficulty, and what the child's interests at school are. Information the child provides may help the teacher better understand the assessment results and may give the teacher new insights about how to translate them into learning experiences.

INTEGRATING ROLES AND TEACHER DEVELOPMENT

Being mindful of these five roles in the Bridging assessment process is not a trivial task for any teacher. It is a developmental process. Most of the professional literature acknowledges that teacher development takes time: experience is the best teacher after the initial preparation course work and student teaching. However, the teaching profession has now also come to recognize that experience alone does not develop more effective practice. Teachers also need to reflect on and think about their teaching practice. Teachers need to interact with other professionals who can challenge their thinking, provide new and interesting ways to view problems, and suggest ways to modify or change their methods given new insights from research.

Thus the teaching profession has become proactive in recognizing that ongoing professional development is a critical and necessary component in the life of professional teachers to support and strengthen their work.

Bridging has been designed with the professional development needs of teachers in mind. The ideas presented in this book can certainly be read and used by individual educators, but the benefits of what it has to offer the individual multiply when used in the context of teachers working together on a regular basis over part or all of the school year. Working with colleagues using the ideas presented in *Bridging* broadens and deepens discussions about children's learning and the process of teaching. Teachers report that their own practices and ideas change as a result of the interaction with those they stand to learn the most from: their peers. Like children when they are uncovering new challenges and concepts, teachers also need time when they can try out ideas, discuss their initial efforts with others, practice skills, prepare for new areas of learning, and get plenty of advice, modeling, and coaching from other teachers. Colleagues can often become one of teachers' greatest sources of support and guidance in growing in the various roles.

Given the importance of the multidimensional roles for teachers in Bridging assessments, we have designed professional development opportunities to help both preservice as well as currently practicing teachers to deepen their thinking and practice regarding these roles. For the past six years, we have been working with early childhood teachers in yearlong, inservice teacher professional development programs studying and implementing Bridging assessment and curriculum activities. The Facilitator's Guide at the end of the book introduces several professional development formats for using Bridging as an integral part of teacher professional development, both preservice and inservice.

BRIDGES TO EFFECTIVE TEACHING

When we began to teach, we wanted to be proficient and skilled in our daily work. We participated in student teaching and watched more-expert teachers carry out lessons. In our early years of teaching, we often found ourselves feeling frustrated at not being able to put into practice the many details in our minds. Too often these details felt like a jumble of educational goals, images of effective practice, advice from colleagues about managing immediate situations with children, and what our own experiences suggested we try. We often had difficulty articulating what was not working and why. We were not always sure what would help to close the gap between our less-skilled attempts to teach and the work of experienced teachers who made teaching look almost easy. We know that such feelings are common among beginning teachers.

One of the reasons why we developed Bridging is to make visible what effective teaching looks like with young children day by day in classrooms. We hope that by simulating the work of skilled teaching in each subject area, we will help novice teachers find a recognizable path for moving toward the proficiency they long for, and we will help more-experienced teachers to fine-tune, reflect on, and articulate what makes their work effective and what they are working to develop further.

We began with the knowledge that in the mind of a skilled teacher, assessment, teaching, and learning are happening in synchrony with what is unfolding in front of them. Effective teaching happens when children engage with content knowledge through methods of teaching that provide a good fit with the needs of the students in the moment. When in the presence of a skilled teacher, an observer is struck by how much the teacher can see and respond to in an instant: having an engaging way to gather up children's attention for the task at hand, knowing when to rearrange materials to facilitate children's efforts, asking a question of a child or group to further their thinking, and being able to talk with an observer about what multiple children are doing. Skilled teachers know what is going on all around them; they see a purpose in it all!

As Lee Schulman first described in 1986 and the National Academy of Education reiterated in its 2005 report, written by Linda Darling-Hammond and Joan Baratz-Snowden and titled *A Good Teacher in Every Classroom: Preparing the Highly Qualified Teachers Our Children Deserve*, effective teaching builds on three interacting bases of knowledge: (1) knowledge of the content area being taught, (2) knowledge of students and their thinking and learning as a group and individually, and (3) a repertoire of teaching methods appropriate for the subject matter and the needs of students. Each of these areas of knowledge embodies rich and complex thinking and skills, which teachers may spend a lifetime developing. Bridging operationalizes and integrates the three areas of effective teaching in the carrying out of assessment activities for teaching and learning. The activities in this book exemplify the thinking of skilled teachers as they consider the multiple domains of knowledge that effective teaching draws from.

We chose the name *Bridging* for this assessment instrument because it is an action word that describes a dynamic process and a series of actions aimed at building bridges. There are many critical elements that need linking to achieve success in educating young children. Our work with early childhood teachers aims to build bridges

- Between children's curiosity, interests, and the intellectual demands of the school;
- Between what children learn and how they learn;
- Between a child's current developmental progress and his or her future developmental paths within and among curricular areas;
- Between child development knowledge and key concepts in school subject areas; and
- Between the assessment of children and curriculum development and implementation.

Building these bridges is challenging; it requires teamwork and commitment. Teachers are at the center of the process. It is the teacher who has the responsibility to coordinate various assessment components: conduct the activities skillfully, and link the assessment results to curriculum planning and instructional practice. Bridging can be a valuable resource for teachers, a tool they can use in the classroom every day to support their teaching becoming more effective. Bridging has as its goal helping teachers recognize and meet the needs of all children and helping children develop their full potential in the integrated and reciprocal processes of assessment and teaching embodied in Bridging activities.

SECTION II

Implementation of Assessment Activities

Gillian Dowley McNamee and Jie-Qi Chen, with
Ann Masur, Jennifer McCray, and Luisiana Melendez

7

Implementing Bridging

Bridging is a flexible assessment instrument tool and process to be used by classroom teachers in the context of their ongoing teaching. It requires teachers to make decisions that may well change at each point of the implementation process during the school year. Although sharing many implementation features with other classroom-based assessment instruments, Bridging also presents unique logistical requirements. Understanding these logistics and the rationale behind them is a prerequisite for effective implementation of Bridging. This chapter discusses teacher implementation decisions that ensure Bridging's usefulness in the context of their particular classrooms.

IMPLEMENTING BRIDGING IN THE CLASSROOM CONTEXT

The context for implementing Bridging assessments is the classroom. Classrooms vary by the needs of students, the teacher-student ratio, teachers' instructional space, schedule, materials, and preferences regarding teaching with small groups or the whole class. Bridging is designed to accept the opportunities and constraints of diverse classroom contexts while at the same time calling for rigor and accuracy in the assessment process.

Given diverse classroom situations, Bridging provides guidelines to help teachers implement the assessment process efficiently and effectively. It also encourages teachers to make choices to best serve their particular needs, including the time of the year to start and repeat the assessment process, the number of children to focus on for detailed observation, whether a particular activity ought to be implemented in large, small, or dyadic situations, and which areas and activities to choose for assessment if time is an issue. The flexibility that Bridging permits invites the teacher to be a partner and decision maker in the implementation process rather than a mechanical user.

Bridging does not impose a standardized, one-size-fits-all implementation procedure for teachers. Instead, it requires teachers to carefully study the activity protocols and rubrics to gain a deeper understanding of the development of key concepts and skills in relation to children's performance levels. Bridging values teacher expertise and experience in setting expected performance levels for their students and in guiding them to accept challenges beyond their current level of development. Bridging's goal is improved student learning and teacher practice; reflecting on assessment results and planning curriculum is an integral part of the assessment process.

BECOMING FAMILIAR WITH ACTIVITY PROTOCOLS

The activity protocols provide a detailed description of each of the 15 Bridging assessment activities. In preparing to implement Bridging, teachers first review all 15 activities to determine how many are already a part of their classroom routine. Teachers will find that many of the activities are familiar, but some may be new. Those activities that are new warrant closer review so that the teacher can decide how to incorporate them into the classroom (see Table 7.1).

The Bridging activities are grouped into five subject areas addressed in most school curricula: language arts and literacy, visual arts, mathematics, sciences, and performing arts. We introduce each subject area with three questions: What do we know about development in this area? What does Bridging provide? Why are these three activities selected? Rather than providing a comprehensive view of the subject area and rationale for each of the Bridging assessment activities, we highlight basic pedagogical principles essential to the development of children's knowledge, skills, and abilities in that area.

Table 7.1   Becoming Familiar With Bridging Assessment Activities

1. **R**eview the 15 Bridging activities to determine how many are already part of your regular classroom activities.

2. **L**ist all of the Bridging activities that are not part of your curricular repertoire and think about how to incorporate them.

In the area of language arts and literacy, for example, research tells us that young children learn to speak, listen, read, and write by actively participating in conversational and book-related activities with adults and peers. Three basic principles guide the process of early literacy development: it begins early; it relies on symbols; and it builds on an awareness of language sounds. We include three activities in this area: children reading books, dictating stories, and acting out their stories. These activities provide dynamic and compelling contexts for teachers to observe young children's evolving concepts of narrative, print conventions, and the communicative power of written language.

Following the introduction to the subject area is a table of the national learning standards for the curricular area and the specific Bridging activities that relate to them. Viewing the table, teachers clearly see the content standards and key concepts that children work on when engaging in particular Bridging activities. For each standard and its key concepts, we provide a brief definition and then refer to them when we describe each Bridging activity. Each activity protocol includes five types of information: activity reference, activity description, list of needed materials, step-by-step implementation procedures, and curriculum extensions.

Activity Reference

In a box at the top of the first page of every protocol, the activity reference identifies the primary subject area(s) reflected in the activity, key concepts and skills to be assessed in that subject area, and recommended social arrangements for conducting the activity in the classroom (see Figure 7.1).

If more than one subject area is listed, the first one is the primary subject area. For example, for Creating Pattern Block Pinwheels, mathematics is the primary subject area with visual arts as the secondary subject area.

Key concepts and skills are listed to help teachers focus on what will be assessed during the activity. Each key concept for the various activities is defined in detail in the introduction to each curriculum area. The key concepts addressed in Creating Pattern Block Pinwheels, for example, include children's understanding of matching shapes and sizes, creating patterns, and constructing radial symmetry.

Social arrangements for the various activities include large group, small group, child-child, or teacher-child interactions. Depending on factors such as the quantity of materials needed or characteristics of the activity, the protocol lists some groupings as "recommended" options and others as "viable" options.

Activity and Goal

Usually one sentence, this description provides an overall picture of the nature of the activity along with its specific goal. For example, the activity description for

Figure 7.1   The First Page of an Activity Protocol

Creating Pattern Block Pinwheels		Procedure

Subject Areas
  Mathematics
  Visual arts

Social Arrangements
  Recommended: small group
  Viable: individual, large group

Key Concepts and Skills
  Matching shape and size
  Creating pattern
  Constructing symmetry/radial symmetry

Activity and Goal

Children view and discuss examples of "pattern block pinwheels" showing radial symmetry; participate in construction of a pattern block pinwheel with teacher guidance; and then produce their own pattern block pinwheels.

Materials

Examples of radial symmetry

Ample supply of pattern blocks

Camera (optional)

Large flat surface to work on

Large (11" × 17") sheets of black construction paper—one for each child (blocks look best on black paper)

If introducing this with a large group, use the following for demonstration:

Overhead projector

Pattern block transparencies (blocks will work, but color will be lost)

Playing an Instrument says, "A group of children explore rhythm instruments and create a musical accompaniment to recorded music." The activity description offers the teacher a quick view of what the activity entails and helps her link the activity to events and ideas that are part of the children's current classroom life. For example, when reading the description of the Pattern Block Puzzles activity, a teacher might think, "Working with puzzles is a frequent activity of children during choice time in my classroom, so this activity will not be hard for most of my children, and it may provide them with an interesting challenge."

Materials

The list of materials itemizes exactly what teachers need to conduct the activity. Bridging uses three types of materials: (1) materials commonly available in the classroom, (2) materials that can be easily and inexpensively obtained, and (3) recycled materials (see Table 7.2). Materials commonly available in the classroom include crayons, paper, picture books, and math manipulatives. Given that these materials can be found in almost all early childhood classrooms, they take little time to gather and prepare. In contrast, recycled materials such as cardboard containers and jar lids, as well as objects from the natural environment such as pine cones and shells, take time to collect and therefore require planning ahead. Inviting parents to assist in this effort over a period of weeks is an effective strategy. Materials that can be easily and inexpensively obtained include flashlights and some simple musical instruments.

Table 7.2   Three Types of Materials for Bridging Activities

Bridging Activity	Material Required to Conduct the Activity
Activities Using Materials Commonly Available in the Classroom	
1. Reading a Book	Children's picture books, familiar and new to the children
2. Dictating a Story	Paper and pencil
3. Acting Out a Story	
4. Experimenting With Crayon Techniques	Paper and crayons
5. Drawing a Self-Portrait	Paper and pencil
6. Making Pattern Block Pictures	Pattern blocks with a variety of colors and shapes; construction paper
7. Creating Pattern Block Pinwheels	Pattern blocks with a variety of colors and shapes; construction paper
8. Solving Pattern Block Puzzles	Pattern blocks with a variety of colors and shapes
9. Exploring Number Concepts	Mathematics manipulatives, such as small plastic bears and chips
10. Assembling a Nature Display	A paper or plastic bag; construction paper
11. Moving to Music	Tape or CD player; tapes or CDs of different kinds of music
12. Playing an Instrument	CD player; CDs of different kinds of music; music instruments (can be homemade)
13. Singing a Song	Something representing a microphone
Activity Using Material Easily and Inexpensively Obtained	
14. Exploring Shadows and Light	Flashlights; an overhead projector (optional); a bag with different materials for each child
Activity Using Recycled Materials	
15. Building a Model Car	A variety of recycled materials

Step-by-Step Implementation Procedures

Bridging procedures are brief descriptions of how to conduct the activity. They are not meant to be a script for activity implementation. Rather, they pinpoint the steps and prompts for carrying out the activity as an assessment, as opposed to teaching, opportunity. Teachers introduce Bridging activities by connecting them to the experiences and interests of children in their classroom.

There are several ways Bridging procedures support implementation of activities. First, immediately following the steps for carrying out the activity is a performance rubric to help the teacher keep in mind the developmental path for skills and concepts in that activity for children ages three to eight. It is followed by two recording sheets that teachers use to document their observations of what the child does during the task and his or her working approach.

Extensions to Curriculum

Each activity protocol concludes with a Bridge to Curriculum, which provides questions to guide the teacher's interpretation of children's performance levels and suggests ways to extend and further develop children's work in a particular area in relation to the key concepts and skills in the subject area. The goal is to support teachers' thinking about what they are learning when carrying out an activity and how to link assessment results to planning for the upcoming days and weeks.

PLANNING THE ASSESSMENT

Once a teacher is familiar with the protocols for each activity, it is important to consider the details involved in implementation in order to get the most out of the assessment process. Of particular importance to this planning process is to consider factors including how many children to assess, whom to focus on, when to assess, where to assess, and which activities to choose. Each of these factors is discussed below.

How Many Children to Assess

One of the practical advantages of Bridging is that many of the assessment activities can be conducted with more than one child at a time. Although not a requirement of the Bridging assessment process, we recommend that teachers carry out all of the Bridging activities or a majority of them with all the children in the classroom. Fifteen activities for 20 to 30 children? Is this possible? At first glance, our suggestion may not seem realistic. A closer look at the Bridging activities, however, shows how assessment of all children is possible and desirable.

As described earlier, most of the Bridging activities are familiar early childhood curricular activities, such as reading books, playing math games, dictating stories, moving to music, and drawing pictures, to name a few. These activities are carried out in almost all early childhood classrooms because children benefit from the varied and rich experiences they offer. Teachers provide time for such experiences because they motivate and engage children in school learning. For the Bridging assessment process, teachers carry out these activities as they always have, but in a more deliberate way so as to gain a deeper understanding of what and how individual children are learning.

This does not mean, however, that we ask a teacher to create detailed assessment records for every child in the class. This is an unrealistic expectation, especially if there is only one teacher in the classroom. For detailed, complete documentation, we recommend that teachers choose two to four children in their classroom at one point in time. For this small group, the teacher generates a learning profile for each child using a summary sheet and graph for expected outcomes for the child's grade level as described in Chapter 2. As second-grade student teacher Ms. Danner describes, focusing the detailed assessment and documentation on two to four children is manageable.

> I was overwhelmed when first introduced to the Bridging assessment process. After learning that I needed to focus on only two to four children for detailed documentation, I was both relieved and a bit skeptical. Two children? How could that tell me the story of other children in my class? I have 25, not just two! I was surprised by how much I learned from the detailed assessment of the two children—not only about these two children but also about my curriculum and teaching practices—what I am good at and what I have been consciously or unconsciously trying to avoid!

While carrying out a Bridging activity with all children, the teacher as an assessor purposefully watches the two to four preselected children in the context of the larger group. As a teacher focuses on particular children, he or she makes a mental note of what is happening with the other children that is interesting or warrants further attention and investigation. This makes assessment seamless with teaching, and it makes it possible to carry out performance assessments in the context of ongoing teaching and learning processes.

Whom to Focus on for Detailed Assessment

Which two, three, or four children are the best candidates for a teacher to focus on for the detailed documentation process? To answer this question, a teacher may ask, "Which children puzzle me the most right now? Which children am I particularly interested in learning more about? Which children would I like to focus on so that I can work more effectively with them?" In response to these questions, many teachers will identify children who raise concerns for either academic or social reasons. Bridging is designed to help teachers more succesfully reach these children by providing detailed information about what they know and how they learn. Teachers are then in a stronger position to plan learning experiences that match individual children's needs and strengths (see Table 7.3).

It is important to note that however challenging some children are, they are not the only ones of interest to teachers and therefore should not be the only focal group. Bridging can also be used to effectively assess children who are shy, quiet, and reserved, or children who show special interest and talent in a particular area.

Table 7.3   Selecting Children to Assess

1. **W**hich children puzzle me the most right now?

2. **W**hich children would I like to learn more about so I can work more effectively with them?

3. **W**hich children seem to have learning difficulties?

4. **W**hich children offer the opportunity for contrast?

5. **T**hink about how many children you would like to conduct all 15 Bridging activities with and keep detailed documentations.

In selecting children for detailed documentation, it is also important to consider the value of contrast—knowing how much can be gained from choosing children that are different from one another, different from our expectations, and different from the group. We recommend that teachers take into account gender and age differences as well as differences in working approaches. For example, a teacher may want to select a child with known strengths in one area, such as drawing and pretend writing, to compare to a child who is reluctant to take a writing tool into her hand. Such a contrast helps make the problem-solving processes and skills involved in mastering a subject area more visible to teachers and potentially more accessible to other children.

When to Assess

As a performance-based assessment, a unique feature of Bridging is its flexibility. It can be carried out at any point after children are settled into the routines of the school year and used as often as the teacher needs assessment data. For example, if teachers want to check on children's progress in learning to read, they can conduct the two Reading Books activities as often as every week or two, or they may use them at longer intervals.

To gain the full benefits of Bridging, teachers need to carry out the assessment process with the selected children at least twice and preferably three times during the school year. The first assessment occurs after six to eight weeks of school, the second in February, and the third in April or May, toward the end of the school year. This timing helps teachers systematically track the development of children's skills and knowledge over the year (see Table 7.4).

Table 7.4   Thinking About When to Assess

---

1. **A**ssessment of specific curricular areas can take place as frequently as the teacher needs data to inform the teaching and learning process.

2. **A**ssessment of selected children using all 15 Bridging activities is best done two or three times a year, in October, February, and May.

For both preservice and inservice teachers, identifying a child's areas of strength and challenge at the beginning of the school year gives teachers a basis to adjust classroom routines and plan the curriculum to fit the needs of individuals and the whole group. Assessment in the middle of the school year helps the teacher document and notice the nature and extent of a child's change during the school year. By compiling the learning profiles of selected children and comparing them to profiles from the beginning of the year, teachers can reflect on many aspects of the children's performance. For example, in which areas is a particular child making the most progress and why? To what extent does the child's progress reflect the content of the curriculum and instructional methods used? What information is most critical for supporting the child's further learning and development? What information might be given to parents? What information might be given to next year's teacher?

How to Assess

Table 7.5 presents suggested social arrangements for each of the Bridging activities. Many activities can be implemented in more than one way, depending on the kind of assessment data the teacher wants to collect and the space available in the classroom.

Table 7.5   Suggested Social Arrangements for Bridging Activities

Area	Activity	Social Arrangement
Language Arts and Literacy	Reading a Book Dictating a Story Acting Out a Story	One-on-one One-on-one Small or large group
Visual Arts	Experimenting With Crayons Drawing a Self-Portrait Making Pattern Block Pictures	Small or large group Small or large group Small or large group
Mathematics	Creating Pattern Block Pinwheels Solving Pattern Block Puzzles Exploring Number Concepts	Small or large group Small or large group One-on-one
Sciences	Exploring Shadows and Light Assembling a Nature Display Building a Model Car	Small or large group Small or large group Small or large group
Performing Arts	Moving to Music Playing an Instrument Singing a Song	Large group Large group Large group

In general, large-group activities can be conducted as part of a regular group time in the classroom. Although all children participate in these large-group activities, the teacher focuses observations on the children selected for detailed documentation. Small-group and one-on-one activities are carried out in relatively quiet places, such as in the reading corner or at a quiet table in the classroom, while the rest of the class is involved in other activities.

In principle, the small group configuration is usually better for assessing children since it allows teachers to gather more detailed information. However, with Bridging activities, several factors influence the choice of social arrangements. These factors include (1) the nature of the activity and materials, (2) competencies and working approaches of the children, and (3) the dynamics of group life in the classroom. Each of these factors is briefly described below to assist teachers in making decisions on how to assess.

The first factor concerns the nature of the activity and materials. When considering choices regarding social arrangements for assessment and teaching, teachers consider the following kinds of questions. What amount of instruction do children require to start the activity? What type of interaction between teacher and child is needed during the activity? What quantity of materials is needed and available? For example, the large-group format is a good choice for the Acting Out Stories and Moving to Music activities because they require no materials for individual children to handle and little instruction from the teacher. Once a few children catch on to the goal of the activity, the rest usually join in to participate. A large group is also more likely to create momentum and inspiration for all those participating. In contrast, one-to-one interactions are better for the Reading a Book and Dictating a Story activities. While both of these activities often take no more than two or three minutes per child, the one-to-one interaction allows the teacher to listen closely to individual children and keep a detailed record of each child's narrative.

Second, children' competencies and working approaches affect teachers' decisions on how to group as well. Small groups are ideal when children of differing abilities work together cooperatively. More-competent children can often boost the performance of their less-competent peers by suggesting ideas, offering help, and modeling how to complete a project. On the other hand, if a child is hesitant to begin an activity, or shows impulsive behavior, the teacher may need time to engage the child one-on-one to promote the child's best work.

An additional factor for teachers to consider is the dynamics of group life in the classroom. If children are accustomed to working together—with each child used to learning from and with others in a group process—small group and large group social arrangements will work well for most activities. Also, if a classroom has one teacher with 30 students, the majority of Bridging activities can be conducted in a large group. Although not always ideal, many public school teachers have successfully used the large group format for all Bridging assessment activities.

In sum, teachers vary in how they carry out the activities as assessments. Some are able to dedicate a whole week to the assessment process; others spread the activities out over a two-week period. The order for presenting the activities is not important, and a teacher may include as many different assessment activities in a day as time permits.

Which Activities to Choose

Some teachers ask, "Which Bridging assessment activities are essential? If I can do only a few, which activities should I choose?" In the Bridging assessment process, we give equal value to each activity; no one or two activities are more important than others in portraying a child's learning profile. We choose a wide range of activities in five curricular areas because we want to emphasize that activities in all subject areas represent important avenues for problem solving and the expression of complex ideas. A teacher may not cultivate the potential of children in all subject areas with equal attention, but to overlook a subject area is to risk leaving out channels for thinking and expression that may be important, or even essential, to some children. Sampling a wide range of areas is a prerequisite for identifying diverse strengths in young children and building on these strengths to further learning.

In practical terms, we are keenly aware of the time constraints every teacher encounters. If a choice has to be made, we recommend that teachers consider the following options: (1) include activities in the areas you are most concerned about for your children; (2) include activities in the areas where you have little knowledge of children's thinking, skills, and interest; (3) include activities representing subject areas *you* know the least about; or (4) focus on activities in one particular area, such as mathematics or sciences, for a period of time (see Table 7.6).

Table 7.6   Deciding Which Activities to Focus On

---

1. **W**hich Bridging activities are not part of my curricular repertoire yet that I would like to include this year?

2. **I**n which areas do I need to know more about these children?

3. **W**hich activities represent subject areas I know the least about?

4. **W**hich areas would I like to focus on to improve my teaching this year?

How to Identify Expected Performance Level

As described in Chapter 2, Bridging does not provide age norms for use in assessing children's performance and interpreting assessment results. Rather, teachers assume responsibility for identifying expected performance levels for a given group of children during a particular period of time. This requires teachers' expertise and experience. To ensure an appropriate level is identified, it is vital that teachers carefully study the rubrics for the selected activities in relation to the children served in the school community. Working with colleagues in determining the expected performance levels helps clarify uncertainty and furthers understanding of the rubrics.

Determining expected outcome levels for a class of children and individuals is the work teachers do to establish children's zones of proximal development for learning. In Chapter 2, we introduced Vygotsky's important contribution to education and child development: the idea that professionals need to look for two levels of development when assessing children. The first level, the actual level, describes those mental processes that are fully developed and evident in children's independent activity—the things they can do by themselves. The second level of development is the potential level, which includes those processes and skills still in the process of developing that are evident in activities children can participate in with help and support from others. The expected performance level in the Bridging assessment process is the second level Vygotsky describes. When instruction takes place between the child's actual level and potential or expected level, it holds the greatest benefit for children.

There are two critical ideas to remember in setting expected levels of development with Bridging tasks. First, there is likely to be variability across teachers who are working at the same grade level in different communities. Why is this likely to be so? Does it mean that some teachers may have lower expectations for their children? No, the different expected performance levels reflect the work teachers are doing to juggle three sources of information: (1) what they know about the specific children they are teaching, (2) the curriculum concepts for children's learning across school subject areas, and (3) state and local learning standards. When teachers consider these three sources of information, they may come to expected performance levels that differ from those set by colleagues in other schools or communities.

This brings us to the second critical detail about expected levels of performance: They are not static during a school year. Expected levels of performance are subject to change over time just as children's developmental levels (reflected in rubric scores) are changing. Teachers need to be readjusting their estimate of children's potential level as the children progress through the school year. In other words, to describe children's development in the Bridging assessment process, teachers are utilizing knowledge of learning standards, knowledge of key concepts and skills in each subject area, *and* knowledge of the children in their classrooms. When teachers keep sight of these three components in identifying expected levels, it sets the stage for appropriate and effective teaching.

Page 95 presents Figure 7.2, the sheet that teachers use to identify the expected performance level for students before the assessment begins. Ideally, if more than one teacher at the same grade level engages in the Bridging assessment process, these teachers can work together, comparing the expected levels they set, discussing differences, and making adjustments. If this is not possible, the teacher sets the expected level based on knowledge of activity rubrics, the children in the classroom, and standards. As the assessment begins, the teacher collects data and compares the expected level with the child's actual performance scores. If the expected level appears either too high or too low, the teacher can adjust the expected level and reflect on reasons for the mismatch between expected and actual levels. "Is it because I don't fully understand the activity rubric? Did I set the expectation too low for my students? Why do students perform better than what I expected in some areas but not in others?" Thinking through these sorts of questions helps the teacher set a more accurate expected performance level.

CONDUCTING BRIDGING ACTIVITIES

The teacher's primary tasks when assessing a child are observing and recording, not instructing or facilitating the child's performance (see Table 7.7). The focus of assessment is to learn about the child's actual performance level independent of adult support. If the child is having difficulty, becomes frustrated with the activity, and stops trying, the teacher notes the difficulty and then provides the necessary support to encourage the child to continue. The child's unassisted performance level is what the teacher scores. As Vygotsky's concept of the zone of proximal development reminds us, in subsequent uses of the activity, the teacher's interactions will focus on guidance and coaching in the area that proved to be difficult in order to promote the child's "potential development."

Table 7.7   Steps to Prepare for and Conduct Bridging Activities

1. Create a Bridging folder for each child. Staple a summary sheet and chart inside the folder.

2. Decide which activity to carry out first. Read the procedures and imagine conducting it.

3. Read the activity's rubric and review the recording sheet. Look for ways the recording sheet helps to organize observations so that they can later be translated into a rubric score.

4. Gather needed materials, including camera if desirable, and have the recording sheet ready.

5. Decide on which social arrangements to use for the activity and plan to introduce it in relation to previous activities/events/ideas in the classroom.

6. Conduct the activity, completing the recording sheet and working approach form during the assessment.

7. Assign a rubric score to the activity.

Teachers complete two recording tasks for the Bridging assessment process: (1) observing, taking notes, and recording the child's working approach during the activity; and (2) scoring the performance level when the child completes the activity. The forms used to record this information follows the description of each activity.

Recording Sheets

All Bridging activities include a recording sheet on which the teacher can make notes while the child is engaged in an activity. For most activities, recording sheets provide space for teachers to jot down their observations of the child's behavior during the activity and to record the products of the activity such as the text of a dictated story or a sketch of a completed model car. For some activities, the recording sheets include a checklist in addition to space for writing notes. In the case of teacher's choice of book reading activity, the checklist prompts the teacher to note various aspects of the child's book knowledge and reading ability, such as voice intonation, the position of the child's hands, eye movement, and reading fluency (Figure 7.3, page 96). The recording sheet preserves detailed data that help teachers understand both the development of skills and concepts in subject areas and also the working approach of individual children.

Scoring

Page 97 presents Figure 7.4, the sheet for documenting a child's learning profile summary, including both rubric scores and working approach scores. Before scoring, it is important to read the rubric and the description of working approaches carefully to become familiar with performance indicators at each developmental level. We recommend that teachers score working approaches while children are carrying out the activity, and score the child's performance level as soon as the child completes the activity. Immediate scoring is particularly important if the activity has no durable product. It helps to ensure accuracy in terms of capturing what a child said, did, and how he or she interacted with the materials and other children. For activities that lead to a visible product (for example, Creating Pattern Block Pinwheels, Making Pattern Block Pictures, Building a Model Car, Assembling a Nature Display), we recommend using a camera to record an image of the child's work.

Teachers who have implemented Bridging activities have commented that when a child does not participate in an activity, the assessment rubric calls for scoring it "0." Such a score seems negative, which is not usually how the child or teacher views the action. This raises an important issue about any assessment and its interpretation. In the Bridging assessment process, as in any assessment, no performance or no participation does not mean no development. It means only what it is—no participation. This becomes interesting "data" to think about alongside other information a teacher is gathering on a child, and provides a good opportunity for questions. Was the nonparticipation a one-time occurrence? Is nonparticipation the child's usual response to this particular activity? Does a particular type of material affect the child's participation or the grouping situation for the activity? Does the child prefer other types of activities for self-expression and participation?

Nonparticipation, then, like any other rubric score, becomes an opportunity to consider what the information gathered can tell us about the child and how he or she benefits from an activity. A child can benefit enormously from watching others dramatize a story as opposed to acting in one. The question for the teacher then becomes "How can I use this information to better understand the child?"

INTERPRETING THE ASSESSMENT RESULTS

After finishing all 15 activities, the next step is to create a learning profile for each focal child using the summary sheet previously mentioned (see Figure 7.4, page 97). The summary sheet includes spaces to record the social arrangements for each activity, the child's rubric score, and the child's working approach. When the summary sheet is completed, the teacher charts the child's performance scores on the graphic chart (see Figure 7.5, page 98). Each teacher will have already charted the expected performance level for children in the class as a whole. Now the teacher compares the child's actual performance levels to the expected levels. When the actual and expected performance levels are charted on a single graph, teachers can study the patterns and variations in a child's performance across assessment activities in order to generate questions as well as hypotheses about the child's learning in school.

From Bridging's point of view, a jagged or uneven learning profile is to be expected. Contrast and discrepencies between activity performances give teachers new ways to look at where and how a child can excel. They also suggest possibilities for building on identified strengths and using strengths to develop skills in areas of challenge.

Children's performance on an activity can change dramatically given the presence or absence of help from teachers or peers. As indicated earlier, the Bridging activity rubrics are designed to help teachers locate, on a developmental continuum, what children can do without assistance and what they can do with help from others. The area of thinking and skill between what a child has mastered independently and what is still in the process of developing is precisely where the child stands to benefit the most from support and practice in order to continue developing.

Analysis of the frequently divergent assessment results in each child's summary profile requires time, questioning, and thinking. To assist with this review and analysis process, we suggest teachers consider the questions listed in Table 7.8. The questions are related to the three types of information appearing on the summary sheet, namely, social arrangements of the activity, the child's performance levels, and observed working approaches when the child engages in the activity.

Effective teaching takes into account a continually updated understanding of what is challenging for children and what their learning needs are. When creating learning profiles for individual children, a teacher will want to compare the Bridging assessment data with knowledge of the children from observations in ongoing classroom activities because no one source of information provides a complete understanding of a child. Effective use of Bridging findings includes considering information gathered from other sources in order to assemble a more complete picture of a child's learning profile in school.

Equally important is engaging in a collaborative assessment process—discussing findings and observations with other teachers, the school principal or director, the child's parents, and the child, too! The teacher and the child have everything to gain as the teacher broadens the sources of insight he or she taps, including both the child's performance on a wide variety of activities and the knowledge of a wide variety of people who are committed to the child's success and learning in the classroom.

Table 7.8   Reflection Questions for Interpreting the Assessment Results

---

Reflecting on Social Arrangements
- What is the range of social arrangements in which this child has participated?
- Which were chosen by the teacher and which by the child?
- Is there a possible relationship between the child's performance levels and the social arrangements used to engage the child?
- Does social setting affect the child's working approach?
- For small-group activities, what is the basis for putting this particular group of children together?

Reflecting on a Child's Performance Levels
- Does the child demonstrate a "jagged profile" of high and low rubric scores?
- Does the variability in performance levels point to a pattern of strengths and vulnerabilities?
- How does the variability revealed by a particular child compare to that of other children in the class?
- How does a child's variability compare to what you expect of other children at this age and grade level?

Reflecting on Working Approach (Evaluative and Descriptive Qualities)
- Is the child's working approach consistent across diverse subject areas?
- Does the child use particular working approaches in areas of strength and other working approaches in areas of vulnerability?
- What does it mean when a child receives high evaluative working approach scores for an activity on which the child has a low rubric score?
- What does the information contained in the descriptive working approaches suggest about how a child is most productive when working?

LINKING ASSESSMENT TO TEACHING

The purpose of the Bridging assessment is to enhance teaching and learning. A vitally important step to achieving this goal is the process of linking the Bridging assessment findings to curriculum planning and classroom teaching. During the process of implementing Bridging activities, documenting results, and interpreting the findings, teachers always maintain an active stance toward listening to and wondering about specific children, their unique talents, their possibly heretofore unknown, and perhaps more hidden, strengths. Effective teachers indeed always interpret the assessment findings in relation to questions such as "What does it mean?" and "What can I do to respond to this child's needs, this particular issue, or this interesting phenomenon?" To facilitate and strengthen this process of reflection that leads to planning for future curriculum, each Bridging activity is accompanied by a Bridge to Curriculum, which offers teachers two kinds of help as follow-up to the assessment process: reflecting and planning.

Reflecting

The first support in the Bridge to Curriculum is a reminder of the key concepts and skills at play in the activity the teacher just observed. This emphasis once again asserts the critical role of the key concepts and skills in the Bridging assessment process: they are the focus of the activity's goals, the backbone of the performance rubric levels, and the link between what is assessed and what will be the focus of instruction in the following weeks and months. Of critical importance to the effective use of Bridging is teachers' deepening understanding of key concepts and skills in varied subject areas.

Following a list of key concepts and skills is a review of the factors that might contribute to a child's performance, including working approaches and activity parameters such as materials, social arrangements, and activity structures. Questions are posed to encourage teachers to think about the possible connections among the child's performance, the child's working approaches employed during the task, and the child's patterns of interaction with various activity parameters.

With the activity parameters in mind, teachers are further asked to reflect on different underlying issues associated with the child's particular performance rubric level. For example, does the child understand the goal of the activity? Has the child developed the initial skills essential to carrying out the activity? Does the child simply need practice with certain key skills before attempting a higher level of the task? Why is this activity so attractive to the child? These types of questions encourage teachers to think not only about what a child did but also about how and why the child may have responded in a particular way.

In the process of reflecting, the teacher carefully reviews the data, ponders the facts, and explores the possible factors that promote or hinder the child's performance on a particular task. Some of these factors are associated with the child, others concern the nature of the activity, and still others are teacher related. Once again, the conceptual framework of Bridging is useful in this process. Having a clear understanding of the sources for the child's performance becomes the prerequisite for helping the child to advance.

Planning

The Planning section is the logical follow-up of Reflecting, and it is also the ultimate goal of the Bridging assessment process. Planning links the child assessment results to curriculum and classroom teaching. To assist teachers with this process, this section provides a set of ideas for teachers to consider carrying out with children to further their explorations and understanding of the subject area concepts and skills. The ideas are not meant to prescribe a particular way of teaching and instructing. Rather, they are suggestive, serving as guidelines for teachers' innovation.

In summary, the Bridge to Curriculum is designed to support teachers' thinking in relation to two types of questions: (1) What does the child's performance and approach to Bridging activities tell me about this specific child's strengths? (2) What can I do to support this child's further learning and development in this area as well as other subject areas? The Bridge to Curriculum mirrors the conceptual framework for assessment: viewing the children's activity performance as a function of what the child brings to the situation, the teacher's decisions about social arrangements and framing of the activity in the classroom setting, and the materials and procedures of each task which embody intellectual challenge and skill for the child. In the Bridging process, the assessment of children, teacher reflection, and future teaching-learning dynamics are linked by the continuous flow of classroom activities that provide the stage for assessment and teaching. The teacher furthers the nature of challenges children meet each day as well as the discourse that connects all participants over time. Bridging assessment provides a road map to this ever-growing complex work.

Figure 7.2   Expected Performance Levels

Grade level: PreK   K   1   2   3

Time of the year: Fall   Winter   Spring

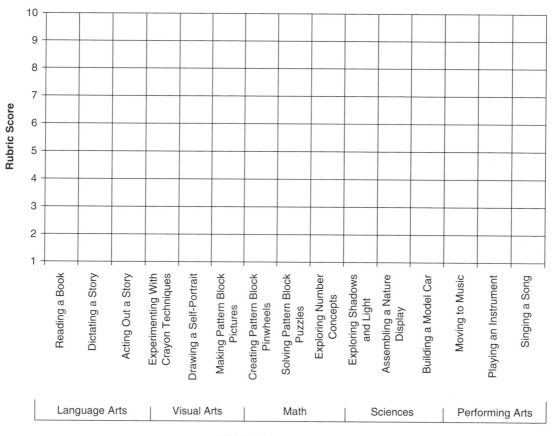

Bridging Areas and Activities

Figure 7.3   Sample Recording Sheet

Reading a Book-Teacher's Choice	**Recording Sheet**

Child's name _____   Assess date _____ Assessor _____

Book level _____ Text title _____ Rubric level _____

Discrepancies

between level of book picked by the child and the level of book picked by teacher:

☐ yes   ☐ no

Book Knowledge

Picks up book and orients to front cover:

☐ yes   ☐ no   ☐ needs help

Knows how to open book and turn pages:

☐ yes   ☐ no   ☐ needs help

Knows where the story begins:

☐ yes   ☐ no   ☐ needs help

Voice

☐ Describing/labeling pictures

☐ Wording/intonation story-like

☐ Sounds like "reading"

Hands

☐ Points to pictures

☐ Uses fingers to track print

Eyes

☐ Watches pictures

☐ Watches print

Reading Proficiency
(only if child is reading conventionally)

☐ Choppy

☐ Word by word

☐ Fluent

Reading Behaviors

(describe what child says and does on each page)

Title Page: _____

Page 1 _____

Page 2 _____

Page 3 _____

Page 4 _____

Figure 7.4 A Child's Learning Profile Summary

Child:		Language Arts			Visual Arts			Math			Sciences			Performing Arts		
		• Reading a Book	• Dictating a Story	• Acting Out a Story	• Crayon Techniques	• Self-Portrait	• PB Pictures	• PB Pinwheels	• PB Puzzles	• Number Concepts	• Shadows & Light	• Nature Display	• Model Car	• Moving to Music	• Music Instrument	• Singing a Song
Age:																
Gender:																
Date																
Social Structure																
Rubric Score																
Evaluative	Initial engagement															
	Focus and attention															
	Planfulness															
	Goal orientation															
	Resourcefulness															
	Cooperation															
Descriptive	Chattiness															
	Pace of work															
	Sense of humor															
	Social referencing															

Note: PB = Pattern Block

Figure 7.5   Summary of Child's Bridging Assessment Performance Scores

Child's Name:

Age:

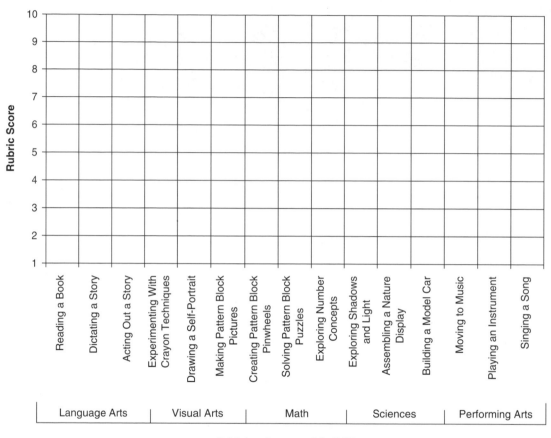

Bridging Areas and Activities

Activities

Language Arts and Literacy

WHAT WE KNOW

Research recognizes a paradox in young children's developing language and early literacy skills: children learn to speak, listen, read, and write by actively participating in daily conversations and activities involving reading and writing with family members, caretakers, and teachers. Home, school, and community settings provide a continuum of literacy opportunities for eager young learners where they can discuss, debate, recount experiences, argue, persuade, joke, entertain, and console one another in spoken and written language.

Children's homes and community settings vary enormously in the nature of the experiences they provide. Early childhood classrooms, however, actively engage children in practicing their emerging language and literacy skills and initiate them in understanding the discourse patterns of schooling. Early childhood classrooms offer children opportunities to become familiar with, and proficient in, the many skills involved in speaking, listening, reading, and writing.

Basic principles guide the process of early literacy development:

- *It begins early.* Learning to read and write begins long before a child enters kindergarten; it begins in activities that do not look like conventional, mature forms of reading and writing.
- *It relies on symbols.* All children between the ages of one and five develop the ability to use symbols to represent ideas through talking, drawing, pretend play, and pretend reading. These symbol-using abilities provide the foundation for a child's development as a reader and writer.
- *It builds on an awareness of language sounds.* Young children's learning to speak involves experimenting with making sounds and playing with sound patterns in words and phrases. The more adults help children notice and enjoy sound sequences in words, rhymes, songs, poems, and stories, the better prepared children are for paying conscious attention to sound conventions represented in the alphabet and print conventions that reading and writing depend on.

WHAT BRIDGING PROVIDES

Bridging's language arts and literacy activities provide a window to the child's developing language and literacy skills from ages three to eight. The activities engage children in reading books and composing ideas in writing for their peer group. For the child, the activities make tangible the previously invisible mental processes called reading and writing. In these activities, they experience an emerging understanding of how reading and writing processes work to communicate ideas, and they practice the skills needed to achieve this goal.

WHY THESE THREE ACTIVITIES

The three Bridging language arts and literacy activities include Reading a Book, Dictating a Story, and Acting Out a Story. These activities build on the research literature that emphasizes the need for young children to experience being read to and to have adults (and older children) write down their ideas to model the mental processes that readers and writers develop. The three Bridging activities—children reading books, dictating stories, and acting out their stories—provide dynamic and compelling contexts in which to see young children's evolving concepts of narrative, print conventions, and the communicative power of spoken and written language. By asking each child to read a favorite storybook, as well as picking an unfamiliar text for the child to read, a teacher can better determine which skills and understandings a child has mastered and which are in the earlier stages of development. The contrast in performance in these two activities guides the teacher in making decisions about the level of instruction and practice that will best meet a child's specific needs.

The storytelling and story acting activities included here derive from the work of Vivian Paley (1981, 1990, 2001), who has demonstrated the power of these activities in all types of early childhood classrooms. These activities (one a language arts, and the other a performing arts, activity) provide a powerful entry point for young children to master many of the key concepts and skills identified by national standards for language arts and literacy such as learning about language (oral and written) as a means for communication and as a rule-governed symbol system, and learning about the close connections between speech and text.

The storytelling and story dramatization activities invite children to participate in the mental processes of good writers: learning to envision a scene, the characters, the plot, and resolution of a problem. The task does not focus attention on the mechanics of writing, such as handwriting, spelling, and punctuation. Instead, the goal is helping children learn to organize ideas and compose cohesive, logical, and creative narratives. Becoming aware of and practicing the conventions of writing are more effectively addressed after children are familiar with the writing process and are motivated to create their own texts to share with others.

Dramatization is one of the best instructional and assessment contexts for literally seeing how young children interpret print. When they put characters' actions and affect into body movements and facial expressions, young children demonstrate logic, comprehension, and their particular interpretation of story events. Acting out stories is a close relative of another form of symbolic activity that young children are familiar with—pretend play. Acting out stories is fun and motivating for young children and allows teachers to see what kinds of thinking are going on as children interpret and comprehend written texts.

A number of basic skill areas in literacy development are not directly assessed in Bridging activities. These include children's emerging skills in phonemic awareness (knowledge and awareness of sound sequences) and phonics (letter-sound correspondence), as well as fine motor skills needed to write letters and words. There are several reasons why these skill areas are not assessed here. While the skills and concepts in these areas are of critical importance in early literacy development, there are numerous assessment tools now available to educators that target these specific skills and in the specific age periods when their development is salient. Also, a distinguishing feature of all Bridging assessment is the observation of skill and concept development in the context of an activity that is meaningful and purposeful from the child's point of view, and in an activity that remains constant from ages three to eight. Phonemic awareness and phonics do not lend themselves to this kind of single steady activity. Consistent with this principle, Bridging's assessment of children's language arts and literacy skills focuses on what children do as they interact with books and stories.

Relationship Between Standards and Bridging Activities in Language Arts and Literacy Area

	Bridging Activities		
Standards for Language Arts and Early Literacy	*Reading a Book*	*Dictating a Story*	*Acting Out a Story*
Language as Communication			
• Language as Communication	√	√	√
• Language as a Rule-Governed Symbol System	√	√	√
• Multiple Purposes of Communication	√	√	√
• Language and Culture			
• Relationships Between First and Second Languages			
• Language and Literacy Communities	√	√	√
Reading			
• Multiple Purposes of Reading	√		
• Speech-Text Connection	√	√	√
• Invariability of Text	√	√	√
• Reading (Decoding) Strategies	√		
Writing			
• Multiple Purposes of Writing		√	√
• Speech-Text Connection		√	√
• Writing Strategies		√	
Structure and Elements of Literary Texts			
• Conventions of Print	√	√	
• Structure and Conventions of Text		√	
• Characteristics of Narrative Text	√	√	√
• Characteristics of Informational Text	√	√	
Literacy and Process of Inquiry			
• Literacy and Research			
• Literacy and Technology			

Standards listed here are a combination of those defined by National Council of Teachers of English and the International Reading Association (available at http://www.reading.org/resources/issues/reports/learning_standards .html) and the Illinois State Board of Education (available at http://www.isbe.state.il.us/ils/ela/standards.htm).

Definition of Language Arts and Early Literacy Standards

Language as Communication

- **Language as Communication** Ideas, feelings, and stories can be communicated through spoken, written, and visual (signed) language.

- **Language as a Rule-Governed Symbol System** In speaking, listening, reading, and writing, knowledge of grammar and sentence structure, vocabulary, and conventions for expression and emphasis are essential for understanding and communication.

- **Multiple Purposes of Communication** Spoken, written, and visual language may be used to accomplish different purposes: for learning, enjoyment, persuasion, exchange of information, communication of ideas. Also to recognize, interpret, and apply connections between information and ideas.

- **Language and Culture** Language is a medium of cultural expression. Languages and dialects, like cultures, are diverse in their conventions for what members of a group can say to one another, when, and how.

- **Relationships Between First and Second Languages** First language may be used to develop competency in a second language and to develop understanding of content across the curriculum.

- **Language and Literacy Communities** Participation in distinct literacy communities includes reflective, creative, and critical uses of language and literacy.

Reading

- **Multiple Purposes of Reading** Reading a wide range of print texts in a wide variety of literary genres supports building vocabulary skills; acquiring new information; generating ideas for responding to the needs and demands of society and the workplace; finding personal fulfillment; and building an understanding of the many dimensions of the human experience.

- **Speech-Text Connection** There is a connection between speech and text; text can be read out loud with voice intonation supporting the meaning of text. Yet text and speech are also inherently distinct.

- **Invariability of Text** The actual words, sentences, and paragraphs that make up a particular text do not change from one reading to the next.

- **Reading (Decoding) Strategies** Knowledge of letters and sounds, sight words, illustrations, and context can be used to help a reader decode text and improve understanding and fluency. Readers also draw on their prior experiences and their interactions with other readers to help them decode text.

Activities: Language Arts and Literacy

(Continued)

(Continued)

Writing

- **Multiple Purposes of Writing** Working to convey ideas in writing in various genres supports clarifying and refining one's knowledge and understanding of ideas, as well as assists with the development of new ideas.

- **Speech-Text Connection** There is a connection between speech and text; speech can be rendered into a written form.

- **Writing Strategies** Writers can make use of a range of resources to assist them in the writing process, including getting help from others, building on their prior experiences, and relying on their knowledge of words, letters and sounds, and syntax.

Structure and Elements of Literary Texts

- **Conventions of Print** There is a set of conventions observed in print regarding grammar, spelling, punctuation, and usage. They are constant and particular to a language.

- **Structure and Conventions of Text** Knowledge of language structure (syntax), language conventions (spelling and punctuation), and understanding of figurative language and genre can be used to create, critique, and discuss print.

- **Characteristics of Narrative Text** Narrative text follows a logical sequence around one or more central ideas or events that lead to a resolution or climax; characters' motivations and actions contribute to the development of these central ideas or events, which occur in a particular setting.

- **Characteristics of Informational Text** Informational text is usually organized around a central idea or topic, and its primary purpose is the communication of facts and information.

Literacy and Process of Inquiry

- **Literacy and Research** Research on issues and interests begins with generating ideas and questions, and by posing problems. Language and literacy are used to gather, evaluate, and synthethize data from a variety of sources and to communicate discoveries in ways that fit the purpose and audience.

- **Literacy and Technology** A variety of technological and informational resources (libraries, databases, computer networks, video) can be used to gather, synthesize, and communicate information.

Reading a Book: Child's Choice*   Procedure

Subject Area	Key Concepts and Skills
• Literacy **Social Arrangements** • *Recommended:* teacher-child, child-child • *Viable:* small group (2–3 children)	• Understanding of books and reading • Concepts of story: elements and structure • Print conventions—left to right orientation, word spacing, punctuation • Relationship between illustrations and text • Reading intonation • Decoding strategies

Activity and Goal

A child picks a book that is available in the classroom, one that the child likes and wants to read to the teacher. This task elicits a child's knowledge of books and reading skills in relation to a familiar and favorite book.

Materials

- A comfortable, quiet place for reading
- A variety of children's books in the classroom library that have a written narrative

   Note: To maximize opportunities to observe reading skills, teacher will want to exclude alphabet books, pop-up books, vocabulary books, and books from languages the child doesn't speak.

   Note: If reading level of the book can be determined, note it on record sheet.

Procedure

1. Ask the child to pick a book from the classroom collection that the child likes and that he or she wants to read to you. Ask to see and hold the book.

2. In a quiet and comfortable place, set the book on the table or floor face down and at a sideways angle. In a friendly way, invite the child to read the book: "Now, read your book to me." It is important to say the word "read" so that what follows is the child's effort to read as opposed to talking about pictures or the story.

3. Often a young child will say, "I can't read" or "I don't know how." When this happens, encourage the child by saying, "Well, pretend you can. Pretend-read it to me."

4. Observe how the child picks up the book and orients to it.

5. When the child starts reading, record the child's related reading behavior, including handling the book, turning pages, eye movement, tone of voice, and way of using fingers and hands in relation to print and pictures. A teacher only needs to spend two to four minutes listening to a child read in order to identify the stage of the child's reading. If the child picks a book that is lengthy, have the child read only a few pages.

6. If a child picks a book that is too difficult to read and says he or she can't read, try to elicit the child's knowledge of print awareness through questions such as: Do you know any of the words here on this page? Any letters? What do you think this might say?

*Adapted from Sulzby (1985).

Reading a Book: Child's Choice — Recording Sheet

Child's name _____ Assess date _____ Assessor _____

Book level _____ Text title_____ Rubric level _____

Reading Behaviors (describe what child says and does on each page)

Book Knowledge

Picks up book and orients to front cover:

☐ yes ☐ no ☐ needs help

Knows how to open book and turn pages:

☐ yes ☐ no ☐ needs help

Knows where the story begins

☐ yes ☐ no ☐ needs help

Voice

☐ description/labeling pictures

☐ wording/intonation story-like

☐ sounds like "reading"

Hands

☐ points to pictures

☐ uses fingers to track print

Eyes

☐ watches pictures

☐ watches print

Reading Proficiency (only if child is reading conventionally)

☐ choppy

☐ word by word

☐ fluent

Text title

_____

Page 1

_____

Page 2

_____

Page 3

_____

Page 4

_____

Reading a Book: Child's Choice   Evaluative Working Approach Rubric

Circle the number that best describes the child's evaluative working approach in this activity.

Child's Name:
_____

Initial Engagement: How does the child initially respond to the activity?

Hesitant _____ **Eager**

1	2	3	4	5
very hesitant or unwilling to begin activity		becomes involved on his or her own		eager to begin activity

Focus, Attention: How on task is the child throughout the activity?

Distractable _____ **Attentive**

1	2	3	4	5
very easily distracted by other children, events, or materials		attentive some of the time		sustained, absorbed attention to activity

Goal Orientation: How clear is the child working toward the activity's goal?

Personal goal _____ **Activity goal**

1	2	3	4	5
works on personal goal rather than activity goal		child's work vacillates between personal goal and activity goal		works efficiently toward activity goal

Planfulness: How organized is the child in working toward task completion?

Haphazard _____ **Organized**

1	2	3	4	5
random or impulsive; no evidence of organization of materials or approach		organized some of the time		well-organized, methodical in approach or with materials

Resourcefulness: What does the child do when stuck?

Helpless _____ **Resourceful**

1	2	3	4	5
does not ask for help; unable to use help when offered		moves forward a step when help is given		seeks help and makes good use of it to figure out challenges

Cooperation (for group activities): How does the child work with peers to accomplish task?

Difficulty working with others _____ **Helpful to others**

1	2	3	4	5
has difficulty sharing materials or attention, taking turns, supporting the efforts of others		gets along with other children		helps other children with activity, materials, or as a mediator; models ideas for others

Activities: Language Arts and Literacy

Reading a Book: Child's Choice   Descriptive Working Approach Rubric

Circle the number that best describes the child's descriptive working approach in this activity.

Child's Name:

_____

Chattiness: How much of the child's talk is unrelated to the activity?

Very quiet _____ **Very chatty**

1	2	3	4	5
little conversation and self-talk throughout the activity		talks from time to time		constantly talks about unrelated topics

Pace of Work: What is the child's pace of work?

Slow _____ **Fast**

1	2	3	4	5
slow to start and carry out the activity		moderate pace throughout the activity		quick start and quick finish

Social Referencing: How often does the child check with teachers or peers?

Little interaction _____ **Constant checking**

1	2	3	4	5
focuses on own work		attention to others' work and checks with others about own work occasionally		frequently asks teacher or peer if own work is on track

Playfulness: How animated, lively, or happy is the child during the activity?

Serious _____ **Playful**

1	2	3	4	5
mood/demeanor is serious and cheerless		business-like with activity		cheerful and sense of humor related to activity

Reading a Book: Child's Choice

Performance Rubric

Level	Name	Performance Indicators*
0	Child does not participate	• Child declines to participate in activity.
1	Attending to pictures, not forming stories	• Child looks at pictures but does not say anything. • Child is "reading" by looking at the storybook pictures; conversation is about the pictures in view. Comments about what is in the pictures are not necessarily related to each other. • "Reading" consists of labeling and commenting on individual story pictures (for example, pointing out a ball, naming animals).
2	Attending to pictures, forming oral stories	• Child is "reading" by looking at the storybook pictures; the child's speech weaves a story across the pages, but the wording and intonation are like those of someone *telling* a story, either like a conversation about the pictures or like a story relayed in a conversation. • Listener often must see the pictures to understand the child's story.
3	Attending to pictures, forming written language-like stories	• Child is "reading" by looking at the storybook pictures, and the child's speech sounds as if the child is reading, both in wording and intonation. • Listener does not need to look at the pictures at all, or only rarely, in order to understand the story.
4	Reading verbatim-like story	• Child is "reading" the text with fluency from memory; reading is a memorized rendition of the text. • Child is not able to decode the print and must look at the pictures (and sometimes the print) in order to "read."
5	Refusal to read	• Child may refuse to read for print-related reasons. Also, the child may show some awareness of letters in words or awareness of certain words. The child is aware that reading means decoding the print, which the child recognizes he or she cannot do yet. • The child may refuse to read, but may pretend-read with prompting.
6	Initial attending to print	• Child can figure out some of the words using one strategy or other; for example, using picture information or certain print features to recognize some letters or words.
7	Attending to print: strategies imbalanced	• Child reads by trying to decipher the print; may not have decoding and meaning-making coordinated. • Reading is choppy, may not respond to punctuation.
8	Mastering reading behaviors	• Child uses one strategy (phonics, picture cues) with some consistency. • Child's reading has some inaccuracies; child is not always using strategies flexibly or effectively. Child may sound out some words, leave "nonsense" words uncorrected, omit unknown words, and/or depend on predictable or remembered text rather than the written text. • Reading is choppy, but child can decode most words on a page.
9	Reading for meaning: beginning fluency	• Reading is accurate; several strategies are used. • Child reads for meaning, showing fluency in sentence phrasing
10	Reading for meaning: independent reader	• Child is able to read book fluently, with appropriate intonation and with little or no help on difficult words. • Child can problem solve new vocabulary.

Adapted from Sulz by (1985) and Fountas and Pinnell (1996).

Activities: Language Arts and Literacy

Reading a Book: Teacher's Choice*   Procedure

Subject Area	Key Concepts and Skills
• Literacy	• Understanding of books and reading
Social Arrangements	• Concepts of story: elements and structure
• *Recommended:* teacher-child	• Print conventions—left to right orientation, word spacing, punctuation
	• Relationship between illustrations and text
	• Reading intonation
	• Decoding strategies
	• Characteristics of informational text

Activity and Goal

The teacher asks a child to read a story. While the child reads, the teacher makes a running record of the child's reading behaviors. This activity offers the opportunity to contrast the child's reading of a familiar, favorite book with one that the teacher believes is at the child's instructional level. It elicits a child's interpretation of reading and the child's level of reading proficiency using a teacher-chosen text.

Materials

- Comfortable, quiet place for reading
- Leveled books (NOTE: Use a book with a simple narrative text such as *The Carrot Seed* for the youngest children. Do not use a book with pictures only or with pictographs.)
- Tape recorder (optional but useful)

Procedure

1. Select a book for the child to read and invite the child to "read" the book to you. Document exactly what the child says when reading, through use of a running record.

2. When selecting a book (see guidelines below), the goal is to find a text the child can read with a 90% accuracy rate. For younger children who are not yet reading conventionally, choose a book with a simple narrative text such as *The Carrot Seed*. If a child is reading, pick a book at a level that the child is likely to read with 100% accuracy. Proceed to higher levels of text until the child's reading accuracy falls below the 90% level.

3. In a quiet and comfortable place, set the book on the table or floor face down. In a friendly way, invite the child to read the book: "Now, read the book to me." It is important to say the word "read" so that what follows is the child's effort to read as opposed to talking about pictures or the story. If a child says, "I can't read," encourage the child by saying, "Read the book in whatever way you can."

4. While the child is reading, sit next to the child and record his or her exact reading behaviors, or only those words and phrases that do not match the text. Teachers may use the conventions for taking a running record as described by Fountas and Pinnell (1996, Chapter 7).

5. Compute accuracy of child's reading using formula described in Fountas and Pinnell (1996, p. 90): Number of words in the text being read minus the number of errors divided by the number of running words multiplied by 100.

*Adapted from Fountas and Pinnell (1996).

Overview of Leveled Book Characteristics*

Book Level	Characteristics of the Book Level	Sample Book Titles
A–B	<ul><li>A single idea</li><li>Few words per page</li><li>Direct correspondence between text and pictures</li><li>Language with naturally occurring oral syntactic patterns</li><li>Layout of print in same place on each page</li><li>Ample layout of printed words so that children can point and read</li></ul>	<ul><li>*Rain; Freight Train; The Harbor* by Donald Crews</li><li>*Where's Spot?* by Eric Hill</li><li>*May There Always Be Sunshine* by Jim Gill</li><li>*Hats Around the World* by Liza Charlesworth</li></ul>
C–I	<ul><li>Familiar story lines and topics</li><li>Concepts within children's experience</li><li>Print appearing on both pages</li><li>Increasing amount of text</li><li>Full range of punctuation</li><li>Stories with more complexity, more events</li><li>Expanding repertoire of reading vocabulary</li><li>Fiction and nonfiction</li></ul>	<ul><li>*The Carrot Seed* by Ruth Krause</li><li>*It Looked Like Spilt Milk* by Charles Shaw</li><li>*Brown Bear Brown Bear* by Bill Martin</li><li>*Are You My Mother?* by P. D. Eastman</li></ul>
I–M	<ul><li>Represent a variety of types of texts and genres of literature</li><li>Have a variety of lengths and variety in vocabulary</li><li>Have fewer pictures; they are moving toward chapter books</li><li>Cannot always be read in one sitting</li><li>Have concepts and themes reflecting children's life experiences or experiences from prior reading</li><li>Have multiple episodes</li><li>Are mostly read silently</li><li>Use pictures that are suggestive, not as directly supportive of reading</li><li>Use more sophisticated language structures</li><li>Explore character and plot development</li></ul>	<ul><li>*Little Bear* by Else Minarik</li><li>*Frog and Toad*, series by Arnold Lobel</li><li>*Henry and Mudge*, series by Cynthia Rylant</li><li>*George and Martha*, series by James Marshall</li></ul>
M–P	<ul><li>Have complex ideas and topics</li><li>Have long stretches of text only</li><li>Provide opportunities to explore story from a variety of perspectives</li><li>Involve subtleties in characters and actions</li><li>Use more complex vocabulary</li><li>Include a great range of genres</li><li>Require using background knowledge to interpret</li></ul>	<ul><li>*George's Marvelous Medicine* by Ronald Dahl</li><li>*Aunt Flossie's Hats* by Elizabeth Howard</li><li>*Cloudy With A Chance of Meatballs* by Judi Barrett</li><li>*The Box Car Children* by Gertrude C. Warner</li></ul>

*Adapted from Fountas and Pinnell (1996).

Activities: Language Arts and Literacy

Reading a Book: Teacher's Choice   Recording Sheet

Child's name _____ Assess date _____ Assessor _____

Book level _____ Text title _____ Rubric level _____

Reading Behaviors (describe what child says and does on each page)

Book Knowledge

Picks up book and orients to front cover:

☐ yes   ☐ no   ☐ needs help

Knows how to open book and turn pages:

☐ yes   ☐ no   ☐ needs help

Knows where the story begins:

☐ yes   ☐ no   ☐ needs help

Voice

☐ description/labeling pictures

☐ wording/intonation story-like

☐ sounds like "reading"

Hands

☐ points to pictures

☐ uses fingers to track print

Eyes

☐ watches pictures

☐ watches print

Reading Proficiency (only if child is reading conventionally)

☐ choppy

☐ word by word

☐ fluent

Text title

_____

Page 1

_____

Page 2

_____

Page 3

_____

Page 4

_____

Reading a Book: Teacher's Choice   Evaluative Working Approach Rubric

Circle the number that best describes the child's evaluative working approach in this activity.

Child's Name:

_____

Initial Engagement: How does the child initially respond to the activity?

Hesitant				Eager
1	2	3	4	5
very hesitant or unwilling to begin activity		becomes involved on his or her own		eager to begin activity

Focus, Attention: How on task is the child throughout the activity?

Distractable				Attentive
1	2	3	4	5
very easily distracted by other children, events, or materials		attentive some of the time		sustained, absorbed attention to activity

Goal Orientation: How clear is the child working toward the activity's goal?

Personal goal				Activity goal
1	2	3	4	5
works on personal goal rather than activity goal		child's work vacillates between personal goal and activity goal		works efficiently toward activity goal

Planfulness: How organized is the child in working toward task completion?

Haphazard				Organized
1	2	3	4	5
random or impulsive; no evidence of organization of materials or approach		organized some of the time		well-organized, methodical in approach or with materials

Resourcefulness: What does the child do when stuck?

Helpless				Resourceful
1	2	3	4	5
does not ask for help; unable to use help when offered		moves forward a step when help is given		seeks help and makes good use of it to figure out challenges

Cooperation (for group activities): How does the child work with peers to accomplish task?

Difficulty working with others				Helpful to others
1	2	3	4	5
has difficulty sharing materials or attention, taking turns, supporting efforts of others		gets along with other children		helps other children with activity, materials, or as a mediator; models ideas the for others

Activities: Language Arts and Literacy

Reading a Book: Teacher's Choice   Descriptive Working Approach Rubric

Circle the number that best describes the child's descriptive working approach in this activity.

Child's Name:

_____

Chattiness: How much of the child's talk is unrelated to the activity?

Very quiet _____ **Very chatty**

1	2	3	4	5
little conversation and self-talk throughout the activity		talks from time to time		constantly talks about unrelated topics

Pace of Work: What is the child's pace of work?

Slow _____ **Fast**

1	2	3	4	5
slow to start and carry out the activity		moderate pace throughout the activity		quick start and quick finish

Social Referencing: How often does the child check with teachers or peers?

Little interaction _____ **Constant checking**

1	2	3	4	5
focuses on own work		attention to others' work and checks with others about own work occasionally		frequently asks teacher or peer if own work is on track

Playfulness: How animated, lively, or happy is the child during the activity?

Serious _____ **Playful**

1	2	3	4	5
mood/demeanor is serious and cheerless		business-like with activity		cheerful and sense of humor related to activity

Reading a Book: Teacher's Choice*   Performance Rubric

Level	Book Levels	Name	Performance Indicators*
0	NA	No participation	• Child declines to participate.
1	A or B books	Attending to pictures, not forming stories	• Child is "reading" by looking at the storybook pictures; speech is only about the pictures in view. The child is not "weaving a story" across the pages. • "Reads" by naming/commenting on pictures (for example, pointing out a ball, naming animals). • Child views pictures, no words spoken but seems to "read" pictures in his or her mind.
2	A or B books	Attending to pictures, forming oral stories	• Child is "reading" by looking at the pictures; the child's speech weaves a story across the pages, but the wording and intonation are like those of someone telling a story, either like a conversation about the pictures or like a story relayed in a conversation. • Listener often must see the pictures to understand the child's story.
3	A or B books	Attending to pictures, forming "written" stories	• Child is "reading" by looking at the storybook pictures, and the child's speech sounds as if the child is reading, both in wording and intonation. • Listener does not need to see the pictures at all, or only rarely, to understand story.
4	A or B books	Reading verbatim-like story	• Child "reads" with fluency from memory; reading is a memorized rendition of text. • Child cannot decode print and must look at pictures (and sometimes print) to "read."
5	A–C books	Initial attending to print	• Child refuses to read for print-related reasons. The child is aware that reading means decoding the print on the page, which the child recognizes he or she cannot do yet. • The child responds to the task, "I can't" or "I don't know how to read."
6	A–C books	Emergent reader	• Child primarily uses information from pictures. • Child may attend to and use some features of print. • Child may know some words. • Child uses the language pattern of books. • Child responds to text by linking meaning with his or her own experiences. • Child begins to make links between his or her own oral language and print.

*Adapted from E. Sulzby (1985) and Fountas and Pinnell (1996).

(Continued)

Activities: Language Arts and Literacy

(Continued)

Level	Book Levels	Name	Performance Indicators*
7	B–I books	Early reader	• Child relies less on pictures and uses more information from the print. • Child recognizes several frequently used words automatically. • Child has several ways to figure out words. • Child reads familiar texts with phrasing and fluency. • Child exhibits strategic behavior such as monitoring, searching, cross-checking, and self-correction.
8	I–M books	Transitional reader	• Child has several ways to figure out words (pictures, context, decoding, syntactic). • Child integrates the use of cues. • Child recognizes a greater number of frequently used words automatically. • Child notices pictures but relies on them very little to read the text. • Child, for the most part, reads fluently with phrasing.
9	M–P books	Self-extending reader	• Child is using well-developed reading strategies to tackle longer texts with abstract concepts and themes. • Child is comfortable reading more difficult, content-specific vocabulary. • Child reads texts at this level with fluency and phrasing.
10	P–S books	Independent reader	• Child uses all sources of information flexibly. • Child solves problems in an independent way. • Child reads with phrasing and fluency. • Child extends understanding by reading a wide range of texts for different purposes. • Child reads for meaning, solving problems in an independent way.

Activities: Language Arts and Literacy

Reading a Book: Child's and Teacher's Choice   Bridge to Curriculum

Reviewing: Key Concepts and Skills Exercised in the Activity

- Understanding of books and reading
- Concepts of story: elements and structure
- Print conventions—left to right orientation, word spacing, punctuation
- Relationship between illustrations and text
- Reading intonation
- Decoding strategies

Reflecting: Questions Related to Child's Performance Child's Working Approach

- Do any Evaluative Working Approaches stand out from the others?
- Are there Working Approach behaviors that seem to be contributing to or hindering the child's performance?
- Can you attribute the behaviors that stand out to any of the activity parameters: materials, key concepts, social arrangements, or activity structure?

Task Parameters

Materials

- Is the child familiar with the book?
- Is the book too complex for child's reading level?

Social Arrangements

- Would the child feel more comfortable in a small group or reading to a friend?

Child's Performance

Rubric Levels 1–3	<ul><li>Is the child using pictures to construct a page-by-page rendition of the text?</li><li>Is the child using pictures to weave a version of the text that has some continuity? (Is there some kind of narrative or central theme that extends through the child's reading?)</li><li>Is the child using a "reading" voice?</li></ul>
Rubric Levels 4–6	<ul><li>Is the child rendering a memorized, verbatim version of the text?</li><li>Is the child aware that the text on the page has specific and unvariable meaning that the child is not yet able to decode?</li><li>Is the child using illustrations to help?</li><li>Is the child recognizing and/or pointing out letters in the text?</li><li>Is the child using knowledge of letters and sounds to try and decode words and text?</li><li>Is the child reading high-frequency words?</li><li>Is the child using knowledge of other familiar sight words to decode text?</li><li>Is the child using previous knowledge and experience with narrative text to help her read?</li><li>Is the child using previous knowledge and experience with informational text to help her read?</li></ul>

(Continued)

Activities: Language Arts and Literacy

(Continued)

Rubric Levels 7–10	• Is the child using knowledge of sound symbol relationships to decode text? • Is the child using knowledge of word structure to decode text? • Is the child using knowledge of word families to decode text? • Is the child using knowledge of syntax and sentence structure to decode text? • Is the child using context to decode text? • Is the child using punctuation to support her reading? • Is the child adjusting her voice to match the meaning of text? • Is child reading fluently and without hesitation, so decoding strategies are practically invisible?

Planning: Linking the Assessment Result to Curriculum Ideas

The following guidelines for curriculum planning reflect a balanced literacy approach that advocates teaching and guiding children's development as readers and writers with differing degrees of support and help from a variety of sources. The balanced literacy approach describes a continuum of support beginning with the maximum amount of help as exemplified in reading aloud to children to the least support as reflected in children's independent reading. Bridging's assessment activity analyzes the child at the independent reading level while the curriculum planning considers the developmental continuum where the child is learning to be an independent reader while benefiting from the help of others—teacher as well as peers.

Reading Aloud to Young Children: Children as young as one or two years old as well as those in elementary school benefit from hearing fluent expressive reading of all kinds of genres including story books (picture books as well as chapter books), fairy tales and folk tales, poetry, and the wide variety of informational texts that enrich young children's lives. It provides them with exposure to and emersion in the fully developed forms of thinking and reflection that good readers experience. When teachers, older school children, and peers read to and with one another, they lay the foundation for the experience we so long for our young children to become proficient in.

Guidelines for teachers when reading to young children include the following:

- Read often throughout the school day and read from a variety of genres.
- Before reading a book, ask children what they think the book might be about when seeing the cover page and hearing the title. For example, "I wonder what this story is about. What do you think?" When possible, do a picture walk through the book to elicit predictions about text. "What do you see here? What's happening? I wonder what is going on here."
- Don't be afraid to read some books several times, even many times! This is how children develop favorites, and frequent readings allow them to memorize the text—an important achievement before they independently read the text.
- Discuss vocabulary that is relevant to the story.
- While reading, read continuously and expressively. Modulate your reading voice to emphasize the meaning conveyed in the text. As a general rule, try not to stop and ask questions during the reading.
- After reading, ask children questions that explore the story's meaning in an open-ended way, meaning there is no one answer, just different points of view on understanding characters and what is happening. Ask questions that explore the reasons for characters' actions, why certain events take place. A good starting point for questions is, "I wonder why . . . . What do you think?" You might want to compare children's thinking to their initial predictions. You might also relate the story to other books you have read and then to the children's own lives.

- When revisiting a storybook, point out words that are salient in the text.
- Introduce children to different versions of the same story. Compare/contrast the various stories in ongoing discussions.

Shared Reading/Choral Reading: In this reading format, teachers display the words of a song, poem, nursery rhythm, or story excerpt on a chart, or read from a big book format or other visual display of the text. The teacher guides the group in reading along with him or her as a group so that they experience the rhythms and pacing of expressive reading as well as enjoy the text together.

- In the beginning, select song lyrics and texts that are predictable, repetitive, and full of fun rhyming words. Nursery rhymes and simple songs such as "Hickory Dickory Dock" provide wonderful opportunities for children to practice phonemic awareness as well as phonics skills.
- In the latter part of kindergarten and the primary grades, have children find salient letters and words after reading the text together.
- As a follow-up activity, cut the chart into sentence strips or even words of the song or poem and have students rearrange them in the appropriate sequence.
- There are many games that can help children explore spelling patterns, such as playing "Hangman" in small or large groups. Put lines on the blackboard corresponding to the number of letters in a word that you are thinking about; for example, _ _ _ _ _ . Children take turns guessing possible letters in the word. As the teacher confirms letters, children study the pattern of what is there until they guess the word. For example: _ o o _ s becomes b-o-o-k-s.

Guided Reading: For primary grade children, teachers will want to work with small groups of children throughout the week who are working on approximately the same kind of reading skills. These small group formats are a good opportunity for teachers to get close to children's reading and assist them in learning and practicing comprehension and decoding strategies.

- During guided reading, explicitly encourage students to use their knowledge about word structures, word families, syntax, punctuation, and the pictures to decode text.
- Provide strategies to help children connect word analysis skills with the text they are reading.
- Provide access to increasingly complex texts.

Independent Reading: As soon as babies are able to hold a book, they are old enough to begin independent reading. When young children are exposed to the pleasures of books through being read to, their interest and curiosity is awakened to explore what they can find and "read" in books. It is very important that teachers set the expectation that everyone will read books at a predictable time of the school day to both get in the habit of picking up different kinds of books to read and practice their emerging reading skills, no matter what their age. To facilitate independent reading, you will want to:

- Maintain an inviting and interesting collection of books in your classroom that represents the full range of genres of interest to young children, including fantasy and fairy tales, poetry, realistic stories (picture books and chapter books), and stories from far away and long ago (historical novels, stories set in different cultures). Include informational texts that communicate concepts, facts, and skills about the world around us and human experiences including biographies and autobiographies, books about times and places near and far, and science books reflecting various areas of animal and plant life, earth sciences, and astronomy.
- Have recorded versions of many favorite books available for independent listening.
- Provide child with opportunities to read for a variety of purposes (for example, have children read to peers; use books to gather information for a project, as well as reading for pleasure).

Dictating a Story*

Procedure

*Adapted from Paley (1981, 1990, 2001).

Subject Area	Key Concepts and Skills
• Language arts and literacy	• Visualizing a scene and conveying it to others in words
Social Arrangements	• Use of language to convey ideas and feelings
• *Recommended:* teacher-child, child-child	• Concept of story: elements and structure
• *Viable:* large group	• Print convention

Activity and Goal

The teacher writes down individual children's dictated stories in each child's notebook/journal and then facilitates dramatization of each story at a group time. Children's stories might be original or the retelling of a familiar book.

Materials

- A notebook for each child or a sheet of paper
- Pencil and markers

Procedure

1. Select a time during the school day when you can be available to write down stories that children dictate individually. To initiate storytelling, the teacher can watch the children at play and invite children to develop one of their play ideas into a written story that will be acted out. Teachers can also read a story from a child in another classroom as an example of a story that can be told and then acted out.

2. Select a table where 3 to 5 children can gather to work on drawing, writing, or just listening and talking to others as dictation takes place.

3. Establish a routine where children take turns dictating stories, perhaps using a sign-up sheet or using the class roster and going down the list to give each child a chance to dictate.

4. To begin the dictation process, sit with the child, pencil ready to record. If the child needs a prompt to get started, ask, "How does your story begin?" or "What happens in your story?" Children may tell an original story or retell a familiar one.

5. During dictation, if a child pauses for 5 seconds or more, or says he or she is stuck, intervene with the following succession of prompts:
   - Repeat the last sentence that the child dictated and then wait to see if that jump starts the child to continue;
   - If that is not helpful, ask, "What happens next?"
   - If that does not help, ask, "Is there anything more in your story?" in order to find out if the child is finished.
   - Reread the whole story and ask if there is anything else the child wants to add.

6. If a child demonstrates a motion or action to be included in the story, ask, "How can you put that into words?" or "How shall I write that in your story?"

7. As the child's dictation gets near to the end of the paper, tell him or her to think of a good ending as there is room for only one or two more sentences. Limit all stories to writing on one side of a 5" × 7" sheet of paper (3 to 5 sentences). Dictation will take approximately 1 to 5 minutes per child. As children grow older and comfortable with more detail, you can expand the story paper to 8.5" × 11".

8. Plan to dramatize children's stories later the same day.

Dictating a Story

Recording Sheet

Child's name _____ Assess date _____ Assessor _____ Rubric level_____

Note any observations of child during the activity and record (or staple) child's dictated story here.

Story Source

☐ Original story

☐ Retelling of a familiar story

Child begins story easily

☐ no

☐ with prompting

☐ yes

Child can bring story to conclusion

☐ no

☐ with prompting

☐ yes

Dictating a Story

Evaluative Working Approach Rubric

Circle the number that best describes the child's evaluative working approach in this activity.

Child's Name:
_____

Initial Engagement: How does the child initially respond to the activity?

Hesitant _____ **Eager**

1	2	3	4	5
very hesitant or unwilling to begin activity		becomes involved on his or her own		eager to begin activity

Focus, Attention: How on task is the child throughout the activity?

Distractable _____ **Attentive**

1	2	3	4	5
very easily distracted by other children, events, or materials		attentive some of the time		sustained, absorbed attention to activity

Goal Orientation: How clear is the child working toward the activity's goal?

Personal goal _____ **Activity goal**

1	2	3	4	5
works on personal goal rather than activity goal		child's work vacillates between personal goal and activity goal		works efficiently toward activity goal

Planfulness: How organized is the child in working toward task completion?

Haphazard _____ **Organized**

1	2	3	4	5
random or impulsive; no evidence of organization of materials or approach		organized some of the time		well-organized, methodical in approach or with materials

Resourcefulness: What does the child do when stuck?

Helpless _____ **Resourceful**

1	2	3	4	5
does not ask for help; unable to use help when offered		moves forward a step when help is given		seeks help and makes good use of it to figure out challenges

Cooperation (for group activities): How does the child work with peers to accomplish task?

Difficulty working with others _____ **Helpful to others**

1	2	3	4	5
has difficulty sharing materials or attention, taking turns, supporting the efforts of others		gets along with other children		helps other children with activity, materials, or as a mediator; models ideas for others

Dictating a Story

Descriptive Working Approach Rubric

Circle the number that best describes the child's descriptive working approach in this activity.

Child's Name:
_____

Chattiness: How much of the child's talk is unrelated to the activity?

Very quiet _____ **Very chatty**

1	2	3	4	5
little conversation and self-talk throughout the activity		talks from time to time		constantly talks about unrelated topics

Pace of Work: What is the child's pace of work?

Slow _____ **Fast**

1	2	3	4	5
slow to start and carry out the activity		moderate pace throughout the activity	quick start and quick finish	

Social Referencing: How often does the child check with teachers or peers?

Little interaction _____ **Constant checking**

1	2	3	4	5
focuses on own work		attention to others' work and checks with others about own work occasionally		frequently asks teacher or peer if own work is on track

Playfulness: How animated, lively, or happy is the child during the activity?

Serious _____ **Playful**

1	2	3	4	5
mood/demeanor is serious and cheerless		business-like with activity		cheerful and sense of humor related to activity

Activities: Language Arts and Literacy

Dictating a Story*

Performance Rubric

Adapted and modified from Applebee (1978).

Level	Name	Performance Indicators*
0	No participation	• Child declines to participate in activity.
1	One-word narrative	• Child says one or more words, but without any connections among the words. • Child may scribble on paper and give one word label or name (for example, dad, doggy, flower).
2	Heap	• Story can sound like a list of items or events. • Story is one sentence (for example, "A mermaid swims in the water"). • Child does not attempt to relate events or words together. • There is no single idea or character at the center of the story.
3	Sequence	• Story is a collection of ideas/objects/associations linked by some concrete similarity. • Story elements share a common core because of some visible similarity (for example, a certain action repeated over and over or an "events of the day" story).
4	Primitive narrative	• There is a core idea or character at the center of the story. • Relations among characters and actions are not fully developed. • The links among the characters and actions are based on practical experience in the here-and-now. The links are concrete rather than conceptual.
5	Unfocused chain	• Story line is tenuous and often gives way to another topic. • Story events lead from one to another but links may shift (settings may blur, characters may come and go). • Story lacks a conflict or problem that is central to plot. • Story might contain very little detail or be a string of associations.

Level	Name	Performance Indicators*
6	Focused chain	• Story proceeds with a set of events and characters around a central idea or conflict that is concrete rather than conceptual. • Stories are of a "continued adventures of _____" type.
7	Elaborated narrative	• Story proceeds with a set of events and characters around a central idea with consistent forward movement toward problem resolution at a conceptual level. • Story has a climax where there is a change in character or circumstances as a result of events or character actions.
8	Complete episodes	• All criteria for Level 7 plus • Story includes some description of characters' motivations or setting. • Story includes overt indicators of changes in time/space.
9	Complex episodes	• All criteria for Level 7 plus • Story includes some description of both characters' motivations and setting.
10	Interactive episodes	• All criteria for Level 7 plus • Story includes some description of both characters' motivations and setting. • Story contains two parallel, interactive episodes.

Activities: Language Arts and Literacy

Dictating a Story Bridge to Curriculum

Reviewing: Key Concepts and Skills Exercised in the Activity

- Understanding of books and reading
- Concepts of story: elements and structure
- Print conventions—left to right orientation, word spacing, punctuation
- Relationship between illustrations and text
- Reading intonation
- Decoding strategies

Reflecting: Questions Related to Child's Performance Child's Working Approach

- Do any Evaluative Working Approaches stand out from the others?
- Are there Working Approach behaviors that seem to be contributing to or hindering the child's performance?
- Can you attribute the behaviors that stand out to any of the activity parameters: materials, key concepts, social arrangements, or activity structure?

Task Parameters

Social Arrangements
- Would the child work better one-on-one?

Child's Performance

Rubric Levels 1–2	• What is the child conveying in naming objects and people?
Rubric Levels 3–6	• Do characters enter and exit the story without being fully developed? • Can the child tell a story that revolves around a central character or characters? • Can the child use characters' actions to tell a story? • Can the child generate dialogue for what story characters say to one another? • Does the child develop several events in the story? • Can the child tell a story that revolves around a central event or conflict?
Rubric Levels 7–10	• Does the child use characters' motivations and feelings to tell a story? • Do characters' feelings and motivations evolve or change in the course of the story? • Does the child's story have a climax or resolution? • Does child place his or her story in particular time and/or place? • Does the child use dialogue in his or her story?

Planning: Linking the assessment result to curriculum ideas

Story dictation is an opportunity to cultivate children's narrative skills and transform them into those of writers. Children benefit from the frequent experience of others, both teachers and their peer group, being interested in the ideas they are developing long enough to write them down carefully, line by line. The classroom becomes a laboratory for expressing and revising ideas in writing when serious attention is given to this activity in young children's school day.

The benefits of this activity for young children begin when the teacher creates space and time for dictation.

Time. Dictation requires no more than 2 to 4 minutes per child. A teacher spends time with an individual child taking dictation while the other children are engaged in productive activity–play time, activity time in centers, or when they are working on other assignments in the primary classroom. Children need to know when to expect the opportunity to dictate stories and know the routines for indicating their wish to do so through a sign-up sheet or other system that the teacher will create with the class.

Place. Dictation represents one medium available to children for the expression of their ideas. It becomes effective when associated with a particular place in the classroom: a writing (and drawing) table that is equipped with pencils, markers, erasers, scissors, rulers, crayons, and a variety of types of paper available to children to choose from when creating and composing a piece of writing, a drawing, or a mixed-media piece. For all young children, the more resources available in an inviting and efficient way, the more likely children are to explore and use the materials in new ways. Teachers will want to align story dictation with this location of resources for creative expression. Tell children that when you take down children's stories, you will sit at the story-writing table and work with individual children as their turn comes up.

Another important aspect of this arrangement is that other children can readily sit at the table and listen in on a child's dictation, get ideas for their own stories, as well as offer ideas to the child dictating (who always has the choice of taking editorial suggestions or not!). Teachers will want to encourage this kind of listening, borrowing, and use of ideas among the children to create a literary community that benefits from and uses the ideas of others to try out a new story idea or point of view.

Scribe. Many teachers feel that their time is too limited and stretched across many responsibilities to regularly take dictation, and at the rate children will want once they discover the intense satisfaction that comes from an adult listening attentively to their ideas. This is an area where teachers can strengthen the activity by getting parent volunteers, other school staff, and even older children in the school, 5th grade and above, to come in on a regular basis to take down children's stories. This can create a broader and richer concept of the classroom as a writers' workshop. All children through third grade benefit from regular opportunities to develop their ideas for a written story without having to focus on the mechanics of the task.

Strengthening story dictation in preschool, kindergarten, and the primary grades. Story dictation contributes to the building of a literary community among children and teachers in a classroom implementing a balanced literacy approach. Story dictation, along with its extensions to writer's workshop and independent self-initiated writing experiences, creates the balance to the reading components described in the planning for book-reading activities. Teachers can further children's development as writers in the following kinds of ways:

- Read often and from a wide variety of genres. Read different versions of the same story that allow children to compare and contrast the texts. All of these narrative forms provide bridges to becoming good readers and writers.

- Help stories live in your classroom in as many different ways as you can: pretend play, creating puppets for puppet plays, having books on tape in a listening center, having a felt board with felt characters for telling stories along with story dictation.

(Continued)

(Continued)

- Have lots of conversations with children where you frequently ask them to recount their experiences from the past, from a variety of situations, and reflecting a variety of emotions. These conversations can be a place where you and they begin to recognize what will make good subjects to dictate or write a story about.

- Encourage children's pretend play. Help children make connections between the story ideas they play out with peers and the stories they can dictate to be dramatized. You may spot a good story in the making during an activity time and might encourage a child who has not yet dictated a story to let you write it down for the group to enjoy later when stories are acted out.

- After stories have been dictated and acted out, talk with the children as a class about the kinds of ideas you notice that are emerging in their stories. Discuss characters and settings in their stories, the kinds of problems they encounter, and how they are solving them. You might explore who likes to tell particular kinds of stories—for example, those who like animal adventure stories, those who like fairytale themes, and those who like creating realistic family situations. This helps children notice both what they have been doing and other story forms that they might want to try out.

- Children can be encouraged to write and illustrate their own stories at the same table where dictation is taking place.

Acting Out a Story*   Procedure

*Adapted from Paley (1981, 1990, 2001).

Subject Area	Key Concepts and Skills
• Language arts and literacy	• Concept of story in body, mind, and voice
Social Arrangements	• Elements and structure of story as portrayed in physical actions
• *Recommended:* large group	• Development of imagery, action, and character
• *Viable:* small group	• Understanding of dramatic necessity, causal sequence

Activity and Goal

A small or large group of children act out stories composed by individual children during the story-dictation time. Dramatization takes place at a small or large group time on the same day a story is dictated.

Materials

- Children's dictated stories from earlier in the day
- Open space for the group to gather to dramatize stories
- A defined "stage," often a rectangular space marked with masking tape on classroom floor

Procedure

1. Have children sit in a circle around the edge of a rug or a class meeting area. During this group time, on the same day on which children have dictated their stories, read one story at a time.

2. After reading each story, ask the author to choose a character to portray. The teacher, not the author, then goes around the rug and asks children if they want to play the different characters in the story. The teacher continues offering children a role until all characters have been assigned.

3. If the author of the story does not want to be singled out for acting, use the procedure described above to assign all roles.

4. After roles have been assigned, read the story as written. The teacher's role is that of narrator and stage manager, directing and guiding the children's actions and signaling the beginning and end of the drama.

5. The rules necessary to keeping dramatization safe and productive are:
   - No touching anyone else
   - No leaving the designated stage area
   - Everything is pretend!

6. Dramatization takes about one to four minutes per story.

Activities: Language Arts and Literacy

Acting Out a Story

Recording Sheet

Child's name _____ Assess date _____ Assessor _____ Rubric level_____

Participation

- ☐ by presence alone
- ☐ is present, pays attention, follows action
- ☐ watches others and participates
- ☐ gestures or speaks with prompting
- ☐ gestures or speech appears self-initiated
- ☐ follows group, generally imitates

Body Movement

- ☐ body appears limp
- ☐ uses body dynamically to express action/ feeling of character

Vocal/Facial Expression

- ☐ speech is monotone, facial expression flat
- ☐ speech and facial expression are varied
- ☐ expression used does not correspond to situation/character
- ☐ expression used is accurate, corresponds to character/situation

Social Awareness

- ☐ does not contribute to organization of group presentation
- ☐ contributes to organizing the scenario
- ☐ cues other children to parts/actions

Use this section to describe what the child does and make notes about the child's experience acting out a story.

Acting Out a Story

Evaluative Working Approach Rubric

Circle the number that best describes the
child's evaluative working approach in this activity.

Child's Name:
_____

Initial Engagement: How does the child initially respond to the activity?

Hesitant _____ **Eager**

1	2	3	4	5
very hesitant or unwilling to begin activity		becomes involved on his or her own		eager to begin activity

Focus, Attention: How on task is the child throughout the activity?

Distractable _____ **Attentive**

1	2	3	4	5
very easily distracted by other children, events, or materials		attentive some of the time		sustained, absorbed attention to activity

Goal Orientation: How clear is the child working toward the activity's goal?

Personal goal _____ **Activity goal**

1	2	3	4	5
works on personal goal rather than activity goal		child's work vacillates between personal goal and activity goal		works efficiently toward activity goal

Planfulness: How organized is the child in working toward task completion?

Haphazard _____ **Organized**

1	2	3	4	5
random or impulsive; no evidence of organization of materials or approach		organized some of the time		well-organized, methodical in approach or with materials

Resourcefulness: What does the child do when stuck?

Helpless _____ **Resourceful**

1	2	3	4	5
does not ask for help; unable to use help when offered		moves forward a step when help is given		seeks help and makes good use of it to figure out challenges

Cooperation (for group activities): How does the child work with peers to accomplish task?

Difficulty working with others _____ **Helpful to others**

1	2	3	4	5
has difficulty sharing materials or attention, taking turns, supporting the efforts of others		gets along with other children		helps other children with activity, materials, or as a mediator; models ideas for others

Activities: Language Arts and Literacy

Acting Out a Story

Descriptive Working Approach Rubric

Circle the number that best describes the child's descriptive working approach in this activity.

Child's Name:
_____

Chattiness: How much of the child's talk is unrelated to the activity?

Very quiet _____ **Very chatty**

1	2	3	4	5
little conversation and self-talk throughout the activity		talks from time to time		constantly talks about unrelated topics

Pace of Work: What is the child's pace of work?

Slow _____ **Fast**

1	2	3	4	5
slow to start and carry out the activity		moderate pace throughout the activity		quick start and quick finish

Social Referencing: How often does the child check with teachers or peers?

Little interaction _____ **Constant checking**

1	2	3	4	5
focuses on own work		attention to others' work and checks with others about own work occasionally		frequently asks teacher or peer if own work is on track

Playfulness: How animated, lively, or happy is the child during the activity?

Serious _____ **Playful**

1	2	3	4	5
mood/demeanor is serious and cheerless		business-like with activity		cheerful and sense of humor related to activity

Acting Out a Story

Performance Rubric

Level	Name	Performance Indicators*
0	No participation	• Child declines to participate in activity.
1	Participation by presence	• Child agrees/volunteers to participate in story dramatization and is physically present but the child's part as a character is not actually a part in the flow of the story.
2	Participation by attention	• Child is physically present in acting out the story but does not make any gestures. • Child does not speak but appears attentive to what is going on; lets narrator convey the child's story part.
3	Participation with prompting	• Child is attentive and focused. • Child makes a few gestures with prompting. • Child repeats the lines of her character timidly, tentatively when prompted to do so. • Movement, facial expressions, and intonation may not totally correspond to character or situation. • Timing of playing out a character's part is not quite in sync with the storyline.
4	Participation in a flow	• Child follows the group rhythm, imitating other children to portray character, part, or lines. • Speaks lines of character eagerly
5	Participation with listening and awareness	• Child watches other children as a reminder of the child's own lines or part, or as a way to gauge own actions. • May or may not need prompts.
6	Acting— Beginner without prompting	• Child recognizes own part and acts out lines and actions without step-by-step prompting. • Child's speech tends to be in conversational voice; facial expressions are limited.
7	Acting— Intermediate	• Child uses movement elements (for example, timing, spacing, and/or body shape) and varied facial expressions during the dramatization. • Child may use lively character voice and highly expressive intonation. Sound effects may be included.
8	Acting—Fully developed	• Child effectively uses a wide range of movement elements, facial expressions, and lively character voice.
9	Acting with social awareness	• Child uses a wide range of movements, facial expressions, and lively character voice. • Child contributes to organizing the scenario and has an awareness of the presentations and actions and other characters.
10	Acting, social awareness and coaching	• Child uses a wide range of movements, facial expressions, and lively character voice. • Child contributes to organizing the scenario. • Child cues other children to their parts/actions.

Activities: Language Arts and Literacy

Acting Out a Story **Bridge to Curriculum**

Reviewing: Key Concepts and Skills Exercised in the Activity

- Concept of story in body, mind, and voice
- Elements and structure of story as portrayed in physical actions
- Development of imagery, action, and character
- Understanding of dramatic necessity, causal sequence

Reflecting: Questions Related to Child's Performance Child's Working Approach

- Do any Evaluative Working Approaches stand out from the others?
- Are there Working Approach behaviors that seem to be contributing to or hindering the child's performance?
- Can you attribute the behaviors that stand out to any of the activity parameters: materials, key concepts, social arrangements, or activity structure?

Task Parameters

Activity Structure

- Does the child feel uncomfortable with the open-ended nature of the task?

Social Arrangements

- Is the child intimidated by performing in front of a large group?

Child's Performance

Rubric Levels 1–2	<ul><li>Can the child attend to the story as it is being read?</li><li>Does the child understand that he or she is expected to assume a role in the story?</li><li>Is the child aware of his or her role even if not acting?</li></ul>
Rubric Levels 3–5	<ul><li>Does the child pay attention to what others are doing to assume his or her own role?</li><li>Does the child use the actions, gestures, or dialogue of others as cues for what to do?</li><li>Does the child imitate the actions, gestures, and dialogue of others in order to assume a role?</li><li>Does the child need prompting in order to assume a role?</li><li>Does the child respond to prompts with any actions, gestures, or dialogue?</li><li>Are responses to prompts adequate for the role?</li></ul>
Rubric Levels 6–8	<ul><li>Is the child able to spontaneously use actions or gestures to assume a role?</li><li>Are these appropriate for the role?</li><li>Is the child able to spontaneously use dialogue to play a character?</li><li>Are these appropriate for the role?</li><li>Does the child use gestures, dialogue, voice intonation, and/or sound effects in a creative manner?</li></ul>
Rubric Levels 9–10	<ul><li>Does the child cue others to help them with their roles?</li><li>Does the child actively engage in sharing a vision for the staging of a story?</li></ul>

Planning: Linking the Assessment Result to Curriculum Ideas

Early childhood classrooms are a sea of movement. Acting out stories, role playing problems, and possible ways to manage the details of living and working among a large group of peers are the logical and optimal ways to make conscious ways of thinking and moving that are conducive to learning for all. Movement and gesture are the first signs of life and liveliness in an infant and are among the first signals caregivers learn to read when meeting the needs of an infant. Gesture and movement are universal means of communication and are ready media for young children to examine the logic and meaning of stories they write as well as those that authors have written that the teachers read to them or that children read to themselves.

Logistics for story acting. A few simple guidelines make story acting one of the easiest and most satisfying activities in an early childhood classroom. First, there needs to be a defined space that has clear physical boundaries; it can be marked by a rug or by masking tape laid down in a square denoting the stage and allowing the children in the audience to sit around. When children are acting in the story, they can never leave the stage.

Second, no props or furniture are used ever. The activity is far more effective if every story idea has to be imagined and translated into physical positions and gestures.

Third, a no-touching rule is essential. Any idea is safe to act out as long as no one gets hurt. This is ensured by requiring that no one touch another's body.

Developing acting skills. The best way to cultivate skills in acting out a story are to start with the tiniest of stories—nursery rhymes and finger plays. These ought to become the glue of a good day in school. Many teachers recognize the immediate benefit of finger plays and nursery rhymes using hand motions while waiting in line or as a group during a transition point in the day. They readily take children's minds off an unsettled situation and focus them in a physical and mental way on a story idea.

The next building block for dramatization is acting out simple adult-authored story books as a group, such as *The Carrot Seed, The Three Billy Goats Gruff,* or *Where the Wild Things Are.* One half of the class can be one character, such as the billy goats, and the other half of the class can be the other main character: the troll. By doing a group dramatization, children do not have to feel the initial self-consciousness that can come when acting in front of a group in a new setting. They can also watch others and compare their own actions to the possibilities represented in the portrayal of a character's gesture or facial expression by other children. As you guide their acting out of such stories, you can explicitly discuss the kinds of actions, gestures, and dialogue that support the meaning of the text.

When dramatizing a story, poem, or song, encourage children to think about the feelings and ideas they are trying to convey to others. Ask questions such as:

- How can you show everyone that you are scared (or angry, surprised)?
- If you are supposed to be a little puppy (or an angry lion, a powerful dinosaur), how can you let others know that?
- How can you show that you are walking in quicksand (or swimming on the ocean, climbing a mountain)?

Whenever possible, take children to watch theatrical performances and discuss them when you return to the classroom. What characters' ideas did they particularly like in the show? What ideas did they get for their own future stories and acting? Children will also enjoy playing pantomine games like charades whereby children act out one word (perhaps verbs such as the types of movements of different animals or insects, or words depicting different emotions).

Activities: Language Arts and Literacy

(Continued)

(Continued)

Many children will gravitate to puppets as one way to act out events in stories. Puppets can be easily made from socks or brown paper lunch bags, thus letting children create their characters as well as the stories to go with them.

Finally, role-playing real-life dilemmas in the classroom can be a powerful way to integrate the need for problem solving from stories to help children learn to get along well in real life. For example, if children are having trouble sharing blocks for building in the block area, a teacher can create a simple story to be created and acted out by the children at group time. A teacher might say that she has written a story and needs help to finish it.

> Once there was a group of animals who played in the forest: a lion, an elephant, a snake, and a duck. They wanted to build a house together. They found many great logs and tree branches to help them make walls for their house. As they began to build, they began to argue. Lion said, "Put that log over here." Elephant said, "No, I need it here!" Duck said, "No, it isn't supposed to look like that!" Snake said, "I have an idea. Give me all the sticks. I'll show you how to do it!"

The story is not finished. How are these friends going to work out this problem? Show me one way you can imagine them building a house together." The teacher then calls four children up to role-play this initial scenario and one possible next scene.

After one group has role-played their idea, the teacher can call four more children into the circle to stage their image of problem resolution. Thus, story acting can become an ongoing arena for exploring ideas right alongside the acting out of ideas from good story books as well as the children's own stories, making the classroom experience a rich tapestry of written ideas that influence each other.

Activities

Visual Arts

WHAT WE KNOW

The arts in general, and the visual arts in particular, provide children with a variety of ways to explore the world beyond words and numbers. Playing with the possibilities and constraints of line, shape, color, and two-dimensional spatial planes, children develop new and exciting ways of thinking and communicating. Using the resources of different visual arts media, they study the properties of these materials and explore their creative potential for communicating ideas and feelings. Work in the arts develops discipline; control of tools, materials, and techniques; and mastery of their use for creating, understanding, and communicating meaning.

In Chapter 4, we discussed the dilemmas we faced when trying to develop a Bridging assessment activity for children's pretend play and the reasons why it was not possible to do so at this time. Children's play is not one specific activity with a progression of steps in its development. Rather, play is an activity that is multifaceted, and in particular, culturally derived and influenced and therefore specific to a community's beliefs and practices. These same dilemmas hold true for children's work in the visual arts. As systems of symbolic expression, play, language, and the arts have common paths of development in the early months and years of a child's life, which very quickly come into the domain of culturally derived lines of development. As set out clearly in the research work of the National Art Education Association, there are no universal stages of development in the visual arts and no universal criteria for assessing children's work. Assessment and interpretation of artwork, then, is questionable at best.

Artists and educators continue to debate (and appropriately so) criteria to evaluate individual children's efforts in drawing and painting. However, they agree on the benefits of engaging children in the production of visual art works in the classroom and the value and potential of such work to further children's thinking in this domain and other subject areas. In addition, artists and educators agree on the critical importance of engaging children in discussion of their work in relation to each other and to the work of artists from all cultures. Thus, while art education in early childhood classrooms continues to evolve, so too does the debate over how to describe different skill levels and outcomes.

WHAT BRIDGING PROVIDES

Why does the Bridging assessment process include the visual arts, given the thinking of experts in this profession? Why not leave the visual arts to teachers' discretion as to when and how to use them in the classroom? After careful review of the concerns and research surrounding children's development in the area of the visual arts, we have decided to include three activities that are very basic and common in early childhood classrooms precisely because they are so common. In addition, the visual arts are of enormous importance to children, and there are clear curricular paths that can support children's development in the arts even if we cannot evaluate the outcome precisely and "accurately." The visual arts provide inventive and resourceful ways to communicate ideas within the classroom, school, and, eventually, the larger community. The exploration of their own creativity provides young children with the opportunity to develop an appreciation of their own work as well as that of others. This appreciation encourages greater understanding of the roles of culture and personal experience in the creation, as well as the interpretation, of any visual artwork.

Bridging's visual arts activities enable children to demonstrate their creativity and fine motor skills as they develop an understanding of individual expression and artistic representation. Children progress from first exploring the physical properties of several media to exploring various ways to use each medium to produce lines and shapes within the confines of a given space. As children experiment with line, color, pattern, and composition, they develop ways to communicate experiences and ideas through representational and abstract forms of artwork.

We believe that careful observation of children's work in the visual arts and the materials used in the three assessment activities provide important insights to a child's development when viewed in contrast to, as well as in comparison with, work in other subject areas. When a child has artistic skills, interests, or both, they become evident in one of the activities presented here and then can inform a teacher's thinking and discussion with others as to how to support a child's learning in school. Thus, while we acknowledge and recognize the limitations of rubric levels, we think the benefits of giving children and teachers a way to talk about visual representations as constructed in today's schools far outweigh the shortcomings in attempting to do so.

WHY THESE THREE ACTIVITIES

The three Bridging visual arts activities are Experimenting With Crayon Techniques, Drawing a Self-Portrait, and Making Pattern Block Pictures. The first activity examines a child's skill and willingness to experiment in a medium. In this case, the medium used is crayons, the most common artistic tool in early childhood classrooms everywhere. The process of exploring the possibilities and constraints of a medium could be carried out with a variety of media including watercolors, tempera paint, or chalk. We chose crayons to demonstrate how readily key concepts and skills in the visual arts can be assessed and developed in all early childhood classrooms.

The second visual arts activity, Drawing a Self-Portrait, is done with pencil alone and reflects one of the most basic drawing tasks used in classrooms and in many assessments: drawing a person. The task asks children to draw a picture of themselves at home. This elicits the range of skills that are emerging over the early childhood years, both the ability to represent a human figure and the ability to locate the figure in a setting. The choice of pencil alone for this task is intentional. The goal of this task, in contrast to the goal in the Experimenting With Crayon Techniques activity, is to foreground the child's drawing skills. Using a pencil, the child focuses on line and shape rather than color. In addition, the child is less likely to be distracted by the imprecision that can result when using tools such as crayons or paints.

The third visual arts activity stands in great contrast to the first two. The Making Pattern Block Pictures activity offers children a chance to create visual images and be expressive whether they are skilled with a pencil or paintbrush. We have seen many children show skill, creativity, and intense involvement with making a pattern block picture precisely because they could exploit the properties of the blocks to create an image. This effort is akin to building with blocks, an experience that many children find pleasurable and challenging. We selected pattern blocks because we wanted to contrast children's activity with a material commonly used for mathematics in early childhood classrooms with the same material used for more open-ended, creative expression. As a Bridging activity, the use of pattern blocks in the visual arts for creative expression, and in mathematics for a more structured goal, allows teachers to see the effects of activity structure and key concept focus on children's engagement in learning.

Relationship Between Standards and Bridging Activities in Visual Arts Area

Standards for Visual Arts	Bridging Activities		
	Crayon Techniques	Self-Portrait	Pattern Block Pictures
Modalities of Visual Arts			
• Different Modalities	√	√	√
• Application of Techniques and Processes	√	√	√
Materials, Techniques, Processes, and Elements			
• Materials and the Visual Arts	√	√	√
• Techniques and Processes	√	√	√
• Line	√	√	√
• Pattern	√	√	√
• Shapes	√	√	√
• Planes	√	√	√
• Color	√		√
• Representation	√	√	√
• Composition	√	√	√
Meaning in Visual Art Works			
• Visual Arts and Artist's Intention	√	√	√
• Content, Techniques, and Communication of Meaning	√	√	√
Historical and Cultural Contexts and the Visual Arts			
• Connections Among History, Culture, and Visual Arts		√	
• Individual Artworks in Historical and Cultural Contexts	√		
Visual Arts and Other Disciplines			
• Connections Between the Visual Arts and Other Art Disciplines			
• Connections Between the Visual Arts and Other Disciplines in the Curriculum		√	√

Standards listed here are a combination of those defined by the Consortium of National Arts Education Associations (available at http://artsedge.kennedy-center.org/teach/standards.cfm) and the Illinois State of Board of Education (available at http://www.isbe.state.il.us/ils/fine_arts/standards.htm).

Definition of Visual Arts Standards

Modalities of Visual Arts

- **Different Modalities** There are a variety of visual media through which ideas and feelings related to the human experience can be expressed and appreciated. There are essential differences among materials, techniques, and processes used in the different media, and each can be used for different purposes and to elicit different responses.

- **Application of Techniques and Processes** Creating visual artwork entails the use of techniques, materials, processes, and vocabulary associated with a particular modality.

Materials, Techniques, Processes, and Elements

- **Materials and the Visual Arts** A wide variety of materials are used in the visual arts, and each material has properties and limitations that frame its use.

- **Techniques and Processes** Visual artworks are created through the use of a wide variety of techniques and processes, and each technique or process has characteristics and limitations that frame its use.

- **Line** Line is an essential element in any visual artwork. There are many types of lines (vertical, horizontal, diagonal, curved), which may be used in isolation or in relation to one another, at random or purposefully, to achieve a variety of visual effects, forms, and textures.

- **Pattern** Repetition of certain elements may be used in visual art works to create a particular effect or communicate certain ideas.

- **Shapes** Shapes are used in visual artworks to represent a diversity of objects, or to create a desired pattern or design, when communicating an idea.

- **Planes** Lines and shapes may be used in visual artworks to set a baseline; indicate symmetry, size, and spatial relationships between objects; communicate ideas regarding the visual and nonvisual features of objects; or to create a nonrepresentational design.

- **Color** In the visual arts, color may be used deliberately, realistically or not, to create monochromatic or polychromatic representational and nonrepresentational works, or to communicate mood, harmony, and atmosphere.

- **Representation** Representational artwork attempts to match the graphic qualities of different materials and elements, including line, color, pattern, symmetry, and planes, to the visual and nonvisual significant features of objects.

- **Composition** The visual effects of a medium, including line, color, pattern, or symmetry, can be combined and arranged for a variety of purposes.

Meaning in Visual Art Works

- **Visual Arts and Artist's Intention** Visual art works have meaning and content that respond to the artist's intention.

- **Content, Techniques, and Communication of Meaning** Individuals can select and use subject matter, symbols, techniques, media, and ideas to communicate meaning.

(Continued)

Activities: Visual Arts

(Continued)

Historical and Cultural Contexts and the Visual Arts
• **Connections Among History, Culture, and Visual Arts** The visual arts have strong connections to the historical and contextual setting in which they are created.
• **Individual Artworks in Historical and Cultural Contexts** Individual artworks have characteristics that identify them as belonging to particular times, cultures, and places.
Visual Arts and Other Disciplines
• **Connections Between the Visual Arts and Other Art Disciplines** There are strong connections between the visual arts and other art disciplines, such as music, drama, and dance. Their similarities and differences can be used to understand these connections.
• **Connections Between the Visual Arts and Other Disciplines in the Curriculum** There are connections between the visual arts and other disciplines in the school curriculum, such as literature, writing, science, and math.

Experimenting With Crayon Techniques   Procedure

Subject Area	**Key Concepts and Skills**
• Visual arts **Social Arrangements** • *Recommended:* small group, large group • *Viable:* child-child, teacher-child	• Appreciation of how artists produce different effects in one medium • Experimenting with qualities of line • Adapting techniques or media to correspond to one's artistic ideas

Activity and Goal

Children use crayons to experiment with producing different effects and then use these crayon techniques to create a picture.

Note: This activity can take place in two separate work sessions on the same day, or on two separate days. For younger children, it is better to carry out the activity during the course of one day.

Materials

- Paper: two or three sheets (8.5" x 11") for each child
- A variety of crayons: fat and thin, some with paper wrapper torn off
- Two sample crayon drawings including several different kinds of crayon marks created by the teacher: one representational and one nonrepresentational
- Simple flat objects that can be used for rubbings (for example, coins, carpeting, popsicle sticks, sandpaper)

Procedure – Work Session I

1. Introduce children, in small or large group, to the idea of making different kinds of marks on a piece of paper using a crayon. Ask the children, **"What are some different ways you can use the crayons to make marks on paper?"**

2. Give each child one or two single sheets of white paper. Make crayons and sample objects for rubbing available to all. Invite them to use the crayons to experiment with as many different ways of making marks on their papers as they can.

3. After a period of experimentation (10–15 minutes), invite the children to share their discoveries with the group. Some children may demonstrate their discoveries, while others will talk about them.

4. Use the children's language and experiments as a bridge to terms such as *thick, thin, hard, soft, rubbing, curved, straight.* If the children's drawings do not show evidence of these techniques, demonstrate and provide the appropriate vocabulary. From a peer or the teacher, children will see the following:

   Rubbing

   Thin lines (crayon tip)

   Thick lines (crayon side)

   Hard lines (press hard)

   Soft lines (press lightly)

   Wavy lines

   Straight lines

   Dots

(Continued)

(Continued)

5. Show students two sample works that incorporate some of these techniques. One of the works needs to be a recognizable representation, that is, a drawing of something real. The other needs to be nonrepresentational, a design or pattern. Encourage children to identify verbally the techniques they see in the work (for example, rubbing, thick line, etc.).

Procedure – Work Session 2

1. This session can either immediately follow the exploration or occur at a later time.

2. Remind the children of their experiments with crayons. Also, show them the two works of art discussed in Work Session 1, and remind them of the techniques used. Invite children to use crayons to create a picture on their own. Encourage them to work for as long as they can. Say, **"Now it is your turn to make a picture. You can make a design, or you can make a picture of something you are thinking about. Use the crayons in as many different ways as you can."**

3. Observe children closely and listen to what they say for clues about their thoughts and their intentions.

Activities: Visual Arts

Experimenting With Crayon Techniques

Recording Sheet

Child's name _____ Assess date _____ Assessor_____ Rubric level _____

Use this section to describe child's completed Crayon Technique (or attach it) and to make notes about the child's experience creating the picture.

Which techniques does the child try out? (Check all that apply)

☐ Rubbing

☐ Thin lines

☐ Thick lines

☐ Hard lines

☐ Soft lines

☐ Wavy lines

☐ Straight lines

☐ Dots

☐ Variety in these elements

☐ Pattern in these elements

☐ Pattern and variation using several elements

Activities: Visual Arts

Experimenting With Crayon Techniques

Evaluative Working Approach Rubric

Circle the number that best describes the child's evaluative working approach in this activity.

Child's Name:

_____

Initial Engagement: How does the child initially respond to the activity?

Hesitant _____ **Eager**

1	2	3	4	5
very hesitant or unwilling to begin activity		becomes involved on his or her own		eager to begin activity

Focus, Attention: How on task is the child throughout the activity?

Distractable _____ **Attentive**

1	2	3	4	5
very easily distracted by other children, events, or materials		attentive some of the time		sustained, absorbed attention to activity

Goal Orientation: How clear is the child working toward the activity's goal?

Personal goal _____ **Activity goal**

1	2	3	4	5
works on personal goal rather than activity goal		child's work vacillates between personal goal and activity goal		works efficiently toward activity goal

Planfulness: How organized is the child in working toward task completion?

Haphazard _____ **Organized**

1	2	3	4	5
random or impulsive; no evidence of organization of materials or approach		organized some of the time		well-organized, methodical in approach or with materials

Resourcefulness: What does the child do when stuck?

Helpless _____ **Resourceful**

1	2	3	4	5
does not ask for help; unable to use help when offered		moves forward a step when help is given		seeks help and makes good use of it to figure out challenges

Cooperation (for group activities): How does the child work with peers to accomplish task?

Difficulty working with others _____ **Helpful to others**

1	2	3	4	5
has difficulty sharing materials or attention, taking turns, supporting the efforts of others		gets along with other children		helps other children with activity, materials, or as a mediator; models ideas for others

Experimenting With Crayon Techniques

Descriptive Working Approach Rubric

Circle the number that best describes the child's descriptive working approach in this activity.

Child's Name:

_____

Chattiness: How much of the child's talk is unrelated to the activity?

Very quiet _____ **Very chatty**

1	2	3	4	5
little conversation and self-talk throughout the activity		talks from time to time		constantly talks about unrelated topics

Pace of Work: What is the child's pace of work?

Slow _____ **Fast**

1	2	3	4	5
slow to start and carry out the activity		moderate pace throughout the activity		quick start and quick finish

Social Referencing: How often does the child check with teachers or peers?

Little interaction _____ **Constant checking**

1	2	3	4	5
focuses on own work		attention to others' work and checks with others about own work occasionally		frequently asks teacher or peer if own work is on track

Playfulness: How animated, lively, or happy is the child during the activity?

Serious _____ **Playful**

1	2	3	4	5
mood/demeanor is serious and cheerless		business-like with activity		cheerful and sense of humor related to activity

Activities: Visual Arts

Experimenting With Crayon Techniques   Performance Rubric

Level	Name	Performance Indicators
0	No participation	• Child declines to participate in the activity.
1	No picture	• Child uses paper or crayons for activity other than crayon drawing. • Child watches others.
2	Scribble or random	• Child makes marks on the paper but (as far as you can tell) they are unrelated to the techniques discussed and practiced.
3	Experiments with one or two techniques	• Child experiments with one or two techniques. No coherent picture or design—just the process of trying out the techniques.
4	Experiments with three or more techniques	• Child experiments with three or more techniques. No coherent picture or design—just the process of trying out the techniques.
5	Techniques in picture or design: very simple	• Child uses one or two techniques in a simple picture or design (for example, a single figure with thick and wavy lines; an alternating pattern with dots in different colors).
6	Techniques in picture or design: simple	• Child uses three or more of the techniques in a simple picture or design (for example, a single figure with thick, wavy, and dotted lines; an alternating pattern with dots, soft lines, and rubbings).
7	Techniques in picture or design: complex	• Child uses at least two of the techniques in a more complex picture (figure and setting) or design (several repeating elements) that shows two of the following: o Pattern or repetition of line, texture, color, light/dark contrast o Overlapping (for example, one technique on top of another: dots on rubbing, thin lines over thick ones, etc.) o Foreground and background o Variety of sizes and shapes o Variety of colors o Use of whole surface of paper
8	Techniques in picture or design: more complex	• Child uses at least two of the techniques in a more complex picture (figure and setting) or design (several repeating elements) that shows three or more of the following: o Pattern or repetition of line, texture, color, light/dark contrast o Overlapping (for example, one technique on top of another: dots on rubbing, thin lines over thick ones, etc.) o Foreground and background o Variety of sizes and shapes o Variety of colors o Use of whole surface of paper

Level	Name	Performance Indicators
9	Integrated composition	• Child's work meets criteria for Level 8 plus uses a certain crayon technique to communicate a particular quality of picture or design (for example, an elephant is shown as having rough skin, or the techniques are used to indicate symmetry).
10	Artistic expert	• Child's work meets criteria for Level 9 and also shows evidence of at least one of the following: • Perspective (some elements or parts of elements behind others so that picture looks three-dimensional) • Color, line, and/or composition used purposefully to communicate a uniform mood (quiet, energetic, threatening, tranquil, etc.)

Experimenting With Crayon Techniques   Bridge to Curriculum

Reviewing: Key Concepts and Skills Exercised in the Activity

- Appreciation of how artists produce different effects in one medium

- Experimenting with qualities of line

- Adapting techniques or media to correspond to one's artistic ideas

Reflecting: Questions Related to Child's Performance

Child's Working Approach

- Do any Evaluative Working Approaches stand out from the others?

- Are there Working Approach behaviors that seem to be contributing to or hindering the child's performance?

- Can you attribute the behaviors that stand out to any of the activity parameters: materials, key concepts, social arrangements, or activity structure?

Task Parameters

MATERIALS

- Is the child familiar with the use of crayons?

- Does the child need more time to experiment with the different techniques?

SOCIAL ARRANGEMENTS

- Would the child feel more comfortable working alone?

Child's Performance

Rubric Levels 1–4	• Are the child's motor abilities interfering with performance? • Is performance an indication that child is more interested in exploring the relationship between physical gestures and marks?
Rubric Levels 5–8	• Does the child understand the different techniques? • Does the child need more time to experiment with use of line, shape, color, pattern, and planes? • Does the child have enough experience with the process of using line, shape, color, pattern, and/or planes to communicate ideas?
Rubric Levels 9–10	• Can the child integrate the use of technique and color with aesthetics?

Planning: Linking the Assessment Result to Curriculum Ideas

The place and use of crayons in early childhood classrooms is a symbol for a teacher's approach to artistic development in young children's lives and its importance alongside the more academic focus to much of school learning. Our description of the use of crayons applies to the many other visual arts media we hope will be available to children over time, including various kinds of paint (watercolors, tempera), chalk and charcoals, and pencils and pens of different thicknesses. In order for the arts to have a place in early childhood curricula, there needs to be a clearly delineated space for the materials that children can have easy access to. They will want to be displayed in an attractive way that draws attention to the colors and other features they offer. Having the materials and workspace for using them near windows and other sources of light will greatly enhance their use. In addition, teachers will want to provide display space for children's work so that they have an ongoing way to view and revisit ideas they are experimenting with and working to represent.

The steps for the crayon technique activity represent steps in the learning process in the arts, each of which teachers will want to stretch out over many days with each different medium. In this sense, the assessment activity is a condensed form of the full-blown learning process. The learning opportunities that teachers will want to provide for each step of children's work will unfold as follows within each medium.

Exploration and experimentation. Have crayons freely available for children to use in an open-ended way, that is, with there being no expectations or requirements for a particular way of using them. Be particularly conscious of providing opportunities to use vocabulary that helps children recognize and articulate the different techniques they are using.

- Encourage the use of crayons on different kinds of papers (for example, butcher paper, tissue paper).
- Have different kinds of surfaces in the art area, and provide children with opportunities to experiment (for example, wire screen, paper with holes, cardboard).
- Display children's art in the classroom to facilitate discussion of how different techniques can be used for different purposes.

Discussion and closer observation. When working in the arts, it is important not to rush children through "covering" different steps in order to complete a project or product. Process is everything! It will be a welcome contrast to other types of work during the school day when you provide unhurried time to explore a medium and pursue ideas deeply rather than rushing to accomplish more. You can encourage children to see what they are doing by asking them to closely observe their own work and that of others and to talk about what they see. You can invite further exploration and discussion as time goes on.

- Use children's own work, no matter how sketchy and preliminary, as an oportunity to talk about what they are working on and trying out. The issue is not how pretty or recognizable the picture is, but rather what they did to produce the marks on paper that they have tried and what they notice about them. The goal of the discussion is to lead out of the children their own thinking about what's happening rather than to get them to label a finished product or anticipate someone else's thinking.
- Invite children to show their work to one another informally around the art table or at a group time to describe ideas or techniques they are experimenting with. As with dictated stories, presenting work to the group for comment and discussion can inspire others to try out various techniques and contribute to the ongoing classroom climate as a supportive learning environment.

(Continued)

(Continued)

- Use reproductions of artwork from around the world as presented in books, posters, or small reproductions from a library or museum shop to generate discussions about line, shape, pattern, color, and composition in the work of artists. What do they notice in the work of others? How do artists from different cultures and historical periods portray people, landscapes, scenes, perspective? What media do they use to represent ideas and why might they have chosen that one?

Focusing the study of using a medium to express ideas. As children develop a sense of familiarity and comfort in using various media, seek opportunities to focus their attention on developing their skills in representation (creating a picture of something recognizable) in contrast to using the media for nonrepresentational work—more free-form expressions that interest and engage them but that do not have an identifiable end product.

- At different points in time, have children use crayons to draw the same subject with varied techniques. Compare these drawings by calling attention to the similarities and differences in how different techniques can present different effects.

- Have a group of children draw the same object from different points of view. Compare and contrast how the same object is represented from different perspectives.

- Encourage children to use different techniques in a variety of projects, like picking particular ways to illustrate classroom books or poems.

- Visit a local museum. Concentrate on just a few pieces of art that belong to the same style or subject or focus on several works that offer interesting points of contrast. Talk about the artists' techniques and encourage discussion about what kind of message or mood the pictures convey.

- Ask students to create a picture using only one kind of technique (for example, rubbings). Talk about the process and highlight ways in which this limitation might have influenced their choice of subject and/or mood.

- Ask students to create a crayon drawing that conveys a particular mood (for example, calm, hectic). Discuss the process and the results.

- Occasionally limit the availability of art materials to one color (in easel paint, markers, and/or crayons). Discuss and display the monochromatic artworks produced. Emphasize how this constraint affected choice of subject, techniques, and mood of the product.

In summary, plan the school year so that children have exposure to and experiences with a wide variety of art materials. Support their use by providing opportunities for free exploration as well as occasions to work on projects with specific purposes.

Drawing a Self-Portrait

Procedure

Subject Area	**Key Concepts and Skills**
• Visual arts	• Representing human body and setting in two dimensions
Social Arrangements	• Using shape, line, and shading in representation
• *Recommended:* small group, large group	
• *Viable:* child-child, teacher-child	

Activity and Goal

Children use pencil to create a self-portrait showing themselves at home.

Materials

• Paper: one or two single 8.5" x 11" sheets

• Pencils: important that this task is done with **lead pencil only**, not colored pencils

Procedure

1. Give children pencils and paper. Ask them to "draw yourself at home." Emphasize the need to show others where they are in their home and what the room or area looks like.

2. Encourage children to work as long as they can.

3. When child is finished, ask the child to label and describe picture.

Activities: Visual Arts

Drawing a Self-Portrait

Recording Sheet

Child's name _____ Assess date _____ Assessor _____ Rubric level_____

Use this section to describe child's completed Self-Portrait (or attach it) and to make notes about the child's experience when drawing.

Drawing a Self-Portrait

Evaluative Working Approach Rubric

Circle the number that best describes the child's evaluative working approach in this activity.

Child's Name:

_____

Initial Engagement: How does the child initially respond to the activity?

Hesitant _____ **Eager**

I	2	3	4	5
very hesitant or unwilling to begin activity		becomes involved on his or her own		eager to begin activity

Focus, Attention: How on task is the child throughout the activity?

Distractable _____ **Attentive**

I	2	3	4	5
very easily distracted by other children, events, or materials		attentive some of the time		sustained, absorbed attention to activity

Goal Orientation: How clear is the child working toward the activity's goal?

Personal goal _____ **Activity goal**

I	2	3	4	5
works on personal goal rather than activity goal		child's work vacillates between personal goal and activity goal		works efficiently toward activity goal

Planfulness: How organized is the child in working toward task completion?

Haphazard _____ **Organized**

I	2	3	4	5
random or impulsive; no evidence of organization of materials or approach		organized some of the time		well-organized, methodical in approach or with materials

Resourcefulness: What does the child do when stuck?

Helpless _____ **Resourceful**

I	2	3	4	5
does not ask for help; unable to use help when offered		moves forward a step when help is given		seeks help and makes good use of it to figure out challenges

Cooperation (for group activities): How does the child work with peers to accomplish task?

Difficulty working with others _____ **Helpful to others**

I	2	3	4	5
has difficulty sharing materials or attention, taking turns, supporting the efforts of others		gets along with other children		helps other children with activity, materials, or as a mediator; models ideas for others

Activities: Visual Arts

Activities: Visual Arts

Drawing a Self-Portrait

Descriptive Working Approach Rubric

Circle the number that best describes the child's descriptive working approach in this activity.

Child's Name:

_____

Chattiness: How much of the child's talk is unrelated to the activity?

Very quiet _____ **Very chatty**

1	2	3	4	5
little conversation and self-talk throughout the activity		talks from time to time		constantly talks about unrelated topics

Pace of Work: What is the child's pace of work?

Slow _____ **Fast**

1	2	3	4	5
slow to start and carry out the activity		moderate pace throughout the activity		quick start and quick finish

Social Referencing: How often does the child check with teachers or peers?

Little interaction _____ **Constant checking**

1	2	3	4	5
focuses on own work		attention to others' work and checks with others about own work occasionally		frequently asks teacher or peer if own work is on track

Playfulness: How animated, lively, or happy is the child during the activity?

Serious _____ **Playful**

1	2	3	4	5
mood/demeanor is serious and cheerless		business-like with activity		cheerful and sense of humor related to activity

Drawing a Self-Portrait   Performance Rubric

Level	Name	Performance Indicators
0	No participation	• Child declines to participate in the activity.
1	No picture	• Child watches others or makes use of paper and pencil for some other purpose.
2	Scribble or random	• Child makes marks on the page, but with no recognizable representation or naming of figure.
3	Humanoid, fragmented or no setting	• Child draws rudimentary human figure (head with eyes, circle atop two sticks, tadpole-like form, etc.), but there is no setting or objects are scattered around the drawing of a figure.
4	Humanoid in setting	• Child draws rudimentary human figure (head with eyes, circle atop two sticks, tadpole-like form, etc.) located in a setting, engaged in an activity, or in the company of other people
5	Simple human, no setting or fragmented setting	• Child draws human figure with **one or two** of the following: ○ Separate parts for head and body ○ Facial features (at least both mouth and eyes) ○ Hands and/or feet ○ Hair and/or clothing • No setting, or only scattered objects. For example, simple human is near a TV, a bike, multiple items, or other people, but there's no room, house, or yard.
6	Simple human, recognizable setting	• Child draws human figure with **one or two** of the following: ○ Separate parts for head and body ○ Facial features (at least both mouth and eyes) ○ Hands and/or feet ○ Hair and/or clothing • Setting is recognizable as a room, house, yard, etc. Objects are located somewhere in space (TV in room, bike on grass).
7	Complex detailed human, recognizable setting	• Child draws human figure with **three or more** of the following: ○ Separate parts for head and body ○ Facial features (eyes, nose, mouth) ○ Hands and/or feet ○ Hair and/or clothing • Setting is recognizable as a room, porch, yard, etc. Objects are located somewhere in space (TV in room, bike on grass).
8	Complex detailed human, complex detailed setting	• Considerable detail in figure and in setting. Room may be recognizable as kitchen, child in the drawing may be wearing same clothes as the artist, etc. Child is ready to pursue artistic elements as described below.

(Continued)

Activities: Visual Arts

(Continued)

Level	Name	Performance Indicators

9	Complex detailed human, complex detailed setting, some artistic elements	• The drawing is Level 8 and the child shows mastery of **one or two** of the following artistic elements (elements must be present in both the figure and the setting):
		  ○ Shading (to make objects look 3-D or show light source effect on how objects appear)
		  ○ Perspective (shows that objects are behind others or farther away; tries to show depth)
		  ○ Line quality (uses thick/thin, hard/soft, straight/wavy, etc., to indicate mood)
		  ○ Repeated design elements (unifies picture with border; repeats line/texture pattern)
		  ○ Proportions of figure(s) to setting or objects is realistic

10	Complex detailed human, complex detailed setting, many artistic elements	• The drawing is Level 8 and the child shows mastery of **three or more** of the following artistic elements:
		  ○ Shading (to make objects look 3-D or show light source effect on objects' appearance)
		  ○ Perspective (shows that objects are behind others or farther away; tries to show depth)
		  ○ Line quality (uses thick/thin, hard/soft, straight/wavy, etc. to indicate mood)
		  ○ Repeated design elements (unifies picture with border; repeats line/texture pattern)
		  ○ Generally realistic proportions of figure(s) to setting and/or objects

Activities: Visual Arts

Drawing a Self-Portrait

Bridge to Curriculum

Reviewing: Key Concepts and Skills Exercised in the Activity

- Representing human body and setting in two dimensions
- Using shape, line, and shading in representation

Reflecting: Questions Related to Child's Performance

Child's Working Approach

- Do any Evaluative Working Approaches stand out from the others?
- Are there Working Approach behaviors that seem to be contributing to or hindering the child's performance?
- Can you attribute the behaviors that stand out to any of the activity parameters: materials, key concepts, social arrangements, or activity structure?

Task Parameters

Materials

- Is the child used to working with lead pencils?

Social Arrangements

- Would the child feel more comfortable working alone?

Child's Performance

Rubric Levels 1–2	• Does the child lack experience using different media for representational purposes? • Does child's level of motor development interfere with use of the pencil? • Is child's primary focus the physical act of making marks rather than creating a representational product?
Rubric Levels 3–5	• Is the child just starting to use line and shape for representational purposes? • Is the child ready to create more complex representations of the human figure?
Rubric Levels 6–8	• Does the child need more experience with the use of lines, shapes, and planes for representational purposes? • Is the child able to use details to individualize the human figure? The setting?
Rubric Levels 9–10	• Does the child need more experience with using artistic elements in drawings?

Planning: Linking the Assessment Result to Curriculum Ideas

Using a pencil to draw a visual sketch of an object is a learned skill. Frequently young children will come to a situation saying, "I can't draw a house [or an animal or person]. You do it for me." They see drawing skills as something a person has and can do, or does not have. It is very important that teachers convey that drawing skills are learned; that all of us can draw if we take time to practice and learn from experiences of observing and revisiting our drawing efforts with new insights. Like with the crayon technique, it is important to begin by having an environment that values drawings, provides a place to keep pencils and various sizes of drawing paper readily accessible, provides frequent opportunities to draw, and provides frequent opportunities to discuss drawings—one's own and those of others.

(Continued)

Activities: Visual Arts

(Continued)

Guidelines for furthering children's drawing in the classroom include the following:

- Provide multiple opportunities for unstructured drawing with pencil and paper during the school day. This ought to include allowing children to make use of the resources at a drawing/writing table or center in the classroom when they finish other requested tasks.

- Provide systematic support to help children understand that drawings are made by putting together basic shapes and lines. This can be done through mini-lessons that help children take apart sample drawings or by helping children think through how they can represent common objects in their spontaneous drawings.

- Have children draw common objects. Use their drawings to compare/contrast the different ways line and shape are used to represent the same object.

- Have children draw a real object, and contrast this with drawing an object from memory. Compare and contrast the products of both processes.

- Use reproductions of drawings from different artists and different cultures to support children's awareness of how line, shape, and composition are used to represent objects and people.

- Examine drawings of the human figure, and discuss how details are represented with the use of different techniques.

- Provide the children with mirrors as they create a self-portrait so that they can move back and forth between what they see and what they put on paper.

- Your classroom library will have a huge store of opportunities to examine the work of illustrators—all the ways artists have devised to give expression to ideas in a visual, as opposed to verbal, format. You will want to include books in your library collection that are illustrated with pencil drawings. When reading these and other books to the class, discuss the illustrator's style and use of techniques.

- Use both children's work and reproductions of works of art to generate discussions about line, shape, pattern, color, and composition.

- At different points in time, have children use pencils to draw the same subject. Compare these drawings, calling attention to similarities and differences in how they represent the same subject. Pay particular attention to the use of different techniques.

- Have a group of children use pencils to draw the same object from different points of view. Compare and contrast how the same object is represented from different perspectives.

- Encourage children to use different media (pencil, paint, crayon) to represent the same subject. Display these works, and discuss how different materials influence the way objects are represented.

Making Pattern Block Pictures

Procedure

Subject Area	**Key Concepts and Skills**
• Visual arts • Mathematics **Social Arrangements** • *Recommended:* small group, large group • *Viable:* child-child, teacher-child	• Matching shapes • Visual representation • Using colors • Part–whole relations

Activity and Goal

Using pattern blocks on black paper, children construct a representational picture.

Materials

- Containers of traditional pattern blocks

- Large sheets of black construction paper

- Large, flat working surface

- Camera to photograph children's completed pictures

- Blank labels for child's name and title of picture

Procedure

1. Give each child a sheet of black paper and container of pattern blocks and say, **"Use the pattern blocks to make a picture of something. It can be a thing or place or person. When you are done, I will ask you to tell me what it is."**

2. When children are finished, ask for a name for the picture and write it down, along with the child's name.

3. Take a photo of the finished picture.

Activities: Visual Arts

Making Pattern Block Pictures

Recording Sheet

Child's name _____ Assess date _____ Assessor_____ Rubric level _____

Naming Picture *(check one)*

☐ Child does not want to "name" picture
☐ Child "names" as afterthought
☐ Child readily names picture

Plan *(check one)*

☐ Child does not commit to a plan at any point, only explores/plays with blocks
☐ At some point, child seems to represent something in particular

Basic Representation *(check one)*

☐ There is no relationship between picture and name
☐ There is some simple relationship between picture and name
☐ Block shape or color evokes some part of name
☐ There is a complex relationship between picture and name

Objects and Settings *(check one)*

☐ Single object only
☐ Two or more objects, but no relationship between them
☐ Two or more related objects
☐ At least one object and a related setting

Object Types *(check one)*

☐ All are commonly depicted by children or readily suggested by block shapes
☐ At least one object is unusual

Presence of Detail *(check one)*

☐ Objects are very simple; parts of objects only broadly indicated
☐ At least one object is very detailed, or blocks **are** used cleverly

Use of Perspective, 3-D *(check one)*

☐ No apparent use of perspective or three dimensions
☐ Effective use of perspective appears in at least part of the picture

Making Pattern Block Pictures   Evaluative Working Approach Rubric

Circle the number that best describes the child's evaluative working approach in this activity.

Child's Name:

_____

Initial Engagement: How does the child initially respond to the activity?

Hesitant _____ **Eager**

I	2	3	4	5
very hesitant or unwilling to begin activity		becomes involved on his or her own		eager to begin activity

Focus, Attention: How on task is the child throughout the activity?

Distractable _____ **Attentive**

I	2	3	4	5
very easily distracted by other children, events, or materials		attentive some of the time		sustained, absorbed attention to activity

Goal Orientation: How clear is the child working toward the activity's goal?

Personal goal _____ **Activity goal**

I	2	3	4	5
works on personal goal rather than activity goal		child's work vacillates between personal goal and activity goal		works efficiently toward activity goal

Planfulness: How organized is the child in working toward task completion?

Haphazard _____ **Organized**

I	2	3	4	5
random or impulsive; no evidence of organization of materials or approach		organized some of the time		well-organized, methodical in approach or with materials

Resourcefulness: What does the child do when stuck?

Helpless _____ **Resourceful**

I	2	3	4	5
does not ask for help; unable to use help when offered		moves forward a step when help is given		seeks help and makes good use of it to figure out challenges

Cooperation (for group activities): How does the child work with peers to accomplish task?

Difficulty working with others _____ _____ **Helpful to others**

I	2	3	4	5
has difficulty sharing materials or attention, taking turns, supporting the efforts of others		gets along with other children		helps other children with activity, materials, or as a mediator; models ideas for others

Activities: Visual Arts

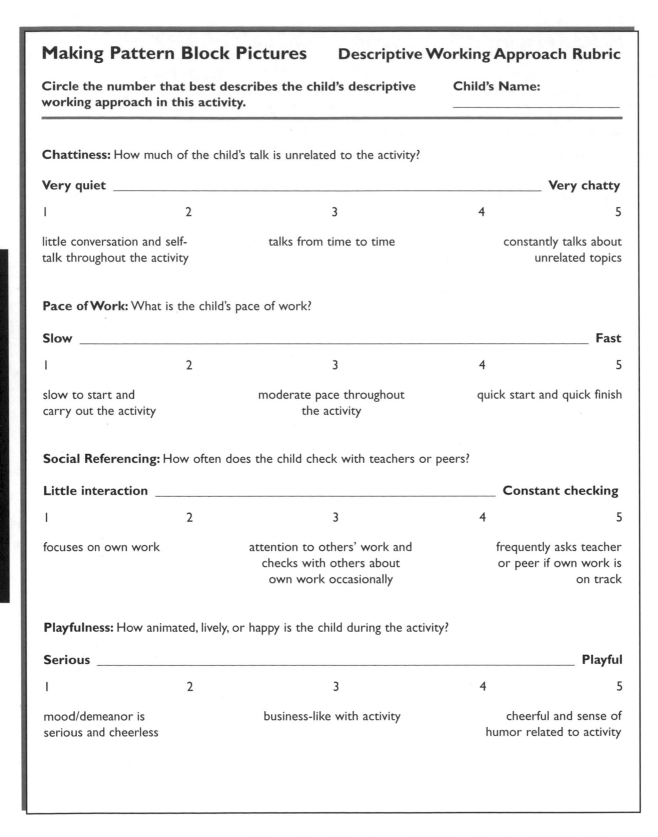

Making Pattern Block Pictures   Descriptive Working Approach Rubric

Circle the number that best describes the child's descriptive working approach in this activity.

Child's Name:
_____

Chattiness: How much of the child's talk is unrelated to the activity?

Very quiet _____ **Very chatty**

1	2	3	4	5

little conversation and self-talk throughout the activity · talks from time to time · constantly talks about unrelated topics

Pace of Work: What is the child's pace of work?

Slow _____ **Fast**

1	2	3	4	5

slow to start and carry out the activity · moderate pace throughout the activity · quick start and quick finish

Social Referencing: How often does the child check with teachers or peers?

Little interaction _____ **Constant checking**

1	2	3	4	5

focuses on own work · attention to others' work and checks with others about own work occasionally · frequently asks teacher or peer if own work is on track

Playfulness: How animated, lively, or happy is the child during the activity?

Serious _____ **Playful**

1	2	3	4	5

mood/demeanor is serious and cheerless · business-like with activity · cheerful and sense of humor related to activity

Making Pattern Block Pictures

Performance Rubric

Level	Name	Performance Indicators
0	No participation	• Child declines to participate in the activity.
1	Block play	• Uses pattern blocks for purpose other than creating a picture.
2	No picture/plan/name	• No apparent plan to make something—blocks are placed and later "named" via free association and only when the experimenter asks for the name; OR • child does not want to name what he or she has created.
3	Basic picture	• Genuine attempt to represent something and the picture is named by the child, and • It is possible to recognize some element of representation—color or shape of some part relates to the picture's name.
4	Simple single object, common subject	• Picture is completed and named by the child, and • Picture's subject is a single object (there is no setting or other object), and • Picture's subject is commonly represented or readily suggested by block shapes (for example, sun, flower, house, person, star), and • There is little detail/complexity—object has few parts.
5	Simple picture	• Picture is completed and named by the child, and • Picture's subject(s) are commonly represented or readily suggested by block shapes (for example, sun, flower, house, person, star), and • There is little detail/complexity—parts of objects are indicated broadly; and • There is either a setting (for example, sun above grass), or there are two objects with a relationship between them (for example, sun and flower).
6	Detailed single object, common subject	• Picture is completed and named by the child, and • Picture's subject is a single object (there is no setting or other object), and • Picture's subject is commonly represented or readily suggested by block shapes (for example, sun, flower, house, person, star), and • There is a lot of detail/complexity—object has many parts or blocks are used in an unusual way.
7	Full, detailed picture	• Picture is completed and named by the child, and • Picture's subject(s) are commonly represented or readily suggested by block shapes (for example, sun, flower, house, person, star), and • Some detail—parts of at least one object are very complex or blocks are used in an unusual way, and • There is either a setting (for example, sun above grass), or there are two objects with a relationship between them (for example, sun and flower).

Activities: Visual Arts

(Continued)

(Continued)

Activities: Visual Arts

Level	Name	Performance Indicators
8	Single uncommon object, well-executed	• Picture is completed and named by the child, and • Picture's subject is a single object (there is no setting or other object), and • Picture's subject is unusual (for example, chair, pair of eyeglasses, fire hydrant), and • Picture clearly evokes the object named.
9	Full picture with uncommon, well-executed subject(s) OR visual sophistication	• Picture is completed and named by the child, and • Picture's subject is a single object (there is no setting or other object), and • Picture's subject is commonly represented or readily suggested by block shapes (for example, sun, flower, house, person, star), and • There is a lot of detail/complexity—object has many parts or blocks are used in an unusual way.
10	Full picture with uncommon, well-executed subjects(s) and visual sophistication	• Picture is completed and named by the child, and • There is either a setting (for example, sun above grass), or there are at least two objects with a relationship between them (for example, sun and flower); and • There is one unusual, well-executed subject (for example, soccer ball, ice cream cone), and • One can see the conscious use of perspective or three dimensionality (for example, one object hidden behind another, chair or table seen at an angle).

Making Pattern Block Pictures   Bridge to Curriculum

Reviewing: Key Concepts and Skills Exercised in the Activity

- Matching shapes
- Visual representation
- Using colors
- Part–whole relations

Reflecting: Questions Related to Child's Performance
Child's Working Approach

- Do any Evaluative Working Approaches stand out from the others?
- Are there Working Approach behaviors that seem to be contributing to or hindering the child's performance?
- Can you attribute the behaviors that stand out to any of the activity parameters: materials, key concepts, social arrangements, or activity structure?

Task Parameters

Materials

- Does the child need more time to explore pattern blocks?

Social Arrangements

- Would the child feel more comfortable working alone?

Child's Performance

Rubric Levels 1–2	• Is child more interested in exploring own ideas than in completing prescribed task? • Does child understand the task?
Rubric Levels 3–5	• Does child need more experience with the use of shapes as building blocks for representing figures?
Rubric Levels 7–10	• Does child need more practice using shapes to represent common objects? • Does child need more practice using shapes to represent uncommon objects?

Planning: Linking the Assessment Result to Curriculum Ideas

Using pattern blocks to create a picture is one way to extend the principles of artistic development represented in the crayon technique activity and self-portrait. In all of the various media children might encounter, the basic principles include nurturing their desire to explore and experiment, seeing how they might use the features of the medium to express ideas, and comparing and contrasting their own efforts to those of others In order to further develop their own sense of the possibilities of the medium for self-expression. As with other media, give children many opportunites to play with the pattern blocks independently and with other children, but without specific teacher direction.

Other possible ways to stimulate their thinking for representation include the following:

- Provide pattern block templates for children to copy or cover with blocks. Begin with templates that have lines to indicate where each kind of block should be placed, and then move on to those templates that have only an external outline. Make sure to include templates that are representational (that is, they portray an object, animal, person). Have children work together or individually to construct a particular object (a fish, a rainbow, a tree).

(Continued)

(Continued)

- Invite pairs of children to work on more complex objects (a chair, a birdhouse). Display, compare, and discuss results.

- Provide sample drawings and/or pictures for children to reproduce using pattern blocks. Discuss with the children how the pictures and drawings can often be broken down into the different shapes that compose them.

- Ask children to represent the same items using pencil, crayons, paint, and pattern blocks. Compare and contrast constraints and advantages of each medium.

- Have children use pattern block stickers (available through most teacher catalogs) to illustrate a story, poem, or song. Assign different pages or parts to different children. Compare and contrast the different representations, perhaps focusing on how a particular character is portrayed on the different pages. Leo Lionni's (1975) storybook *Pezzettino* can be a great resource in carrying out this activity with young children.

- If an overhead projector is available for children' use, provide transparent pattern blocks to be used with the overhead. Encourage free exploration, or assign the creation of a particular picture.

Activities: Visual Arts

Activities

Mathematics

WHAT WE KNOW

Children begin to develop mathematical understandings of number, measurement, pattern, and shape long before they encounter these concepts in more formal math instruction in school. The concepts and skills they are learning in this curricular area develop gradually over a period of years, not months. As in early literacy development, home and community environments present young children with abundant opportunity for observing patterns in their world and for learning about quantities and shapes of objects, and how to measure, compare, and make predictions about these objects. This early math learning is physical—children learn from seeing and manipulating objects and from physically sensing the differences among any number of objects in their hands or pockets. This informally acquired knowledge provides a foundation for learning math concepts and symbols as they continue through elementary school.

Research confirms that children learn best when they understand not only the "how" of math (how to carry out a procedure such as adding or measuring) but also the "why"—the mathematical reasoning that leads to making sense of those relationships in everyday life. For this reason, each of the Bridging mathematics assessment activities invites children to use varied materials to solve problems that draw on key concepts and skills in mathematics. While working on the problems, children wonder, raise questions, try multiple ways of using materials, and follow various paths of reasoning.

WHAT BRIDGING PROVIDES

Bridging takes as its starting point two of the five areas of the mathematical learning standards developed by the National Council of Teachers of Mathematics (NCTM)—number sense and geometry—and provides activities that tap directly into what young children know and how they approach problems in these areas. Plastic bears and "cookies" act as concrete means of exploring children's thinking about quantity and the rules of number use. Small, colorful pattern blocks give children a chance to demonstrate their sense of spatial relationships and shape. Through use of these simple materials, the Bridging mathematics activities address not only the basic tenets of early number sense and geometry but also the concepts of estimation, measurement, algebra, and analytical methods featured in other areas of the NCTM learning standards.

The Bridging activities provide steps that progressively challenge children's mathematical thinking. In addition, they reveal children's current level of understandings and strategies for approaching challenges as they do so. In each of the activities, children first reveal their understandings in the physical manipulation of objects, followed by verbalization, and later, representation on paper—first through drawings and later using progressively more conventional mathematical symbols and equations. This progression in learning reinforces the need for the math curriculum to begin and sustain opportunities for children to have hands-on experiences with manipulatives throughout the early childhood years and, at the same time, make connections between concrete experiences and mathematical symbols and abstract concepts.

WHY THESE THREE ACTIVITIES

The three Bridging mathematics activities are Exploring Number Concepts, Solving Pattern Block Puzzles, and Creating Pattern Block Pinwheels. In the Number Concepts, children's thinking is revealed through a set of four activities, generally done together. The Exploring Number Concepts activities break apart the components of counting, comparing quantities, and manipulating them to help pinpoint a child's understandings and strategies for arriving at solutions. The Bridging Number Concepts activities are carried out within a story that is acted out with little figures of bears and button-like objects that represent cookies. Within the story of bears going on a picnic and needing to pack cookies for everyone, children act out the various mathematical operations constituting number sense: counting, addition, subtraction, estimation, and division, along with their skills at representing these concepts on paper. The procedure for this activity can be thought of as a conversation with the child wherein the teacher initiates a little story with problems that the bears encounter as they prepare for and participate in a picnic with friends. As the child responds, the teacher tracks the child's line of thinking and follows up in responses that draw out a more detailed picture of where the child is on the developmental continuum of fundamental number concepts and skills.

When discussing and developing Bridging's mathematics activities, one of our first choices of material to work with was unit blocks—the hard wood blocks of various sizes and shapes present in some early childhood classrooms that young children readily enjoy playing and building with. However, we recognized that, although universally appealing, unit blocks are not always available in schools, particularly in primary classrooms. We searched for a comparable material that would invite children's exploration of spatial relationships, measurement, and pattern construction and found that pattern blocks are available in most early childhood classrooms. Pattern blocks are commonly made of wood or plastic, and come in large sets containing squares, triangles, trapezoids, rhombuses (diamonds) of two different sizes, and hexagons. Each shape is a different color, so that all hexagons are yellow and all squares are orange, for example. Like unit blocks, they are designed to be proportional to one another, so that, for example, each edge of the triangle block is the same length as the edge of the square block. Each block is about ¼ inch thick, so that they easily combine edge to edge to create two-dimensional displays.

These highly attractive and flexible manipulatives lend themselves to the kind of hands-on play and representation that can uncover children's thinking in the area of geometry and create a window into a more intuitive, less verbally focused mathematical skill set. Children for whom spatial relations and visual displays provide interest can demonstrate growing understandings of part–whole relationships, patterning, and logical-analytical skills. Through the focused attention to a sometimes-neglected area of mathematics these activities provide, Bridging gives teachers an alternative view of mathematical strengths, which is an important counterpoint to the more conventionally assessed number sense.

The two pattern block activities included in the Bridging assessment process utilize these appealing shaped blocks in two very different kinds of ways. Solving Pattern Block Puzzles is a spatial-analytical task in which children are challenged to find the combination of blocks that will completely and exactly cover a shape drawn on paper. Creating Pattern Block Pinwheels, on the other hand, provides an opportunity to demonstrate a sense of pattern and symmetry while creating beautiful, unique, and often elaborate patterned displays. Together these two mathematics activities utilize one material in two very distinct ways: one highly structured and analytical and the other semi-structured and essentially creative. Completing the spectrum, pattern blocks also are used in a very open-ended Visual Arts activity called Making Pattern Block Pictures. By utilizing one set of manipulatives in three ways, Bridging provides a means of examining the salience of activity structure for a child's learning. Assessment of strengths in mathematics, in particular, benefits from the inclusion of tasks with extremely different types of goals since children who struggle with one math pattern block activity can demonstrate competence with the other.

Activities: Mathematics

Activities: Mathematics

Relationship Between Standards and Bridging Activities in Mathematics Area

Standards for Early Mathematics	Bridging Activities		
	Number Concepts	*Pattern Block Puzzles*	*Pattern Block Pinwheels*
Number Concepts			
• Abstraction	√		
• Stable Order	√		
• One-to-One Correspondence	√	√	
• Cardinality	√		
• Order Irrelevance	√		
• Mental Number Line	√		
• Representation of Number	√	√	
• Part–Whole Relations	√		
• Word Problems	√		
Estimation and Measurement			
• Visual Estimation	√		
• Size Match		√	√
• Standard Units in Measurement			
• Unit Size Affects Measurement			
• Estimation versus Calculation			
Algebra and Analytical Methods			
• Operations With Whole Numbers	√		
• Pattern			√
• Commutative Property			
• Associative Property			
• Distributive Property			
• Order of Operations			

	Bridging Activities		
Standards for Early Mathematics	*Number Concpets*	*Pattern Block Puzzles*	*Pattern Block Pinwheels*
Geometry			
• Shape Match		√	√
• Symmetry			√
• Dimensionality			
• Parallelism			
• Perpendicularism			
Data Analysis and Probability			
• Comparison With Numbers			
• Graphs, Tables, and Charts			
• Averaging			

Standards listed here are a combination of those defined by National Council of Teachers of Mathematics (available at http://www.nctm.org/standards/standards.htm) and Illinois State Board of Education (available at http://www.isbe.state.il.us/ils). The first five key concepts in number concepts are adapted from the work of Gelman and Gallistel (1978).

Activities: Mathematics

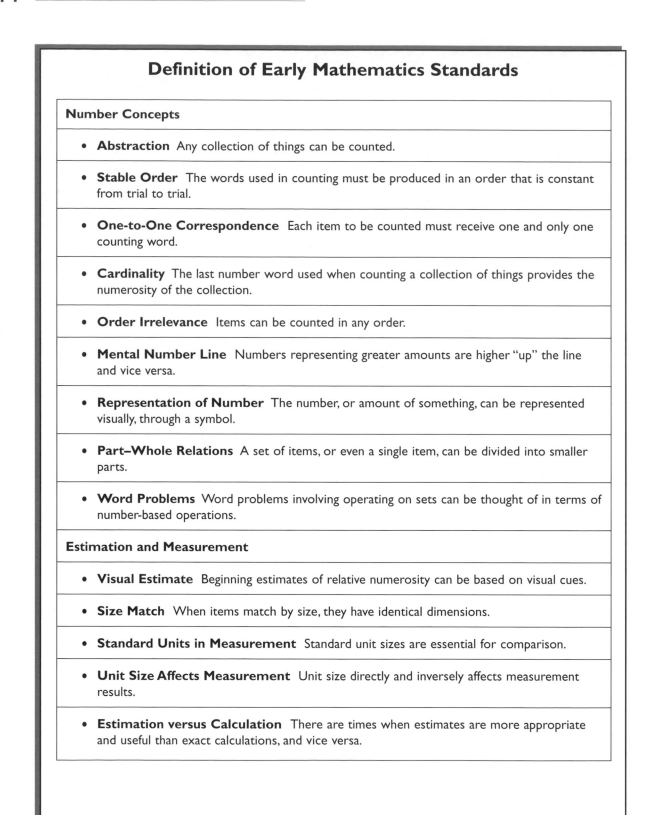

Definition of Early Mathematics Standards

Number Concepts

- **Abstraction** Any collection of things can be counted.

- **Stable Order** The words used in counting must be produced in an order that is constant from trial to trial.

- **One-to-One Correspondence** Each item to be counted must receive one and only one counting word.

- **Cardinality** The last number word used when counting a collection of things provides the numerosity of the collection.

- **Order Irrelevance** Items can be counted in any order.

- **Mental Number Line** Numbers representing greater amounts are higher "up" the line and vice versa.

- **Representation of Number** The number, or amount of something, can be represented visually, through a symbol.

- **Part–Whole Relations** A set of items, or even a single item, can be divided into smaller parts.

- **Word Problems** Word problems involving operating on sets can be thought of in terms of number-based operations.

Estimation and Measurement

- **Visual Estimate** Beginning estimates of relative numerosity can be based on visual cues.

- **Size Match** When items match by size, they have identical dimensions.

- **Standard Units in Measurement** Standard unit sizes are essential for comparison.

- **Unit Size Affects Measurement** Unit size directly and inversely affects measurement results.

- **Estimation versus Calculation** There are times when estimates are more appropriate and useful than exact calculations, and vice versa.

Activities: Mathematics

Algebra and Analytical Methods

- **Operations With Whole Numbers** Numbers can be acted upon and changed through a regular system of rules, and each of these actions can be reversed or negated (for example, $8 \times 10 = 80/10 = 8$).

- **Pattern** A pattern is constructed of repeating elements.

- **Commutative Property** Numbers can be added or multiplied in any order (for example, $4 + 3 + 9 = 9 + 3 + 4$.

- **Associative Property** Numbers can be grouped in any way when computing either a sum or a product (for example, $(5 + 3) + 9 = 5 + (3 + 9)$).

- **Distributive Property** If a term is multiplied by terms in parentheses, the multiplication can be "distributed" over all the terms inside to simplify the problem (for example, $8(5 + 7) = 8 \times 12 = 8 \times 5 + 8 \times 7$).

- **Order of Operations** When expressions have more than one operation, rules are used to govern the order in which they are performed (for example, multiply and divide first, add and subtract second).

Geometry

- **Shape Match** When items match by shape, their dimensions have the same relative proportion to one another.

- **Symmetry** Symmetry is achieved when parts of a single object match one another.

- **Dimensionality** All objects exist in three dimensions while only some can be drawn in two dimensions.

- **Parallelism** Lines parallel to one another will never touch, no matter how far they are extended.

- **Perpendicularism** Lines perpendicular to one another cross at a 90-degree angle.

Data Analysis and Probability

- **Comparison With Numbers** Numbers provide a powerful means for making comparisons between disparate sets of things.

- **Graphs, Tables, and Charts** Pictures, tallies, tables, charts, and graphs can be used to organize number information and make comparisons easier.

- **Averaging** Operations can be used on sets of numbers to determine an "average."

Creating Pattern Block Pinwheels   Procedure

Subject Area	**Key Concepts and Skills**
• Geometry	• Shape match
Social Arrangements	• Size match
• *Recommended:* small group	• Communicating results
• *Viable:* individual or large group	• Pattern
	• Symmetry and Radial symmetry

Activity and Goal

Children view and discuss examples of "pattern block pinwheels" showing radial symmetry, participate in construction of a pattern block pinwheel with teacher guidance, and then produce their own pattern block pinwheels.

Materials

- Examples of radial symmetry (see examples on pages 178 and 179)

- Ample supply of pattern blocks

- Camera (optional)

- Large flat surface to work on

- Large (11" × 17") sheets of black construction paper—one for each child (blocks look best on black paper)

If introducing this with a large group, use the following for demonstration:

- Overhead projector

- Pattern block transparencies (blocks will work, but color will be lost)

Advance Preparation

1. Check to ensure you are using traditional pattern blocks by placing your blocks on Example I on page 178. If blocks used fit the Example dimensions exactly, all your blocks in the set should be of the right size and shape.

2. Determine whether or not you will attempt to preserve pinwheels through photos, a sketch of child's work, or written notes (see Recording Sheet).

3. Prepare to use Examples I and II on pages 178 and 179 by covering outlined pinwheels with actual blocks. Cover with paper to conceal until ready to begin.

Procedure

1. Set the stage for this activity by discussing what a pinwheel is in a way that will make sense to your class.

2. Show examples of pattern block pinwheels using the model pages 178–179. Lead discussion by asking, **"What do you notice about these two pattern block pinwheels?" Or try asking, "What is the same about these two pinwheels?" and "What is different about these two pinwheels?"**

3. Lead children to the following discoveries:

   Each pinwheel has one yellow hexagon in the center.

   Each is basically "round" and looks like a flower, star, or a pinwheel.

4. Lead children in making a pinwheel with radial symmetry together.

   - Start with yellow hexagon.

   - Have children select six blocks of one type and place them around the hexagon.

   - Count each block as it is placed to emphasize that each layer has six blocks. Say, **"There, that's one layer."**

   - Repeat with six blocks of another type.

   - AVOID red (a trapezoid) and white (a rhombus) blocks with younger children, as their shapes are more difficult to work with.

   - If a child makes a placement error (doesn't use six of the same block, makes directional mistakes, etc.), ask **"Is that right?"** Encourage children to correct any misplaced blocks or unfinished layers on their own.

   - Leave this pinwheel in the work area for students to see.

5. Tell students, **"Now you will each make your own pattern block pinwheel."**

   - Leave the group-made model pinwheel visible, but remove Examples I and II during the remainder of the activity; in this way, there will be a helpful example but fewer models from which the children will be tempted to copy.

   - Give each child a sheet of black paper and place a single yellow hexagon at the center.

   - Ensure easy access to the blocks for each child.

   - If a child completes more than one pinwheel, give credit for the highest level achieved.

   - Optional: Write child's name on paper strip and place by black paper—photograph pinwheel.

Pinwheels—Example I

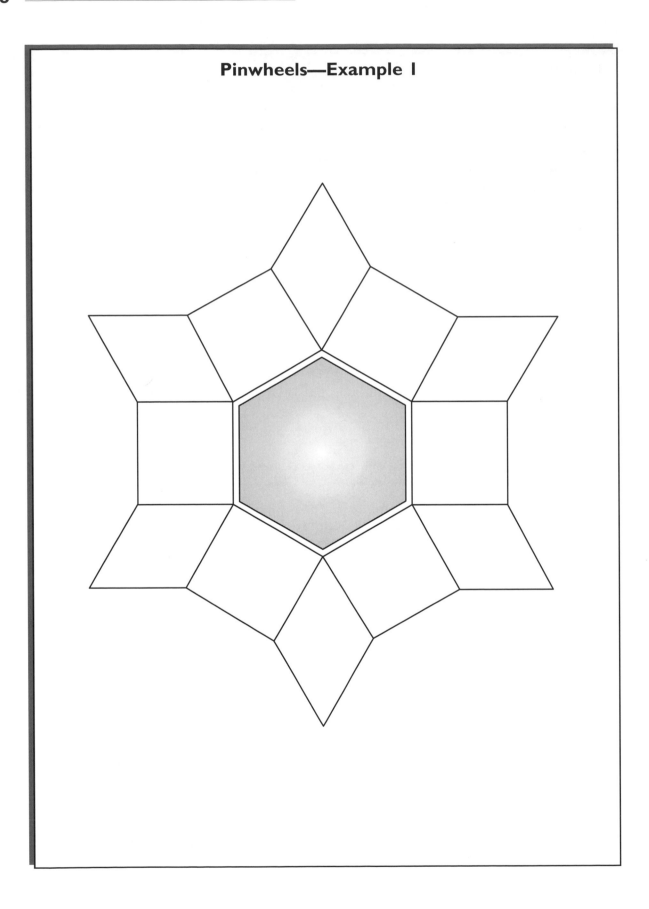

Pinwheels—Example II

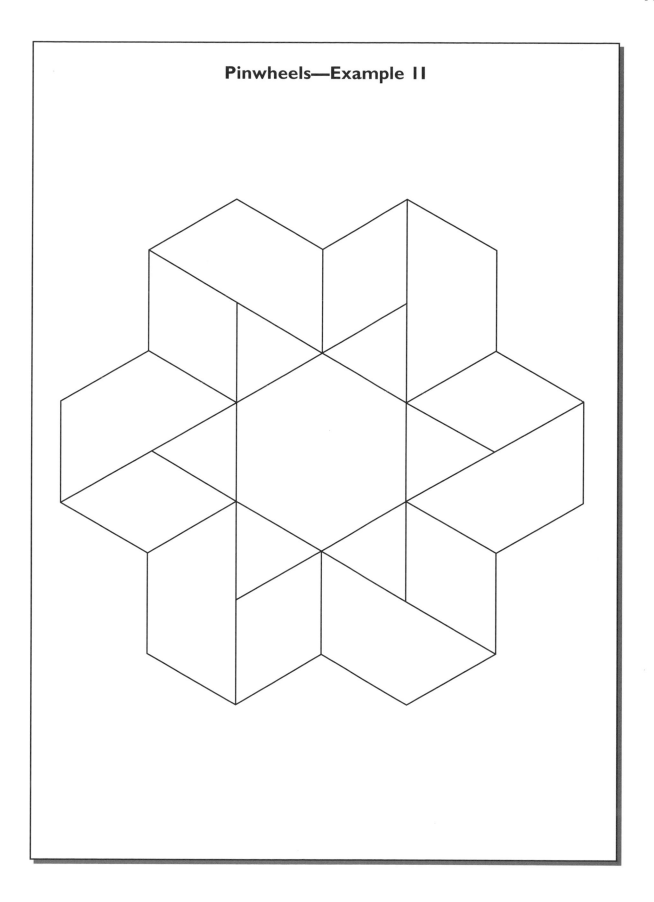

Creating Pattern Block Pinwheels

Recording Sheet

Child's name _____ Assess date _____ Assessor _____ Rubric level _____

If NO radial symmetry achieved, check one on each row below

Note on child's experience with activity

Two-dimensional layout?   ☐ yes   ☐ no

Blocks touch sides of hexagon?   ☐ yes   ☐ no

Blocks generally surround hexagon on all sides? ☐ yes   ☐ no

Sequencing of blocks?   ☐ yes   ☐ no

Bilateral symmetry?   ☐ yes   ☐ no
(Design is identical on two sides of hexagon)

If at least ONE layer of radial symmetry achieved, check all that apply below

☐ one layer copied from model
☐ two layers copied from model

☐ one original layer of radial symmetry
   (design moves out from central hexagon in six identical rays)
   ☐ edges of blocks meet well   ☐ edges don't meet well
   ☐ NO directional confusion   ☐ directional confusion

☐ two original layers of radial symmetry
   ☐ edges of blocks meet well   ☐ edges don't meet well
   ☐ NO directional confusion   ☐ directional confusion

☐ three to five original layers of radial symmetry
   ☐ edges of blocks meet well   ☐ edges don't meet well
   ☐ NO directional confusion   ☐ directional confusion

☐ six to eight original layers of radial symmetry
   ☐ edges of blocks meet well   ☐ edges don't meet well
   ☐ NO directional confusion   ☐ directional confusion

☐ nine or more original layers of radial symmetry
   ☐ edges of blocks meet well   ☐ edges don't meet well
   ☐ NO directional confusion   ☐ directional confusion

Activities: Mathematics

Creating Pattern Block Pinwheels

Evaluative Working Approach Rubric

Circle the number that best describes the child's evaluative working approach in this activity.

Child's Name:
_____

Initial Engagement: How does the child initially respond to the activity?

Hesitant _____ **Eager**

1	2	3	4	5
very hesitant or unwilling to begin activity		becomes involved on his or her own		eager to begin activity

Focus, Attention: How on task is the child throughout the activity?

Distractable _____ **Attentive**

1	2	3	4	5
very easily distracted by other children, events, or materials		attentive some of the time		sustained, absorbed attention to activity

Goal Orientation: How clear is the child working toward the activity's goal?

Personal goal _____ **Activity goal**

1	2	3	4	5
works on personal goal rather than activity goal		child's work vacillates between personal goal and activity goal		works efficiently toward activity goal

Planfulness: How organized is the child in working toward task completion?

Haphazard _____ **Organized**

1	2	3	4	5
random or impulsive; no evidence of organization of materials or approach		organized some of the time		well-organized, methodical in approach or with materials

Resourcefulness: What does the child do when stuck?

Helpless _____ **Resourceful**

1	2	3	4	5
does not ask for help; unable to use help when offered		moves forward a step when help is given		seeks help and makes good use of it to figure out challenges

Cooperation (for group activities): How does the child work with peers to accomplish task?

Difficulty working with others _____ **Helpful to others**

1	2	3	4	5
has difficulty sharing materials or attention, taking turns, supporting the efforts of others		gets along with other children		helps other children with activity, materials, or as a mediator; models ideas for others

Activities: Mathematics

Creating Pattern Block Pinwheels

Descriptive Working Approach Rubric

Circle the number that best describes the child's descriptive working approach in this activity.

Child's Name:
_____

Chattiness: How much of the child's talk is unrelated to the activity?

Very quiet _____ **Very chatty**

1	2	3	4	5
little conversation and self-talk throughout the activity		talks from time to time		constantly talks about unrelated topics

Pace of Work: What is the child's pace of work?

Slow _____ **Fast**

1	2	3	4	5
slow to start and carry out the activity		moderate pace throughout the activity		quick start and quick finish

Social Referencing: How often does the child check with teachers or peers?

Little interaction _____ **Constant checking**

1	2	3	4	5
focuses on own work		attention to others' work and checks with others about own work occasionally		frequently asks teacher or peer if own work is on track

Playfulness: How animated, lively, or happy is the child during the activity?

Serious _____ **Playful**

1	2	3	4	5
mood/demeanor is serious and cheerless		business-like with activity		cheerful and sense of humor related to activity

Level	Name	Performance Indicators
Creating Pattern Block Pinwheels		**Performance Rubric**
0	Child does not participate	• Child declines to participate in the activity.
1	Collection or no interest	• Child's blocks appear unorganized; OR • Child uses blocks in three dimensions (building up) with no pattern of symmetry.

2	2-D, surround only, OR organized, not surrounding	• Child is operating in two dimensions; AND
		  ○ Blocks surround hexagon; OR
		  ○ Design is very organized but does not surround.

3	2-D, surround, and touch OR pattern	• Child is operating in two dimensions; AND
		  ○ Blocks surround hexagon; AND
		  ○ Blocks touch/abut hexagon well; OR
		  ○ Blocks selected maintain hexagon shape; OR
		  ○ Blocks are sequenced/bilaterally symmetric with positioning problems.

4	Copies one layer OR one new layer with problems	• Child has copied one layer of radial symmetry exactly from the model on display; OR • Child created one new layer, but it has placement or positioning problems.
5	Copies two layers OR pattern, but not radial symmetry	• Child has copied two layers of radial symmetry exactly from the model on display; OR • Child created one patterned layer with no placement or positioning problems, but it's sequenced or bilaterally symmetric, not radial symmetry.
6	One new layer OR two new layers with problems	• Child created one layer radial symmetry, no placement or positioning problems; OR • Child created two layers radial symmetry with placement/positioning problems.
7	Two new layers OR three to five new layers with problems	• Child created two layers radial symmetry, no placement/positioning problems; OR • Child created three to five layers radial symmetry with placement/positioning problems.
8	Three to five new layers OR six to eight new layers with problems	• Child created three to five layers radial symmetry, no placement/positioning problems; OR • Child created six to eight layers radial symmetry with placement/positioning problems.
9	Six to eight new layers OR nine or more new layers with problems	• Child created six to eight layers radial symmetry, no placement/positioning problems; OR • Child created nine or more layers radial symmetry with placement/positioning problems.
10	Nine or more new layers, no problems	• Child created at least nine layers radial symmetry, no placement/positioning problems.

Activities: Mathematics

Creating Pattern Block Pinwheels   Bridge to Curriculum

Reviewing: Key Concepts and Skills Exercised in the Activity

- Shape match

- Size match

- Pattern

- Symmetry/Radial symmetry

Reflecting: Questions Related to Child's Performance

Child's Working Approach

- Does any one Evaluative Working Approach quality stand out from the others?

- Is there any one Working Approach behavior contributing to or hindering the child's performance?

- Can you attribute the behavior that stands out to any of the activity parameters: materials, key concepts, social arrangements, or activity structure?

Task Parameters

Materials

- Were there enough blocks so the child was able to make whatever the child imagined?

- Is it difficult for the child to manipulate the blocks?

- Does this child find the blocks particularly attractive and appealing?

- Does the child have enough table space to work out ideas of visual design?

Social Arrangements

- Was the room too noisy or crowded for this child to work well?

- Would or did the child benefit from working next to a friend?

- Would or did the child benefit from working alone and without interruption?

Activity Structure

- Does the creative aspect of this math activity help the child to stay involved?

- Does this child need more structure in an activity in order to be successful?

Child's Performance

Rubric Levels 1–2	• Is the child simply uninterested in the activity? • Can the child match blocks by shape, size, and color? • Does the child need time to explore pattern blocks in his or her own way prior to completing a teacher-directed activity? • Is the child overwhelmed by parts of the pinwheel construction process?
Rubric Levels 3–5	IF child only copied one or two layers: • Does the child need more practice and guidance constructing multiple layers of a pinwheel? • How does the child respond if you suggest using a pattern block shape not used in the model? Does the child want to complete the activity in order to move on to something else? IF child did not copy the model: • Does the pinwheel indicate the child has some understanding of pattern? • Does the child have the counting skills to select six of the same type of block? • Does the child understand the task but choose not to use six of the same type of block, opting instead for doing his or her own thing? • Is the child placing block edges against each other to help organize positioning? • Does the child understand how to position blocks within a pinwheel level the same way each time?
Rubric Levels 6–7	• Is the child placing block edges against each other to help organize positioning? • Does the child understand how to position blocks within a pinwheel level the same way each time?
Rubric Levels 8–10	• What is it about this activity that this child likes? • Does the creative aspect of this math activity help the child stay involved? • Does this child have spatial strengths? • How can this strength be used to help this child with other activities?

Planning: Linking the Assessment Result to Curriculum Ideas

Mathematics learning for young children involves repeated experiences of open-ended exploration of materials. These experiences facilitate the child's connecting concrete manipulation of objects to more abstract rules, understandings, and symbol systems with guidance and instruction from adults in time. Those last two words are very important: in time! Development cannot be rushed and when it is, we shortchange children by preventing them from building a deep understanding of the concepts involved. Even when children are in first and second grade and have had many opportunities to work with pattern blocks, they still need time for open-ended experiences to integrate new insights, practice ideas, and experiment with new possibilities. Therefore, teachers of early childhood classrooms at all levels will want to provide time during the school day for play with these materials: opportunities where children use pattern blocks individually and in small groups to work and build with no set agenda from the teacher. As discussed in Chapter 4, such open-ended play and experimentation ought to be going on with a number of materials in areas around the classroom related to all subject areas. The teacher can always set out pattern blocks as one of the materials available in a center or on a table saying, **"I wonder what you will come up with today as you work with our pattern blocks?"**

(Continued)

Activities: Mathematics

(Continued)

To facilitate children's work with pattern blocks, you may want to give children trays on which to place their pattern block experiments. Trays provide natural boundaries between children's constructions and are an easy way to save a child's work, either to continue working on at a later time or to preserve it so it can be brought to a class meeting for group discussion. You will want to be conscious of the work space that children have available to them; be sure that the table surface is large enough to respond to the needs of children who may prefer a large work surface or to accommodate a number of children working on trays together, while also providing space for children to work alone or with a partner.

In summary, two important ideas are reflected in the time and space that teachers are providing for pattern blocks (as well as with other math materials). One is the importance of time: the development of mathematical concepts takes years, not months. We need to be conscious of children banking long stretches of time for play and manipulation of materials interspersed with more focused discussion, experiments, and studies of children's discoveries and new questions. This is where the assessment process comes in: it provides a window into the particular kinds of questions and experiments the children are ready for at a given point in time. The second important idea concerns space: having some flexibility in the classroom setup is important if the environment is to resemble a laboratory for learning as opposed to a factory model that assumes that all learning is uniform and can be programmed.

Pinwheels: Focused experiences. As you watch children working with pattern blocks, you will begin to notice ways in which you can assist in organizing their experiments to help them explore symmetry and patterning. Two simple ways are to set out large white circular paper plates and invite children to make pattern block designs inside of them. After about a week of such experiments, you can see if any of the children have discovered the possibility of starting with one block in the middle and building a pattern around it. If no one has, you can suggest it but only after allowing a week or so for the children to experiment with the blocks inside of this new and intriguing type of space constraint. The more they have experimented with the material, the farther they will go with a new suggestion like: **"What happens if you put a square in the middle of your paper plate and build around it? See what you each come up with when you start with a square in the middle."**

There are several kinds of experiences that you will want to provide in the classroom that will contribute to the child's explorations of pattern blocks. One is sorting objects and talking about how objects such as pattern blocks, buttons in a jar, colors in a basket of crayons, a collection of counting bears that come in different sizes and colors, or a collection of small random objects in a shoe box, are alike and how they are different. Noticing the properties of objects in all their detail helps prepare children for working with those properties in a disciplined and controlled way. If they have not noticed the features of an object, they are not ready to use those properties in a purposeful way. Asking children to sort pattern blocks—those that are alike from those that are different—can be a nice way to set up a new storage system for your blocks. Having them in clear plastic containers with the six shapes each in their own space, as opposed to all mixed together in one large tub, may engender new ideas among the children. Let the children do the work of sorting them; they will learn a lot by doing so.

A second type of experience that children will benefit from is making and constructing patterns in a wide variety of situations and in using a wide variety of materials. For example, when playing a game of checkers, they will want to notice the patterns on a checkerboard and in the movements that one can make with checker pieces. Stringing beads provides wonderful opportunities for noticing and constructing patterns. There are patterns in music and our movements in response to the patterns in its beat (see Moving to Music activity). There are patterns in the objects we find in nature—the shapes of leaves and the lines in their veins (see Nature Display activity). There are patterns in story themes (the sounds of the billy goats' hooves crossing the bridge in *The Three Billy Goats Gruff* and what they say to the troll as they cross over the bridge).

A third type of experience that will contribute to children eventually noticing patterns in radial symmetry is counting within a pattern—noticing how many objects of a particular color, size, or shape they are working with at any point in time. You can point out and help children notice patterns in everyday objects (clothing, window frames, wallpaper) and make patterns with themselves (sitting boy-girl-boy-girl or red shirt, white shirt, blue shirt, red shirt, white shirt, blue shirt). When laying materials out for children to experiment with, you can challenge them to make patterns of two repeating elements (beads on strings) and move to three repeating elements when ready. Within small and large groups, you can guide children in describing their pattern and counting out the repeated elements.

Pinwheels: Discussion, careful studies, experiments. While providing a rich context for exploring the use of pattern blocks to create patterns, you can also be gathering different examples of radial symmetry in both pattern blocks and other materials. A flower, such as a daisy, a bicycle wheel, and a pizza cut into slices all have radial symmetry. Within small or large groups, you may want to take a pattern block pinwheel that someone has made and discuss what is interesting about it: what do they notice that is special about the placement of blocks? Invite the children to start with a particular piece and try it for themselves. Some children may prefer to copy the one you are presenting for dicussion; this is an effective strategy and a good way to get the feel for how to build a pinwheel. While placing blocks, help children notice positioning with the use of words such as *around, above*, and *below*. Also point out the need to place block edges flat against each other to notice the pinwheel that is emerging. Discuss why is it important to choose six of the same type of block (if starting with the yellow hexagon in the center).

You will want to make sure that this concentrated study and experimentation with pinwheels continues over a period of time—at least a week. If children are building on large paper plates or trays, you can invite them to revisit their constructions over several days to elaborate on them. This is one of the best ways to help children gain new insights: by revisiting their work and participating in discussions with peers where they notice what they are each doing: What is interesting about what Maria did? How are Anthony's and Kiara's pinwheels different from one another? How could we make Alex's pinwheel look like it's spinning?

Part of the experimenting can include a day when you invite children to make a pinwheel using only three block sizes and see what they can create. This is especially effective when pinwheels have become very elaborate and extensive, since it introduces a new constraint and keeps children interested. You can also provide materials for children to make pinwheels using other media and discuss the process and results. For example, have children copy pinwheels with colored pencils on paper; consider providing pattern block stencils; make pinwheels out of unit blocks; decorate a paper plate to make radial symmetry; make pinwheels using a nonhexagon center piece. To check on the question of symmetry, you can invite children to use a ruler, a pencil, or sheets of paper standing on edge to create wedges to compare to see whether they are the same. Finally, you will want to discuss how the ideas and skills used in making pinwheels apply to other activities in mathematics, art, and science, such as matching, balance, counting, and careful observation and experimentation.

Activities: Mathematics

Solving Pattern Block Puzzles   Procedure

Subject Area	Key Concepts and Skills
• Geometry	• Shape match
Social Arrangements	• Size match
• *Recommended:* child-child, teacher-child	• One-to-one correspondence
• *Viable:* small group, large group	• Part–whole relations

Activity and Goal

Children arrange pattern blocks on preprinted puzzle sheets to try to cover successively more difficult puzzle forms.

Materials

- Large, flat work surface—it is important that children be able to lay out and examine blocks
- Six pattern block puzzle worksheets (A–F), one set for each participating child
- Open bin(s) with ample supply of pattern blocks

Procedure

1. Before beginning, check pattern blocks by using them to complete the Puzzle A worksheet. If blocks fit the puzzle, the set of blocks will work for the entire activity.

2. Children sit at a table with pattern blocks within easy reach. Place Puzzle A worksheet in front of each child with the title at the top. It is important that it is easy for children to see, reach, and lay out blocks.

3. Introduce the activity by saying: **"Here are blocks you can use to cover the puzzle on this worksheet. Try to completely fill in this puzzle. Lay the blocks on top of the puzzle."** Feel free to give some help to get the child started, if the child appears hesitant. Stop helping after first puzzle.

4. All children begin with Puzzle A and continue until unable to solve two puzzles (whether consecutive or not) without substantial help. At this point, stop the activity. Also stop activity at any time if a child is unable or unwilling to continue.

5. Attempting each puzzle:

   - If a child cannot solve a particular puzzle independently on his or her first attempt, give help as needed until a solution is achieved. Then move onto the next level unless this is the second puzzle the child has been unable to complete.
   - For puzzles C and D, if the child correctly solves on first attempt, ask the child, **"Is there another way that you can do this puzzle using different blocks?"**
   - If the child cannot provide "another" way, give help as needed until a new solution is achieved.
   - If the child is unwilling to try or is not interested in "another way," move on to the next puzzle.
   - For puzzles E and F, if a child correctly solves on first attempt, note number of green triangles used. If more than one, ask child, **"Can you do this puzzle using only one green triangle?"**

Puzzle A

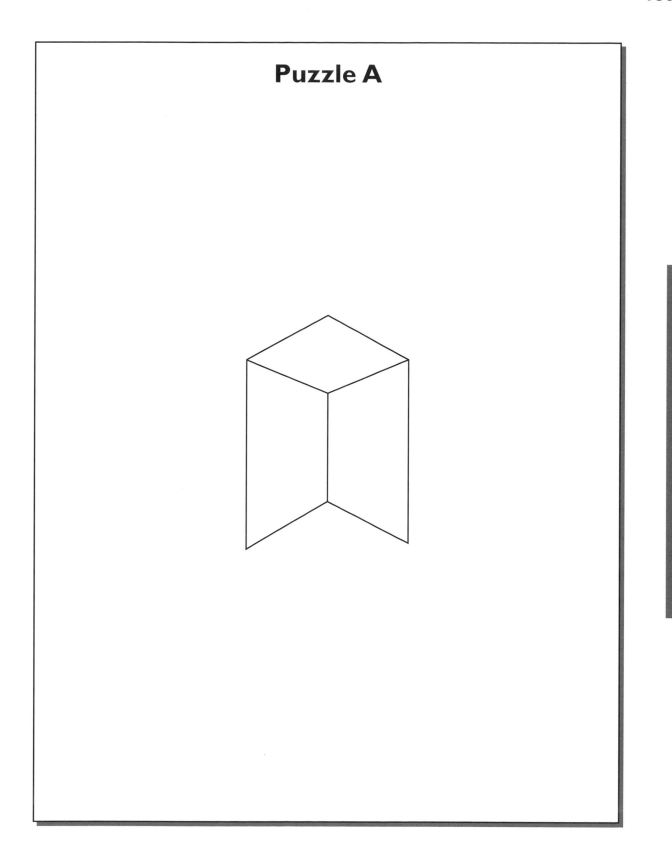

Puzzle B

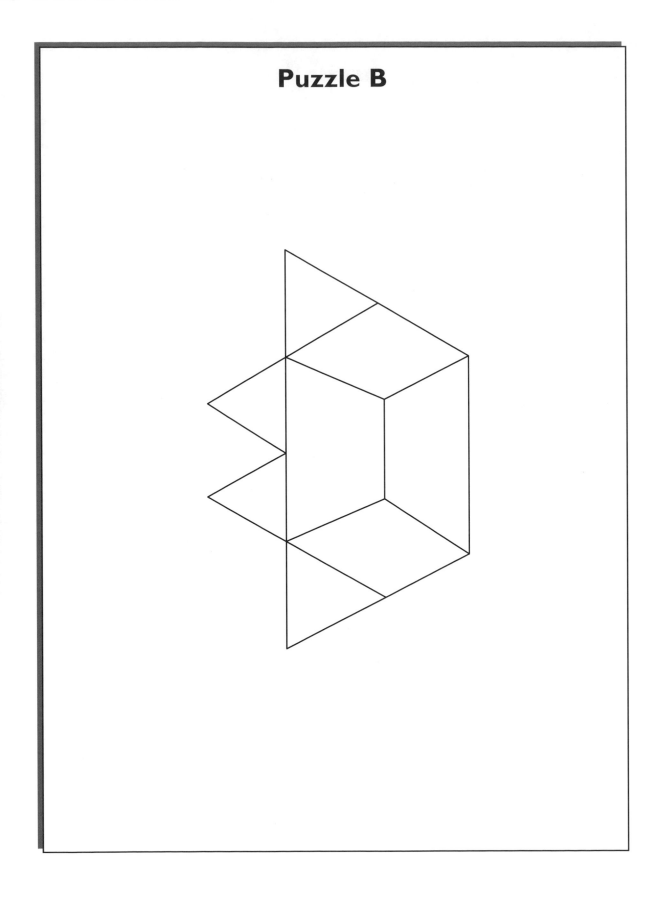

Puzzle C

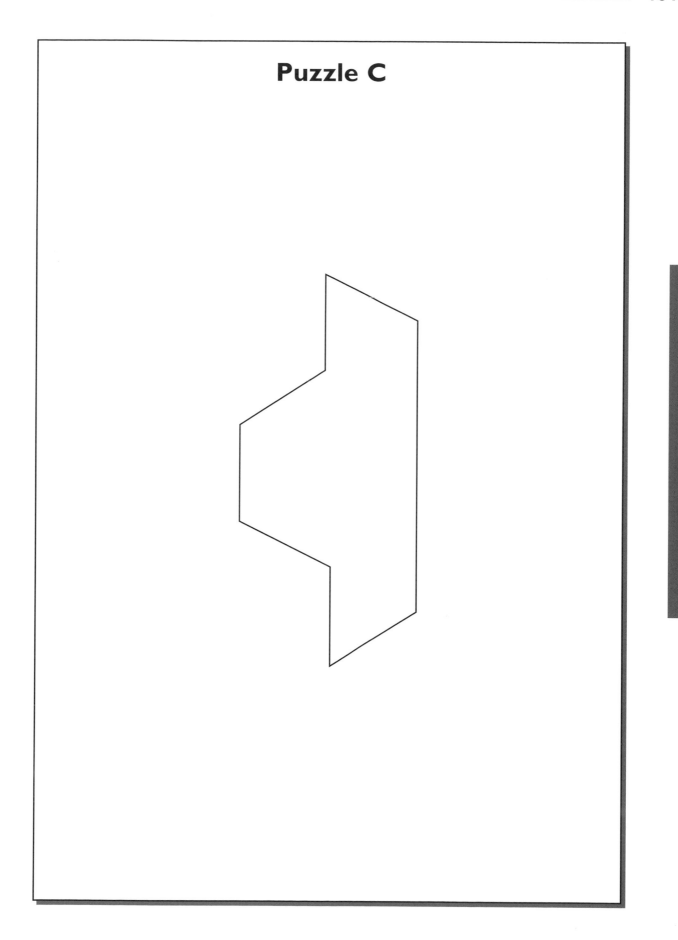

Puzzle D

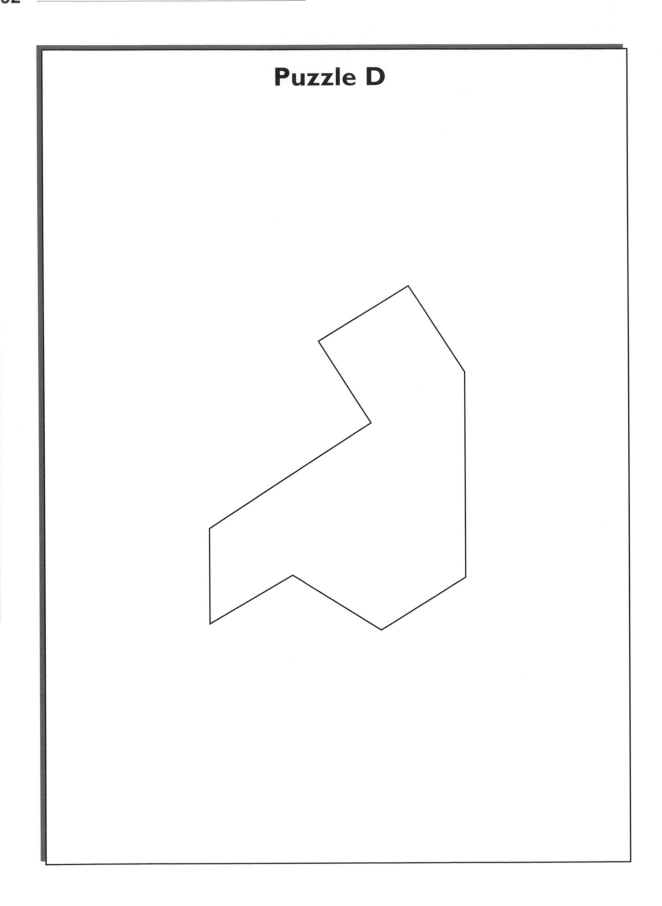

Puzzle E

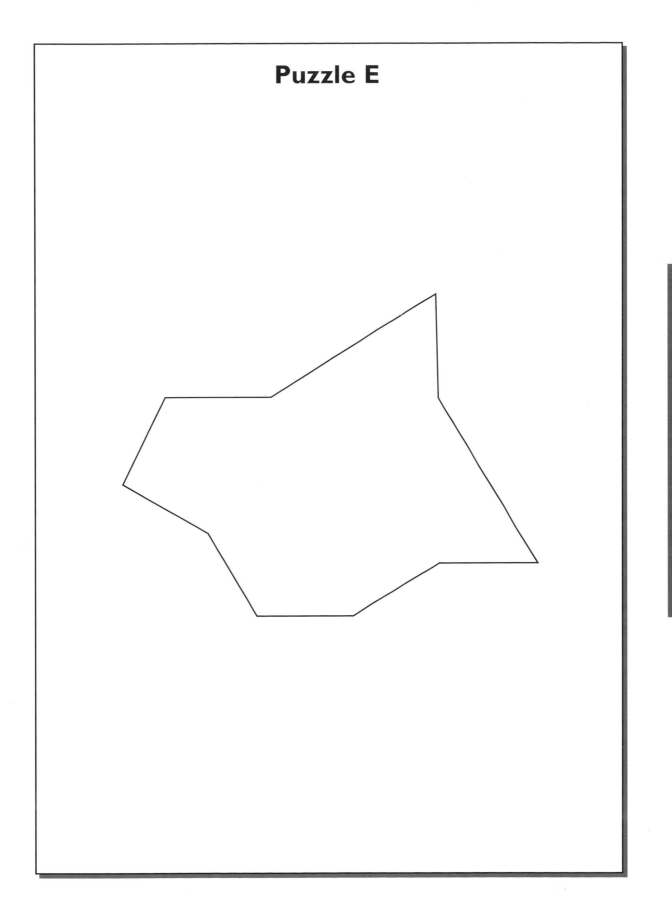

Puzzle F

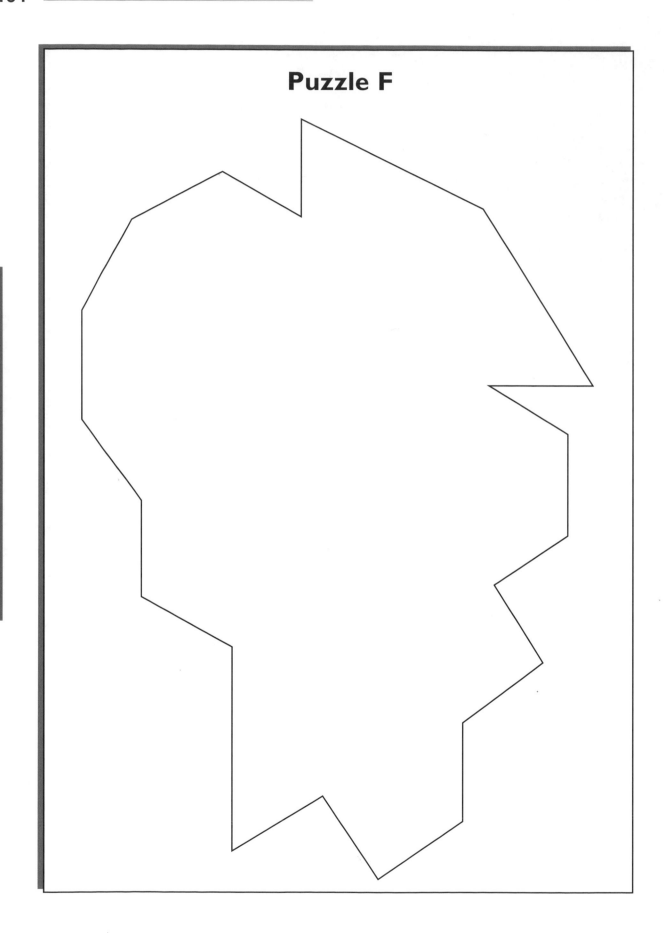

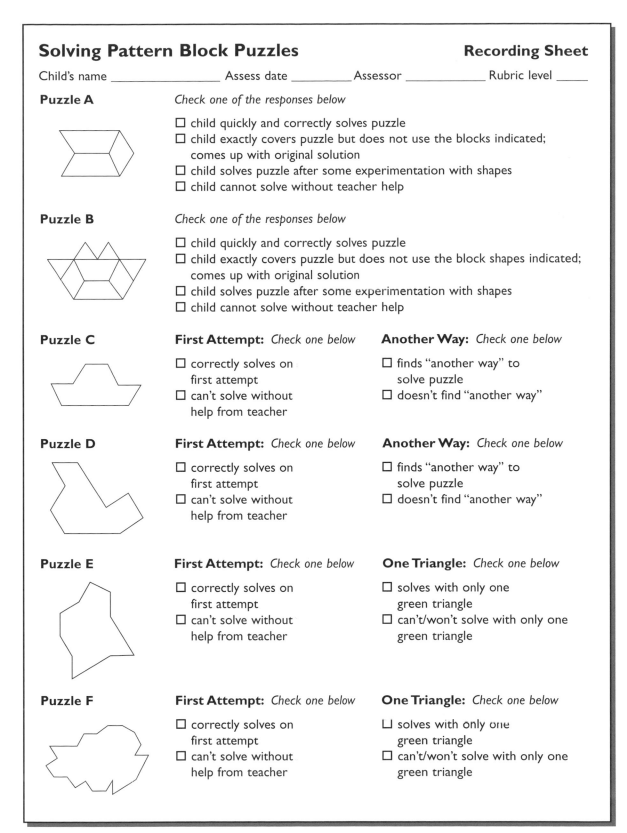

Solving Pattern Block Puzzles   **Recording Sheet**

Child's name _____ Assess date _____ Assessor _____ Rubric level _____

Puzzle A   *Check one of the responses below*

☐ child quickly and correctly solves puzzle
☐ child exactly covers puzzle but does not use the blocks indicated; comes up with original solution
☐ child solves puzzle after some experimentation with shapes
☐ child cannot solve without teacher help

Puzzle B   *Check one of the responses below*

☐ child quickly and correctly solves puzzle
☐ child exactly covers puzzle but does not use the block shapes indicated; comes up with original solution
☐ child solves puzzle after some experimentation with shapes
☐ child cannot solve without teacher help

Puzzle C   **First Attempt:** *Check one below*   **Another Way:** *Check one below*

☐ correctly solves on first attempt
☐ can't solve without help from teacher

☐ finds "another way" to solve puzzle
☐ doesn't find "another way"

Puzzle D   **First Attempt:** *Check one below*   **Another Way:** *Check one below*

☐ correctly solves on first attempt
☐ can't solve without help from teacher

☐ finds "another way" to solve puzzle
☐ doesn't find "another way"

Puzzle E   **First Attempt:** *Check one below*   **One Triangle:** *Check one below*

☐ correctly solves on first attempt
☐ can't solve without help from teacher

☐ solves with only one green triangle
☐ can't/won't solve with only one green triangle

Puzzle F   **First Attempt:** *Check one below*   **One Triangle:** *Check one below*

☐ correctly solves on first attempt
☐ can't solve without help from teacher

☐ solves with only one green triangle
☐ can't/won't solve with only one green triangle

Activities: Mathematics

Solving Pattern Block Puzzles Evaluative Working Approach Rubric

Circle the number that best describes the child's evaluative working approach in this activity.

Child's Name:

_____

Initial Engagement: How does the child initially respond to the activity?

Hesitant _____ **Eager**

1	2	3	4	5
very hesitant or unwilling to begin activity		becomes involved on his or her own		eager to begin activity

Focus, Attention: How on task is the child throughout the activity?

Distractable _____ **Attentive**

1	2	3	4	5
very easily distracted by other children, events, or materials		attentive some of the time		sustained, absorbed attention to activity

Goal Orientation: How clear is the child working toward the activity's goal?

Personal goal _____ **Activity goal**

1	2	3	4	5
works on personal goal rather than activity goal		child's work vacillates between personal goal and activity goal		works efficiently toward activity goal

Planfulness: How organized is the child in working toward task completion?

Haphazard _____ **Organized**

1	2	3	4	5
random or impulsive; no evidence of organization of materials or approach		organized some of the time		well-organized, methodical in approach or with materials

Resourcefulness: What does the child do when stuck?

Helpless _____ **Resourceful**

1	2	3	4	5
does not ask for help; unable to use help when offered		moves forward a step when help is given		seeks help and makes good use of it to figure out challenges

Cooperation (for group activities): How does the child work with peers to accomplish task?

Difficulty working with others _____ **Helpful to others**

1	2	3	4	5
has difficulty sharing materials or attention, taking turns, supporting the efforts of others		gets along with other children		helps other children with activity, materials, or as a mediator; models ideas for others

Solving Pattern Block Puzzles   Descriptive Working Approach Rubric

Circle the number that best describes the child's descriptive working approach in this activity.

Child's Name:

_____

Chattiness: How much of the child's talk is unrelated to the activity?

Very quiet _____ **Very chatty**

1	2	3	4	5
little conversation and self-talk throughout the activity		talks from time to time		constantly talks about unrelated topics

Pace of Work: What is the child's pace of work?

Slow _____ **Fast**

1	2	3	4	5
slow to start and carry out the activity		moderate pace throughout the activity		quick start and quick finish

Social Referencing: How often does the child check with teachers or peers?

Little interaction _____ **Constant checking**

1	2	3	4	5
focuses on own work		attention to others' work and checks with others about own work occasionally		frequently asks teacher or peer if own work is on track

Playfulness: How animated, lively, or happy is the child during the activity?

Serious _____ **Playful**

1	2	3	4	5
mood/demeanor is serious and cheerless		business-like with activity		cheerful and sense of humor related to activity

Activities: Mathematics

Solving Pattern Block Puzzles   Performance Rubric

Level	Name	Performance Indicators
0	No participation	• Declines to participate in activity.
1	Teacher help	• Tries, but cannot complete both puzzles A and B without at least some help from teacher.
2	Puzzle A or Puzzle B	• Completes either Puzzle A or Puzzle B or both without teacher help, but does not complete another puzzle without help
3	Puzzle C, one way only	• Correctly solved Puzzle C on first attempt, but didn't find "another way"
4	Puzzle C, two or more ways	• Correctly solved Puzzle C at least two different ways
5	Puzzle D, one way only	• Correctly solved Puzzle D on first attempt, but didn't find "another way"
6	Puzzle D, two way only	• Correctly solved Puzzle D at least two different ways
7	Puzzle E, two or more triangles	• Correctly solved Puzzle E on first attempt, but did not find a "one triangle" solution
8	Puzzle E, one triangle	• Correctly solved Puzzle E using only one green triangle
9	Puzzle F, two or more triangles	• Correctly solved Puzzle F on first attempt, but didn't find a "one triangle" solution
10	Puzzle F, one triangle	• Correctly solved Puzzle F using only one green triangle

Solving Pattern Block Puzzles   **Bridge to Curriculum**

Reviewing: Key Concepts and Skills Exercised in the Activity

- Shape match
- Size match
- One-to-one correspondence
- Part–whole relations

Reflecting: Questions Related to Child's Performance

Child's Working Approach

- Does any one Evaluative Working Approach quality stand out from the others?
- Is there any one Working Approach behavior contributing to or hindering the child's performance?
- Can you attribute the behavior that stands out to any of the activity parameters: materials, key concepts, social arrangements, or activity structure?

Activity Parameters

Materials

- Were there enough blocks so the child was able to try any solution the child thought of?
- Is it difficult for the child to manipulate the blocks?
- Does this child find the blocks particularly attractive?

Social Arrangements

- Was the room too noisy or crowded for this child to work well?
- Would or did the child benefit from working next to a friend?
- Would or did the child benefit from working alone and without interruption?

Activity Structure

- Does the high level of structure in this activity help the child to stay focused?
- Does this child need more opportunities for creativity in an activity in order to be successful?

(Continued)

(Continued)

Child's Performance

Rubric Levels 0–1	• Can the child match objects by shape? • Can the child match objects by size? • Can the child match objects by color?
Rubric Level 2	IF child follows outlined block shapes • Does the child understand that two blocks together can be used to make a new shape? • Does the child know how to make/recognize a few of the most simple combinations of two blocks? • Is the child noticing symmetrical angles on either side of the puzzle and using matching blocks to cover them? IF child creates original solution (covers puzzle without following outlined block shapes) • Are these early puzzles too simple for this child and lose the child's interest?
Rubric Levels 3–4	• Does the child demonstrate willingness to try new block combinations when the first attempt fails? • Does the child know how to make/recognize a few of the most simple combinations of two blocks? • Does the child use larger, highly salient puzzle angles to select initial blocks and then fit other blocks against these? • Does the child appear to understand how two or more of one type of block can substitute for another (as in two trapezoids for a hexagon)? • Is the child careful to fit block edges flat against one another so the puzzle is filled with precision and remaining puzzle shapes are portrayed accurately?
Rubric Levels 5–6	• Does the child begin a puzzle with those angles that can be filled in the fewest number of alternate ways? • Is the child aware of the slight difference in angle a tan diamond (rhombus) can make?
Rubric Levels 7–10	• Does the child begin at the puzzle's outer edge and move in toward its center? • Does the child understand all the ways green triangles can be used with other blocks to "substitute" (for example, with another green triangle to make a blue diamond, or with a blue diamond to make a red trapezoid)?

Planning: Linking the Assessment Result to Curriculum Ideas

As with the Pattern Block Pinwheels activity, young children need ample time and space to experiment with the pattern blocks before you can expect to see progress in solving puzzles. Shapes, sizes, and spatial relationships are key to any puzzle activity, and children will benefit from opportunities to sort blocks into shape groups, fit them together and observe the results, notice the size relationships between them, and discover on their own how many of one block can "replace" another (for example, six triangles can make a hexagon). Supporting children's exploration of the blocks requires a large work surface, enough blocks to allow children to try out the different ideas that occur to them and sufficient time and repeated exposure for the development of spatial thinking.

Children often also benefit from the provision of a "frame" for their experiments. As mentioned in the activity procedure, the blocks look wonderful on large sheets of black construction paper, though white sheets work well also. Plastic trays, like lunch trays, provide a defined work area and help children control their efforts and minimize possible frustrations. They also allow work to be saved and moved about without disruption, which is crucial to extended exploration and group discussion. Plastic frames, specifically made for pattern block use, come in triangle and hexagon shapes about 10" across, are proportionally sized to allow the blocks to completely fill them, and provide a physical edge within to "construct." If possible, vary the types of "frames" you provide so as to help children notice their possibilities.

Puzzles: Focused Experiences. Pattern block puzzles require children to pay special attention to shape attributes, so activities that help them focus on the "outside edges" of things will be helpful here. Young children often enjoy new words so discussing the pattern block shapes and using the shape names such as "hexagon" and "trapezoid" is a good idea to focus their attention on shape attributes and facilitate discussion of them. You may want to allow children to experiment with the blocks on an overhead projector; since only the shadow of a block is projected, color is absent and shape is emphasized. Children may surprise you by making "stars" and "rockets." For further focus on the shapes of the individual blocks, children can match blocks to the outlined shape of a single block at a time or go on a "pattern block hunt," finding pattern block shapes in the classroom and the school environment. Pattern block stencils are also useful here with children who can use a pencil, allowing them to reproduce and preserve their creations (a precursor of other, more abstract kinds of representation). You can also create "symmetry puzzles" in which a sheet of paper has a line down the middle and an array of pattern block shapes down one side of the line. Children must "mirror" the array on the other side of the line to complete the puzzle. This emphasizes the ability to both match and to rotate shapes in space, an ability that is key to geometric thinking.

To focus more on fitting blocks together, begin with very simple pattern block "puzzles" that utilize only two or three blocks at a time. These puzzles can be provided in two formats: first, with each individual block outlined, and then with only the outer edge of the puzzle provided. As you introduce puzzles with more blocks, provide symmetry in their designs to help children find ways to complete them. Then gradually remove symmetry while keeping the number of blocks the same. Throughout these exercises, use the tan rhombuses only when children are already demonstrating a high level of competence combining sets of other blocks. Because these rhombuses are relatively narrow, they can be difficult to see and isolate within a puzzle shape. The tan rhombuses, however, can also be an important element for keeping more advanced children challenged, so be aware of when and where they are needed to keep exploration exciting. Through these activities, children will begin to get a sense of how different combinations of blocks fill distinct spaces.

Other classroom activities that emphasize shape should also be available. Constructive toys, such as Legos and unit blocks, are great for experimenting with shapes and spatial relationships. Children's puzzles are excellent for emphasizing shape and range from very simple (each puzzle piece lies in its own cut-out space), to moderately complex (5 to 12 pieces combine within a frame to create a picture, and pieces tend to be cut along lines in the visual image), to very difficult (no frame, no relationship between piece shape and visual image). It may be important to provide a range of types of puzzles so children can select those they are ready for.

Activities: Mathematics

(Continued)

(Continued)

Puzzles: Discussion, careful studies, experiments. Children often enjoy seeing how combinations of pattern blocks can "substitute" for other blocks. Large or small group demonstrations that show how a hexagon shape can be filled by a single hexagonal block, two red trapezoids, or three blue rhombuses make quite an impression. Asking children to come up with their own "substitutions" can generate a lot of experimentation and excitement. Allow time for children to bring such discoveries back to the group for sharing and discussion. Focusing on the green triangles, the smallest block in the set, can also be productive: how many other pattern block shapes can be made using only green triangles, and why?

An emphasis on symmetry will give children an additional analytical tool for evaluating shape and space. A good way to provide such an emphasis is to show examples, and discuss and demonstrate what makes them symmetrical or asymmetrical. Then children can be asked to determine whether a puzzle is symmetrical, and to construct their own symmetrical puzzle and bring it back to the group to view and discuss. Errors in constructing bilateral symmetry are not only common, but they tend to illustrate important shape and spatial distinctions that are difficult for many children (and adults!) to notice.

Older children with strong fine motor skills will enjoy making up puzzles for one another. Pattern block stencils help pencil-using children create puzzles in which all blocks are outlined. Harder puzzles, in which only the outside edge is drawn, require careful tracing that doesn't disturb block arrangement. Encourage children to make their own puzzle book, including both less and more difficult puzzles, symmetric and asymmetric.

Another important part of puzzle solving is strategy. Have children work in small groups of three or four students each. Give each group the same puzzle shape to be filled in. After a few minutes, call the class to a large group discussion where the groups pool ideas on how to solve the pattern block puzzle. Using the overhead projector, have children discuss how they are getting started on the task, what they have tried so far, and what they might try next when they return to their small groups. When children are encouraged to discuss their work, strategy is likely to become more visible and available to them. For larger puzzles, children will benefit from demonstrations and discussions of ways to fill in highly distinctive angles and shapes first and working in from the edges.

To make a large puzzle even more challenging, you can limit the number of green triangles that can be used. When children are required to use more of the larger blocks, there are fewer distinct ways to complete a puzzle. This is a terrific exercise for tapping logical thinking along with geometry!

Exploring Number Concepts   Procedure

Subject Area	**Key Concepts and Skills**
• Number Concepts	• Abstraction
Social Arrangements	• Stable order
	• One-to-one correspondence
• *Recommended:* small group, large group (limit 15–17)	• Cardinality
• *Viable:* child-child, teacher-child	• Order irrelevance
	• Operations with whole numbers
	• Mental number line
	• Visual estimate
	• Representation of number
	• Part–whole relations
	• Word problems

Activity and Goal

This activity consists of four related number tasks: counting; subtraction; estimation; and "fair share" (simple division). Children demonstrate mathematical thinking, problem solving, and written representation of problems by responding to a series of game-like tasks using toy counting bears and "cookies." The four activities are best carried out in a single sitting but can also be carried out as discrete activities if it works out better for the child.

Materials

- Two identical clear plastic containers
- Counting bears, all the same size, or some other small object that can represent an animal
- Chips or other disks to represent cookies
- Paper and pencil

Advance Preparation

1. Read through the entire procedure in advance. Think of these various number concept tasks as steps in a dance that children are learning. Experience has shown that children respond well to the sequence of activities, which can take approximately four to five minutes in total to carry out with a child.

2. Once you are comfortable with the flow of the sections, you can be playful in introducing this activity. For example, have one of the bears say, "Hi! Let's go on a picnic! I'll bring some cookies." If the child responds to this, you continue a simple story line about the bears on a picnic. If the child does not seem to engage with the idea of treating the bears as story characters, you can focus on the counting tasks.

3. It is a good idea to pre-count some cookies and "package" them in baggies or on trays so that they do not drop or scatter (see notes on "Number of 'new' cookies for counting on," "Cookies for fair share-no remainder," and "Cookies for fair share-with remainder" below).

4. Prepare for estimation by placing appropriate number of bears in one of the plastic jars (see note on "Estimation # for second jar" below).

Procedure—Counting

Number of bears for counting:

- 3–4 yr olds = 9
- 5–8 yr olds = 23

Note: For remaining number activities (subtraction, estimation, and division), use the number of bears in the highest set the child can count correctly: either 9 or 23.

(Continued)

(Continued)

1. Present the child with the initial set of bears appropriate to his or her age level. Ask child, **"How many bears are there?"** If child does not count correctly, ask child to recount and makes suggestions as appropriate, for example, **"Touch each one when you count it."**

2. If child hasn't explicitly answered, "How many bears are there?" ask, **"How many bears are there altogether?"**

3. If child counts the correct number of bears for age, ask her to keep counting beyond that number, but without any bears (**"How much farther can you count?"**) and ask the child to stop after another 10 numbers or so.

4. If the child can count beyond this point easily, say, **"Wow! Can you start counting at 88?"** and see if the child can count past 100.

5. If the child can count past 100, ask the child to count by 2s or 5s or 10s, and see how high the child can go (stop after 100).

6. Returning to the bears, ask, **"Now these bears are on a picnic. If each bear gets one cookie, how many cookies will we need?"** If child does not respond, or does not respond correctly, place on the table a number of cookies that is greater than the number of bears. Direct child: **"Find out how many cookies we'll need."**

7. If the child is incorrect, try again making suggestions as appropriate, for example, **"How many bears did you say there were?"** or **"Try giving each bear a cookie,"** or **"Does each bear have one cookie?"**

8. If the child cannot figure out how many cookies are needed, even with prompting, skip Step 10 below and continue to **Subtraction**. If the child answers correctly, either by making a one-to-one correspondence or by stating the number, continue in sequence.

9. Give the child a piece of paper, or have the child write on the recording sheet. Ask the child, **"Show me on the paper how many cookies we need if each bear gets one cookie."**

10. **Counting on.** <u>Do the following steps only if the child successfully counts at least half the number of bears expected for that child's age group</u>. Move paper, bears, and cookies out of the way. In a clear space, show new cookies. Point to these cookies and ask the child, **"How many cookies are there here?"** If child doesn't count them correctly, say **"Count with me"** and point/count together.

11. Add cookies. Ask, **"How many cookies are there now?"** Listen and watch for "counting on," the ability to start counting at a number other than one.

Number of "new" cookies for counting on

- 3–4 yr olds = 5
- 5–8 yr olds = 11

Procedure—Subtracting

Note on cookies: Some children understand one-to-one correspondence and will not have distributed cookies to the bears. You may ask them to pass out the cookies at this point. On the other hand, children who are accustomed to using paper and pencil for math computation may not need manipulatives for this section.

Number of bears to "go home" (subtract)

- 3–4 yr olds = 3
- 5–8 yr olds = 5

1. Show appropriate number of bears from counting above and say **"The [9 or 23] bears are still on their picnic, but now [3 or 5] bears decide to go home. How many bears will still be at the picnic after they leave? You can move the bears around if that will help you figure it out."** Repeat the question, if necessary.

2. If the child is incorrect, ask the child to try again and repeat the numerical details, as necessary. If the child is correct, continue to next part of activity.

3. Give the child a piece of paper or have the child write on the recording sheet. Ask, **"Show me on paper how you figured out how many bears would be left."** Repeat the details of the problem the child has just solved.

4. If the child does not write an equation on paper, offer encouragement and ask him or her to show you **"how you figured out the answer to my question about how many bears, since there were [9 or 23] and [3 or 5] left."** Then move on.

Procedure—Estimating

Estimation # for second jar

- 3–4 yr olds = 20
- 5–8 yr olds = 50

1. Put all the bears from **Subtraction** in a plastic jar. In an identical jar, place estimation number of bears. Say, **"In this jar we have the [9 or 23] bears you were just playing with. Look at the bears in both jars and compare them. About how many bears do you think are in this other jar?"**

2. After the child makes an estimate, probe the child's thinking. Ask, **"How did you decide?"**

Procedure—Division

1. **Fair share-no remainder.** Put 3 bears in front of the child. Say, **"I baked [6, 9, or 15] cookies for these bears."** Put this number of "cookie" chips next to the child. Continue, **"I want to give all the cookies to the 3 bears. I want to be fair, so every bear gets the same. How many cookies does each bear get? You can move the bears and cookies around if that will help you figure it out."**

   Cookies for fair share-no remainder

   - 3–4 yr olds = 6
   - 5–6 yr olds = 9
   - 7–8 yr olds = 15

2. If the child does this incorrectly, try again. If child does not succeed on second try, stop here. If the child is correct, proceed to next step. If the child distributes the cookies correctly but does not answer the question, ask again, **"So how many cookies does each bear get?"**

3. **Fair share-with remainder.** Remove the first set of bears and cookies just used. Set out 4 new bears and [10, 14, or 22] cookies. Say, **"Here are 4 bears and [10, 14, or 22] cookies I baked for them. I want to give all the cookies to the 4 bears. I want to be fair, so every bear gets the same number of cookies. How many cookies does each bear get? You can move the bears and cookies around if that will help you figure it out."**

4. Based on what the child does, ask question(s) designed to probe the child's thinking about the remainder. For example,
   - **"What will you do with these cookies?"**
   - **"How come this bear(s) gets extra?"**
   - **"Is that fair for everybody?"**

   Cookies for division-with remainder

   - 3–4 yr olds = 10
   - 5–6 yr olds = 14
   - 7–8 yr olds = 22

Counting

Recording Sheet

Child's name _____ Assess date _____ Assessor _____ Rubric level _____

Strategy (check one)

Child has a strategy for keeping track of which bears have been counted

☐ no

☐ yes, but it doesn't work

☐ yes, and it works

Highest Number

Record highest number

counted in correct sequence:

```
┌─────────────┐
│             │
│             │
└─────────────┘
```

Answer to "How many bears?" (check one)

Child realizes the importance of the last bear counted: that the total number of bears is the same as the last count (for example, repeats "9" or says "9 bears").

☐ no

☐ yes, but but has to recount

☐ yes

One-to-One Correspondence (check one)

☐ None evident

☐ Uses manipulatives: incorrect

☐ Uses manipulatives: correct

☐ Knows the correct answer without manipulatives

Counting on (when adding, starts with known amount and counts up rather than counting all objects)

☐ No

☐ Yes

Observation of Counting

Note what the child does—pay particular attention to hands, eyes, and what the child says.

Written Representation

Attach (or copy here) what the child writes or draws

Counting   Evaluative Working Approach Rubric

Circle the number that best describes the child's evaluative working approach in this activity.

Child's Name:

_____

Initial Engagement: How does the child initially respond to the activity?

Hesitant _____ **Eager**

1	2	3	4	5
very hesitant or unwilling to begin activity		becomes involved on his or her own		eager to begin activity

Focus, Attention: How on task is the child throughout the activity?

Distractable _____ **Attentive**

1	2	3	4	5
very easily distracted by other children, events, or materials		attentive some of the time		sustained, absorbed attention to activity

Goal Orientation: How clear is the child working toward the activity's goal?

Personal goal _____ **Activity goal**

1	2	3	4	5
works on personal goal rather than activity goal		child's work vacillates between personal goal and activity goal		works efficiently toward activity goal

Planfulness: How organized is the child in working toward task completion?

Haphazard _____ **Organized**

1	2	3	4	5
random or impulsive; no evidence of organization of materials or approach		organized some of the time		well-organized, methodical in approach or with materials

Resourcefulness: What does the child do when stuck?

Helpless _____ **Resourceful**

1	2	3	4	5
does not ask for help; unable to use help when offered		moves forward a step when help is given		seeks help and makes good use of it to figure out challenges

Cooperation (for group activities): How does the child work with peers to accomplish task?

Difficulty working with others _____ **Helpful to others**

1	2	3	4	5
has difficulty sharing materials or attention, taking turns, supporting the efforts of others		gets along with other children		helps other children with activity, materials, or as a mediator; models ideas for others

Activities: Mathematics

Counting

Descriptive Working Approach Rubric

Circle the number that best describes the child's descriptive working approach in this activity.

Child's Name:

_____

Chattiness: How much of the child's talk is unrelated to the activity?

Very quiet _____ **Very chatty**

1	2	3	4	5
little conversation and self-talk throughout the activity		talks from time to time		constantly talks about unrelated topics

Pace of Work: What is the child's pace of work?

Slow _____ **Fast**

1	2	3	4	5
slow to start and carry out the activity		moderate pace throughout the activity		quick start and quick finish

Social Referencing: How often does the child check with teachers or peers?

Little interaction _____ **Constant checking**

1	2	3	4	5
focuses on own work		attention to others' work and checks with others about own work occasionally		frequently asks teacher or peer if own work is on track

Playfulness: How animated, lively, or happy is the child during the activity?

Serious _____ **Playful**

1	2	3	4	5
mood/demeanor is serious and cheerless		business-like with activity		cheerful and sense of humor related to activity

Subtracting

Recording Sheet

Child's name _____ Assess date _____ Assessor _____ Rubric level _____

Understanding of Problem

Child understood the problem immediately, teacher did not have to repeat/rephrase

☐ no

☐ yes

Observation of Counting

Note what the child does—pay particular attention to hands, eyes, and what the child says

Written Representation

Attach (or copy here) what the child writes or draws

Activities: Mathematics

Subtracting		**Evaluative Working Approach Rubric**		

Circle the number that best describes the child's evaluative working approach in this activity.

Child's Name:
_____

Initial Engagement: How does the child initially respond to the activity?

Hesitant				**Eager**
1	2	3	4	5
very hesitant or unwilling to begin activity		becomes involved on his or her own		eager to begin activity

Focus, Attention: How on task is the child throughout the activity?

Distractable				**Attentive**
1	2	3	4	5
very easily distracted by other children, events, or materials		attentive some of the time		sustained, absorbed attention to activity

Goal Orientation: How clear is the child working toward the activity's goal?

Personal goal				**Activity goal**
1	2	3	4	5
works on personal goal rather than activity goal		child's work vacillates between personal goal and activity goal		works efficiently toward activity goal

Planfulness: How organized is the child in working toward task completion?

Haphazard				**Organized**
1	2	3	4	5
random or impulsive; no evidence of organization of materials or approach		organized some of the time		well-organized, methodical in approach or with materials

Resourcefulness: What does the child do when stuck?

Helpless				**Resourceful**
1	2	3	4	5
does not ask for help; unable to use help when offered		moves forward a step when help is given		seeks help and makes good use of it to figure out challenges

Cooperation (for group activities): How does the child work with peers to accomplish task?

Difficulty working with others				**Helpful to others**
1	2	3	4	5
has difficulty sharing materials or attention, taking turns, supporting the efforts of others		gets along with other children		helps other children with activity, materials, or as a mediator; models ideas for others

Subtracting

Descriptive Working Approach Rubric

Circle the number that best describes the child's descriptive working approach in this activity.

Child's Name:

_____

Chattiness: How much of the child's talk is unrelated to the activity?

Very quiet _____ **Very chatty**

1	2	3	4	5
little conversation and self-talk throughout the activity		talks from time to time		constantly talks about unrelated topics

Pace of Work: What is the child's pace of work?

Slow _____ **Fast**

1	2	3	4	5
slow to start and carry out the activity		moderate pace throughout the activity		quick start and quick finish

Social Referencing: How often does the child check with teachers or peers?

Little interaction _____ **Constant checking**

1	2	3	4	5
focuses on own work		attention to others' work and checks with others about own work occasionally		frequently asks teacher or peer if own work is on track

Playfulness: How animated, lively, or happy is the child during the activity?

Serious _____ **Playful**

1	2	3	4	5
mood/demeanor is serious and cheerless		business-like with activity		cheerful and sense of humor related to activity

Activities: Mathematics

Estimating

Recording Sheet

Child's name _____ Assess date _____ Assessor _____ Rubric level _____

Estimated Number

Actual number in jar:

Child's estimate:

Observation of Counting

Note what the child does—pay particular attention to hands, eyes, and what the child says

Explanation

Write down what the child says to explain his or her estimate

Estimating

Evaluative Working Approach Rubric

Circle the number that best describes the
child's evaluative working approach in this activity.

Child's Name:

_____

Initial Engagement: How does the child initially respond to the activity?

Hesitant _____ **Eager**

l	2	3	4	5
very hesitant or unwilling to begin activity		becomes involved on his or her own		eager to begin activity

Focus, Attention: How on task is the child throughout the activity?

Distractable _____ **Attentive**

l	2	3	4	5
very easily distracted by other children, events, or materials		attentive some of the time		sustained, absorbed attention to activity

Goal Orientation: How clear is the child working toward the activity's goal?

Personal goal _____ **Activity goal**

l	2	3	4	5
works on personal goal rather than activity goal		child's work vacillates between personal goal and activity goal		works efficiently toward activity goal

Planfulness: How organized is the child in working toward task completion?

Haphazard _____ **Organized**

l	2	3	4	5
random or impulsive; no evidence of organization of materials or approach		organized some of the time		well-organized, methodical in approach or with materials

Resourcefulness: What does the child do when stuck?

Helpless _____ **Resourceful**

l	2	3	4	5
does not ask for help; unable to use help when offered		moves forward a step when help is given		seeks help and makes good use of it to figure out challenges

Cooperation (for group activities): How does the child work with peers to accomplish task?

Difficulty working with others _____ **Helpful to others**

l	2	3	4	5
has difficulty sharing materials or attention, taking turns, supporting the efforts of others		gets along with other children		helps other children with activity, materials, or as a mediator; models ideas for others

Activities: Mathematics

Estimating

Descriptive Working Approach Rubric

Circle the number that best describes the child's descriptive working approach in this activity.

Child's Name:

_____

Chattiness: How much of the child's talk is unrelated to the activity?

Very quiet _____ **Very chatty**

1	2	3	4	5
little conversation and self-talk throughout the activity		talks from time to time		constantly talks about unrelated topics

Pace of Work: What is the child's pace of work?

Slow _____ **Fast**

1	2	3	4	5
slow to start and carry out the activity		moderate pace throughout the activity		quick start and quick finish

Social Referencing: How often does the child check with teachers or peers?

Little interaction _____ **Constant checking**

1	2	3	4	5
focuses on own work		attention to others' work and checks with others about own work occasionally		frequently asks teacher or peer if own work is on track

Playfulness: How animated, lively, or happy is the child during the activity?

Serious _____ **Playful**

1	2	3	4	5
mood/demeanor is serious and cheerless		business-like with activity		cheerful and sense of humor related to activity

---

Division

Child's name _____ Assess date _____ Assessor _____ Rubric level _____

Strategy (check one)

Child has a strategy for sharing the cookies among the bears

- ☐ no
- ☐ yes, but relies on manipulatives
- ☐ yes, and can do it mentally

Remainder (check one)

Child can think of something "fair"

- ☐ no, does not offer a solution at all
- ☐ yes, but is not mathematically fair (for example, "I get the extras," or "throw them away," etc.)
- ☐ yes, and it is mathematically fair (for example, "Cut the extras in x pieces and everyone gets a piece")

Observation of Sharing Equally

Note what the child does—pay particular attention to hands, eyes, and what the child says.

Remainder

Write down what the child says should be done with the remaining cookies.

Division   Evaluative Working Approach Rubric

Circle the number that best describes the   **Child's Name:**
child's evaluative working approach in this activity.

_____

Initial Engagement: How does the child initially respond to the activity?

Hesitant _____ **Eager**

1	2	3	4	5
very hesitant or unwilling to begin activity		becomes involved on his or her own		eager to begin activity

Focus, Attention: How on task is the child throughout the activity?

Distractable _____ **Attentive**

1	2	3	4	5
very easily distracted by other children, events, or materials		attentive some of the time		sustained, absorbed attention to activity

Goal Orientation: How clear is the child working toward the activity's goal?

Personal goal _____ **Activity goal**

1	2	3	4	5
works on personal goal rather than activity goal		child's work vacillates between personal goal and activity goal		works efficiently toward activity goal

Planfulness: How organized is the child in working toward task completion?

Haphazard _____ **Organized**

1	2	3	4	5
random or impulsive; no evidence of organization of materials or approach		organized some of the time		well-organized, methodical in approach or with materials

Resourcefulness: What does the child do when stuck?

Helpless _____ **Resourceful**

1	2	3	4	5
does not ask for help; unable to use help when offered		moves forward a step when help is given		seeks help and makes good use of it to figure out challenges

Cooperation (for group activities): How does the child work with peers to accomplish task?

Difficulty working with others _____ **Helpful to others**

1	2	3	4	5
has difficulty sharing materials or attention, taking turns, supporting the efforts of others		gets along with other children		helps other children with activity, materials, or as a mediator; models ideas for others

Division   **Descriptive Working Approach Rubric**

Circle the number that best describes the child's descriptive   Child's Name:
working approach in this activity.
_____

Chattiness: How much of the child's talk is unrelated to the activity?

Very quiet _____ **Very chatt**

| 1 | 2 | 3 | 4 | 5 |

little conversation and self-   talks from time to time   constantly talks about
talk throughout the activity   unrelated topics

Pace of Work: What is the child's pace of work?

Slow _____ **Fast**

| 1 | 2 | 3 | 4 | 5 |

slow to start and   moderate pace throughout   quick start and quick finish
carry out the activity   the activity

Social Referencing: How often does the child check with teachers or peers?

Little interaction _____ **Constant checking**

| 1 | 2 | 3 | 4 | 5 |

focuses on own work   attention to others' work and   frequently asks teacher
                                       checks with others about   or peer if own work is
                                       own work occasionally   on track

Playfulness: How animated, lively, or happy is the child during the activity?

Serious _____ **Playful**

| 1 | 2 | 3 | 4 | 5 |

mood/demeanor is   business-like with activity   cheerful and sense of
serious and cheerless   humor related to activity

Activities: Mathematics

Counting

Performance Rubric

Level	Name	Performance Indicators
0	No participation	• Declines to participate in activity
1	No counting	• No counting behavior but plays with bears or watches others
2	Counting words	• Knows and uses some counting words; they are either not in order or not enough to count bears
3	Sequence but no strategy	• Uses necessary and correct counting word sequence, but has no strategy for keeping track of which bears have been counted
4	Beginning strategy	• Uses necessary and correct counting word sequence, but strategy is flawed (for example, pointing at bears without organizing or moving them)
5	Count but no cardinality	• Counts correctly, including keeping track of which bears are counted, but does not understand that the last number word used is also the cardinal amount (does not volunteer amount, and when asked "so, how many bears . . . ?" responds by counting again or not answering)
6	Correct counting	• Counts correctly and can answer cardinal amount question (says "9 bears" or "23 bears")

7	Correct counting plus one	• Achieves Level 6 above and **one** of the following:
		  o uses "counting on" to find out how many cookies
		  o can count through 100 with no or very minimal errors
		  o can count by 2s, 5s, or 10s
		  o can write Arabic numerals

8	Correct counting plus two	• Achieves Level 6 above and **two** of the following:
		  o uses "counting on" to find out how many cookies
		  o can count through 100 with no or very minimal errors
		  o can count by 2s, 5s, or 10s
		  o can write Arabic numerals

9	Correct counting plus three	• Achieves Level 6 above and **three** of the following:
		  o uses "counting on" to find out how many cookies
		  o can count through 100 with no or very minimal errors
		  o can count by 2s, 5s, or 10s
		  o can write Arabic numerals

10	Correct counting plus four	• Achieves Level 6 above and **all four** of the following:
		  o uses "counting on" to find out how many cookies
		  o can count through 100 with no or very minimal errors
		  o can count by 2s, 5s, or 10s
		  o can write Arabic numerals

Subtracting   Performance Rubric

Level	Name	Performance Indicators
0	No participation	• Declines to participate in activity
1	No subtraction; guesses or repeats number counted	• Does not engage in subtraction or guesses a number or repeats number of bears counted
2	Manipulatives: counting error	• Takes some bears away, but not the correct number
3	Manipulatives: answers the wrong question	• Counts the correct number of bears to "go home," but says this is the answer to "How many bears are left?"
4	Manipulatives: answers the right question incorrectly	• Takes away correct number of bears, but cannot correctly count number of bears who remain
5	Manipulatives: no number symbols	• Uses manipulatives, answers correctly, but can't/won't represent on paper or offers a scribble or a drawing of bears
6	Manipulatives: no equation	• Uses manipulatives, answers correctly, and uses either tally marks or Arabic numerals, but does not write full, correct equation
7	Mental math: no number symbols	• Solves problem correctly **without manipulatives**, but can't/won't represent on paper or offers a scribble or a drawing of bears
8	Mental math: no equation	• Solves problem correctly **without manipulatives** and uses either tally marks or Arabic numerals, but does not write full, correct equation
9	Manipulatives: written equation	• Solves problem correctly **with manipulatives** and writes full, correct equation using Arabic numerals
10	Mental math: written equation	• Solves problem correctly **without using manipulatives** and writes full, correct equation using Arabic numerals

Activities: Mathematics

Estimating   Performance Rubric

Level	Name	Performance Indicators
0	No participation	• Declines to participate in activity
1	No estimate	• Does not attempt to answer the question
2	Counting	• Thinks counting is the required answer
3	Impossible estimate	• Guesses that the number in the second container is either <u>less than</u> the known number of bears **or** <u>the same</u> as the known number
4	Unreasonably high estimate	• Guess is <u>more than</u> the known number of bears, but is <u>unreasonably high</u>; specifically, 100 or more
5	Unreasonable estimate, with or without justification	• Estimate is <u>outside of the following range,</u> but less than 100: • **for 20 bears, 15–50** • **for 50 bears, 35–80**
6	Reasonable estimate—non-quantity-based justification	• Estimate is within range specified in Level 5 above, but child can't/won't offer a mathematical or quantity-based justification; for example, may say "I don't know" or "I just thought it"
7	Reasonable estimate, NO reference to number	• Estimate is within range specified in Level 5 above, and child gives a vaguely quantity-based justification, for example, "It's a lot more" or "It's heavier"; justification does not make reference to counting, the specifically known number in the other jar, or the use of ratio language
8	Reasonable estimate, decomposition strategy	• Estimate is within range specified in Level 5 above, and child justifies guess by saying he or she "counted" bears in a single layer, counted how many layers of bears there were, and added these layers together to get a number (decomposition and additive strategies)
9	Reasonable estimate, specific reference to known number	• Estimate is within range specified in Level 5 above, and child refers to comparing the second jar to the known number in the other jar; to qualify, child must mention the [9 or 23] bears in the first jar specifically; for example, "It had to be a lot more than 9" or "There's 23 (using hand to show level) and then there's a lot more here"
10	Reasonable estimate, ratio language	• Estimate is within range specified in Level 5 above, and child uses ratio language to describe the relationship between the quantities in the two jars; for example, child says, "There had to be at least <u>twice</u> as many" or "It looks like a little more than <u>twice</u> as much"

Division		**Performance Rubric**
Level	Name	Performance Indicators
0	No participation	• Declines to participate in activity
1	No division	• Does not distribute cookies to bears
2	Unclear	• Does something with cookies, but it's unclear if it has anything to do with "How many cookies does each bear get?"
3	No-remainder: deals or says 3 cookies	• Stops after dealing one cookie to each bear—or says the answer is 3
4	No-remainder: dealing errors	• Deals all cookies, but some bears get more than others
5	No-remainder: counting or cardinal errors	• Deals cookies correctly, but has no answer or an incorrect answer to "How many cookies does each bear get?"
6	No-remainder: corrected errors	• Deals out correct number of cookies to each bear and says correct number of cookies per bear, but only after self-correction or prompts to "try again" from teacher
7	No-remainder correct; remainder errors	• Deals out correct number of cookies to each bear and says correct number of cookies per bear for no-remainder problem, but cannot suggest anything mathematically fair to do with remainder on second problem (for example, may say, "I don't know" or "Have mom bake more")
8	No-remainder correct; fair remainder suggestion; no fractions	• Deals out correct number of cookies to each bear and says correct number of cookies per bear for no-remainder problem, AND has mathematically fair suggestion for dealing with remainder, BUT cannot answer how many cookies each bear gets for remainder problem (2½)
9	Both correct but shows remainder with manipulatives	• Correctly solves both the no-remainder and remainder problems, including stating that "each bear gets 2½ cookies;" but using manipulatives with remainder problems.
10	Both correct, mental math	• Solves remainder problem, including stating that "each bear gets 2½ cookies" **without using manipulatives**

Activities: Mathematics

Exploring Number Concepts   Bridge to Curriculum

Reviewing: Key Concepts and Skills Exercised in the Activity

- Abstraction
- Stable order
- One-to-one correspondence
- Cardinality
- Order irrelevance
- Representation of number
- Operations with whole numbers
- Word problems
- Mental number line
- Visual estimate
- Part–whole relations

Reflecting: Questions Related to Child's Performance

Child's Working Approach

- Does any one Evaluative Working Approach quality stand out from the others?
- Is there any one Working Approach behavior contributing to or hindering the child's performance?
- Can you attribute the behavior that stands out to any of the activity parameters: materials, key concepts, social arrangements, or activity structure?

Activity Parameters

Materials

- Are there other materials this child shows a natural interest in that might motivate better participation?
- Does the child show extra focus or a longer attention span because he or she finds the materials interesting and attractive?
- Are the bears and/or cookies difficult for the child to manipulate?
- Are the bears and cookies too suggestive of pretend play, and therefore distracting to the child?

Social Arrangements

- Would the child do better if working with another child? In a small group?
- Does the child excel in this activity because it provides one-on-one interactions with the teacher?

Activity Structure

- Does the child prefer a more open-ended activity?
- Would the child do better if parts of the activity were conducted on different days?
- Does the heavy use of receptive language skills make this a difficult activity for this child?

Child's Performance

Rubric Levels 0–1	• Does the child know some of the counting words? • Is the child aware that the counting process can be applied to a collection of items?
Rubric Levels 2–3	• Does the child understand that counting words must be used in a stable order? • If it is stable, is the child's sequence of counting words in the conventionally correct order? • If the child has some correct and stable counting words, do they "go high enough" to cover the amount of items presented? • Does the child understand that each item must be counted at least once? • Does the child understand that each item must be counted ONLY once? • Does the child attempt to track which items have already been counted? • Is the attempt to track which items have been counted effective? • Does the child know to use the last number word produced when counting to provide the cardinal measure of amount?
Rubric Levels 4–5	• Does the child know that for each bear to get one cookie, an equivalent number of cookies is needed, or does the child need to match a cookie to each bear and recount to determine the number of cookies? • Does the child appear to understand that objects can be counted in any order, or does the child need to always start with the same object?
Rubric Levels 6–10	• Does the child attempt to use a written Arabic number to visually represent the number of cookies? • When cookies are added, does the child start over from one or begin counting with the known amount of at least one group? • Can the child navigate the transition from 99 through 100 to 101, etc.? • Does the child show evidence of counting bears by grouping them into sets of 2, 5, or 10?

Planning: Linking the Assessment Result to Curriculum Ideas

Much as the classroom should be rich in opportunities for exploring early literacy, it should also be rich in opportunities for experimenting with and thinking about number. This "number richness" requires both thoughtful planning of the classroom environment and activities, as well as the active involvement of teachers who ask questions and encourage the early exploration of relationships between number and quantity.

The general availability of "sets" of like objects is an important attribute of the "number-rich" classroom, since heightened similarity helps children conceive of the idea of groups of things. It is easier to see "threeness" among three identical pencils than among three plants when one is flowering, one a cactus, and one a small tree. One general advantage of objects like the counting bears is that while they are all extremely similar—they lend themselves to groupings by color. Groups or "sets" are clearly alike, since they each contain bears identical in shape, while the distinction of color between sets suggests comparing them and noticing that there are "more" blue bears than yellow bears, for example. Such early comparisons between sets are a crucial underlying basis for understanding cardinal amount.

(Continued)

(Continued)

Young children should also have opportunities to experiment with continuous, rather than discrete, quantity. Continuous quantities are not sets of objects, but amounts of things like sand or water, or ways of describing length or width. Unit blocks provide excellent examples of larger and smaller (or longer and shorter) objects, and sand and water tables are wonderful for giving children the opportunity to experiment with the kinds of "more" and "less" that are not so easily described numerically. While these activities do not feed as directly into competence with number specifically as do activities involving discrete objects, they relate directly to estimation skills and are an important precursor to all types of measurement activities.

Opportunities should also be provided for connecting actual amounts to symbolic representations of amounts. Drawn pictures, dice, and tally marks can all be ways of recording and communicating amount, and the classroom that includes many of these visual displays provides more opportunities for discovering their significance. Arabic numerals paired with either real objects or pictures of objects (the number "5" alongside a picture of five apples) help children understand that the idea of quantity can be represented symbolically. Board games with either dice or numerical spinners help children connect visual representations of amount with a number of spaces moved or tokens taken, enhancing their sense of the quantity each written value represents.

There are many practical and real reasons to count things each day in an early childhood classroom, such as knowing how many children are present each day or finding out how many children want a vanilla, as opposed to a chocolate, frosted cupcake. Demonstrations of counting ought to be a predictable and common part of classroom activities, providing multiple opportunities to see and understand relationships between the string of spoken words we use to track objects or events and the objects and events themselves. There is an element of familiarity and practice in counting and number concepts that the early childhood teacher ought not to neglect. Similarly, exposing children to the idea of dividing a set of objects into several groups, combining groups of objects, or eliminating or taking away objects will provide them with important baseline experiences of quantity that will help them understand more complex numerical relationships later.

Counting: Focused experiences and discussion. Counting experiences can be included in lots of different social settings. Sometimes counting objects together as a large group gets children involved and excited and may put an uncertain child at ease because her efforts are not "in the spotlight." On the other hand, there are times when your one-on-one help counting out the right number of napkins for a table at snack time will be incredibly helpful. Be explicit about counting procedures: each item must be counted AT LEAST once, and each item must be counted ONLY ONCE; effectively combining these two requirements is a difficult early counting challenge. Count things as a group at circle time and discuss strategy: how can you track which items have already been counted? Does it matter which item in a set is counted first? For children who are ready, walk them through the process of "counting on," noting that **"once we know how many are in this set, we can keep going with our string of number words to include the next set as well."** Repeated demonstrations of such techniques that patiently illustrate their reliability will help children to trust and learn to use them. Talk about decade and century transitions—that "one" is tacked on to "twenty" to make "twenty-one" and that this pattern repeats at "thirty" and so on. Older children can practice counting by twos, fives, and tens as a large group; this is often best done while referring to a visual number line.

To work on children's burgeoning sense of cardinality, count both small and large sets. Small-set counting really helps children who are just beginning to understand the relationship between number and amount, since they are more likely to have an intuitive understanding of "three" than of "eight." Provide practice matching equivalent sets of objects together and counting them; this will make the relationship between object-to-object matching and "equal number" ideas more clear.

To address the visual representation of number, demonstrate different ways to indicate number, such as drawings, tally marks, and Arabic numerals. Include numeral stencils and/or examples of numerals at your writing table, so children are encouraged to produce number symbols there. Provide a number line that goes past 100 in your classroom, and use it when counting larger amounts, pointing to each number in turn as it is said aloud. The key is to provide multiple opportunities for children to both become familiar with number symbols and to make connections between numerals and the real amounts they represent.

Subtraction: Focused experiences and discussion. The relationship between cardinal amount and number is central to the ability to "take away" and understand the quantity that remains, so dice and spinner games and other opportunities to count real objects and events provide crucial underlying understandings for subtraction. Keeping running tallies of events, such as how many children walked to school today, and comparing today's results with yesterday's is another good way to help children encounter numerical quantities and think about the relationships between them.

Children will also need help learning which kinds of actions increase the size of a group and which decrease it, so providing lots of "story problems," both verbally and with real objects, is important to their ability to conceptualize "subtraction." Begin with the story, and ask children, **"Are there more or less now?"** Follow up by recreating the subtraction story with real objects. At first, have your real objects exactly match those used in the story; that is, if apples are taken from apples, use real apples to find out whether more or less are left at the end. Later, when children are more comfortable with this process, you can use popsicle sticks or chips to represent the apples, helping children to think about quantity in a more abstract way.

Subtraction strategies are also important, however, so demonstrating different ways to mark or track which items are "taken away" can be very helpful. Have children count a small set and practice taking away a portion of the set in the large group; noticing and figuring out how many are left can be done later. When children seem to have the counting abilities to accomplish this, begin by asking whether the remaining amount is more or less than was there before. If children are not sure, ask how they might find out. By providing these explicit steps, you will help children discover subtraction on their own.

Estimation: Focused experiences and discussion. As in counting and subtraction, the relationship between number and amount is central to being able to estimate. "The Daily Guess" is a terrific activity for enhancing this understanding, as each day you place a number of some type of small object (marbles, dominoes, erasers) into a see-through container and have children guess how many there are. Guesses (or estimates) can be written down prior to counting the objects as you remove them one by one. Give children a chance to explain how they arrived at their guesses, since this will lead to interesting estimation strategy discussions.

Comparison processes are also important to this skill. To help facilitate comparison and link it with number, provide two sets of objects for visual comparison. Count each set in a large group meeting, discuss which one has more, and write the numerical amounts for each down on labels so children can study the relationships between number and amount AND between the two sets throughout the day.

Be sure to include estimates of continuous amount in your studies. Count how many cups of water it takes to fill two different glass jars, and label each for display. Ask children to predict whether the edge of the teacher's desk or the edge of a student's desk can include more unsharpened pencils placed end to end. Have children use real pencils to test their hypothesis and write down the results to label the desks with, being sure to discuss the results. Activities like this will help prepare children to use units of measurement.

(Continued)

Activities: Mathematics

(Continued)

For older children, you can demonstrate relationships between sets of objects in which one set has "two times" or "three times" as much as the other. Count the objects to demonstrate how this relationship is represented in numbers. Ask children, once you know the number in the smaller set, "Can you predict the number in the larger set?" Be sure to record predictions and results and discuss strategies throughout the activity.

Fair Share: Focused explorations and discussion. Since "fairness" is the backbone of a functioning early childhood classroom, there are often many opportunities for helping children think about the distribution of a set of objects. One cookie for each child, or in front of each snack setting, is probably the simplest of these types of activities, though very young children may need help figuring out how to be sure that EVERYBODY gets one, and only one. This type of one-to-one correspondence is an important precursor to the numerical thinking that allows for splitting in half or other ways of dividing sets that are more complex, so lots of practice with it at early ages is very helpful.

Children who are just learning about distributing a set will need practice with small numbers of objects given to even smaller numbers of people, like six similar objects given to three people. Even in this case, the strategy of "dealing" one item at a time to each person until all items are distributed may have to be demonstrated and explicitly talked about before children begin to think of using it. Knowing that with six items and three people, each person should get two is a very advanced skill and not likely to occur before the primary grades.

Also demonstrate and discuss the division of one item that can be divided among several children, like a graham cracker, pizza, or cake, between two or more people. Ask children, **"What would happen if we split the pizza between MORE children—would the pieces be smaller or larger?"** Encourage children to explain their reasoning, and if possible, follow discussion with a real demonstration. When appropriate, introduce fractional language by noting that each of the six people got one sixth of the pizza. As children become somewhat comfortable with fractional language, challenge them to think about how to divide a larger set of objects into a smaller number of proportional amounts; for example, what is one half of 20 pencils?

Activities

Sciences

WHAT WE KNOW

Young children learn the basics of science through activities and experiences that engage them with objects and phenomena in the world around them. At its best, science curricula create experiences that capitalize on children's inclination to wonder, observe, and experiment, alone and with others. Within these experiences, children are linking new information about the organic and physical world to concepts they already have. Teachers play a critical role in engaging, guiding, and coaching children as they develop connections between what they currently know and new concepts they are beginning to consider.

According to the National Science Education Standards, the most important goal of science teaching and learning at any age is participating in and becoming skilled in the processes of inquiry. From the earliest years, children ask questions about the world around them. They bring to school the inclination to gather evidence, formulate hypotheses and explanations, compare new ideas to what they previously knew, and discuss theories that are emerging from their explorations with classmates. Teachers support science learning when they recognize the importance of this active learning process, acknowledge the predisposition of young children to such learning, and provide time, space, materials, and routines for learning. Further, children's science learning becomes rooted in school curricula when teachers model these processes of inquiry and fuel these explorations with content knowledge and open-ended questioning.

Successful science curricula in the early childhood years accomplish the following:

- Provide daily opportunities for children to observe, explore, and ask questions about events and experiences that facilitate their familiarity with important ideas in science and with the process of scientific inquiry;
- Allow children to manipulate materials, explore cause and effect sequences, and study changes that result from their actions;
- Encourage children to focus on transformations while they compare, infer, draw conclusions, and establish connections to previous knowledge;
- Promote children's learning and using vocabulary associated with science content and the process of inquiry; and
- Provide opportunities for children to discuss, revise, debate, display, and present their theories about how phenomena work.

WHAT BRIDGING PROVIDES

In the area of science, the domain is accurately characterized in the plural: sciences. While there is a common base to the process of inquiry in the biological, mechanical, and physical sciences, the content of each domain, the concepts, and procedures for experimentation are distinct and unique to each. There is truly no one activity or assessment that can capture the full breadth of science content knowledge and skills in one experience. The three Bridging science activities provide children opportunities to pursue questions through three distinct lines of inquiry relevant to each branch of science: analytical (physical science), organizational (biological science), and constructive (mechanical science). The activities target key concepts in each content area and involve children in using materials and approaches that encourage them to examine relationships in the physical and living world around them in ways that call for methodical, systematic, and logical thinking.

Through their involvement in these activities, children demonstrate both their interests and understandings to teachers. The goal of science activities and assessments is *not* to ensure that three-, five-, and eight-year-old children develop a conception of the world that mirrors the ideas that adults hold. Rather, science curricula and assessments consist of ongoing opportunities for children to explain how they see the world given their current knowledge base and reasoning skills. Encouraging young children to formulate questions, generate explanations, and connect new concepts to existing theories is the essence of effective science education. As a result of such experiences, children gradually construct successively more complex explanations for phenomena. Bridging offers teachers the opportunity to understand the kind of knowledge children hold about the physical and natural world and to plan subsequent experiences to further children's learning. Bridging helps teachers to realize that their job is not to lead children to the "right answer." Rather the teacher's job is to guide young children to wonder, to ask questions, to experiment, to observe carefully, and to discuss and debate with others the connections between what they have discovered as result of their observations and experimentations and what they knew before.

WHY THESE THREE ACTIVITIES

The three science Bridging activities are Exploring Shadows and Light, Assembling a Nature Display, and Building a Model Car. These activities provide children with opportunities to observe and study phenomena in the physical, natural, and mechanical realms. Exploring Shadows and Light, the physical sciences activity, asks children to exercise analytical and exploratory skills to discover how properties of light and objects interact to determine the quality of shadows. In the natural sciences activity, Assembling a Nature Display, children use the perceptual, structural, functional, and environmental characteristics of materials gathered from the outdoors to organize a nature display that demonstrates their understanding of relationships in the living world. Finally, in the mechanical sciences activity, Building a Model Car, children engage in a creative process to both examine the properties of common recycled materials gathered for their functional, mechanical, and artistic properties and then use the materials to construct a model car that rolls.

All three Bridging science activities serve to expose young children to the discourse, vocabulary, and materials pertinent to each of these areas of study. Each of the activities featured in the science section utilizes materials and experiences that are familiar to many young children. They make it possible for students to revise and expand their knowledge about ideas, such as the relationship between structure and function, the properties of light, or the relationship between organisms and their environment. Each of the assessment activities provides insights into the children's thinking at a moment in time in the context of ongoing experiments. The activities can be sustained over several days, if not weeks, while providing an assessment lens for uncovering each child's level of development and understanding within that area. The three activities allow teachers to see that while some children will show strong analytical and communicative skills across the three activities, others will demonstrate scientific strengths through a deep interest in one particular content area. All three activities are valuable models of early childhood science curricula.

Activities: Sciences

Relationship Between Standards and Bridging Activities in Science Area

Standards for Science	Bridging Activities		
	Shadows and Light	*Nature Display*	*Building a Model Car*
Science as an Inquiry			
• Scientific Inquiry	√	√	√
• Developing a Working Theory	√	√	√
• Communicating Results	√	√	√
Physical Science			
• Makeup of Objects	√	√	
• States of Materials			
• Properties of Objects and Materials	√	√	√
• Relationships Between Structure and Function			√
• Properties of Light	√		
• Shadow Formation	√		
• Position of Objects	√		√
• Objects in Motion			
• Properties of Sound, Heat, Electricity, and Magnets			
Life Science			
• Properties of Organisms		√	
• Environments and Organisms		√	
• Relationships Between Structure and Function		√	
• Interaction Between Cues and Behavior			
• Life Cycles			
• Relationship Between Characteristics of Parents and Offspring			
Earth and Space Science			
• Properties of Earth Materials			
• Changes in Earth Surface			

	Bridging Activities		
Standards for Science	*Shadows and Light*	*Nature Display*	*Building a Model Car*
• Properties of Weather			
• Fossils and Past Evidence			
• Objects in the Sky			
Science in Personal and Social Perspectives			
• Safety and Security			
• Health Needs			
• Human Populations			
• Human Populations and Resources			
• Human Populations and Environments			
• Science and Technology			

Activities: Sciences

Definition of Science Education Standards

Science as an Inquiry

- **Scientific Inquiry** Scientists use different kinds of tools and investigation techniques, such as describing, classifying, and testing, to answer questions about natural and physical phenomena.

- **Developing a Working Theory** Data from scientific inquiry are used to develop hypotheses and theories about physical and natural phenomena.

- **Communicating Results** Information derived from the use of scientific techniques and tools can be communicated through language, drawings, or displays.

Physical Science

- **Makeup of Objects** Objects are made of one or more materials.

- **States of Materials** Materials can exist in different states; some common materials, such as water, can change from one state to another by heating or cooling.

- **Properties of Objects and Materials** Objects and materials have many observable properties, including size, weight, shape, color, and the ability to react with other substances. These properties can be observed, inferred, or measured, and used to describe, group, classify, or organize objects and materials into categories.

- **Relationships Between Structure and Function** Objects and materials have different structures that serve different functions.

- **Properties of Light** Light travels in a straight line until it strikes an object. Light that encounters an object in its path can be reflected, refracted, or absorbed.

- **Shadow Formation** An object blocking a source of light can produce a shadow. Shadows can change in size, shape, and clarity depending on the type of reflection surface and the relative positions of the object, the light source, and the reflection surface.

- **Position of Objects** The position of an object can be described by locating it relative to another object or the background.

- **Objects in Motion** An object in motion can be described by tracing and measuring its position over time. The position and motion of objects can be changed by pushing and pulling, and the size of the change is related to the strength of the push or pull.

- **Properties of Sound** Sound is produced by vibrating objects, and its pitch can be changed by changing the rate of vibration.

- **Properties of Heat** Heat can be produced in many ways and can move from one object to another by conduction.

- **Properties of Electricity** Electric circuits can produce light, heat, sound, and magnetic effects. Electrical circuits require a complete loop.

- **Properties of Magnets** Magnets attract and repel each other and certain kinds of materials.

Life Science

- **Properties of Organisms** Organisms have many observable properties, including size, weight, shape, and color. These properties can be observed, inferred, or measured and used to describe, group, classify, or organize organisms into categories.

- **Environments and Organisms** There is a relationship between the characteristics and needs of organisms and the characteristics of the environments where they develop and live; distinct environments support the needs of different organisms.

- **Relationships Between Structure and Function** Organisms have different structures that serve different functions.

- **Interaction Between Cues and Behavior** The behavior of individual organisms is influenced by internal and external cues; senses help detect these internal and external cues.

- **Life Cycles** Organisms have life cycles that include being born, developing into adults, reproducing, and dying; the details of these life cycles are different for different organisms.

- **Relationship Between Characteristics of Parents and Offspring** Organisms tend to closely resemble their parents because many of their characteristics are inherited from them.

Earth and Space Science

- **Properties of Earth Materials** Earth materials have different physical and chemical properties.

- **Changes in Earth Surface** The surface of the earth changes; some changes are slow processes, such as erosion, and others are rapid, like landslides or volcano eruptions.

- **Properties of Weather** Weather changes from day to day and over the seasons and can be described by measurable quantities, such as temperature, wind direction and speed, and precipitation.

- **Fossils and Past Evidence** Fossils provide evidence about the plants and animals that lived long ago and the nature of the environment at that time.

- **Objects in the Sky** Objects in the sky, such as the sun, moon, stars, clouds, birds, and airplanes, have properties, locations, and movements that can be observed and described.

Science in Personal and Social Perspectives

- **Safety and Security** Safety and security are basic needs.

- **Health Needs** Individuals have some responsibility for their own health; this responsibility includes understanding the role of nutrition and of potentially harmful substances.

- **Human Populations** Human populations include groups of individuals living in a particular location; they can increase or decrease.

(Continued)

(Continued)

- **Human Populations and Resources** Resources come from living and nonliving environments to meet the needs and wants of a population; the supply of many resources is limited.

- **Human Populations and Environments** Environments consist of the space, conditions, and factors that affect an individual and a population's quality of life and their ability to survive; these environments can change naturally or be influenced by humans; changes in environment can differ in quality and speed.

- **Science and Technology** New ways of solving problems and getting work done are constantly emerging. New ideas and inventions have an effect on people and their environments and may not be available to all people in the world.

Exploring Shadows and Light

Procedure

Subject Area	**Key Concepts and Skills**
• Physical science	• Scientific inquiry
Social Arrangements	• Developing a working theory
	• Communicating results
• *Recommended:* small group, large group	• Properties of light, objects, and materials
	• Shadow formation
• *Viable:* child-child, teacher-child	• Position of objects

Activity and Goal

Children are invited to play and explore with a flashlight, using different objects and materials that are either opaque (light cannot pass through: produces dark shadow), transparent (most light can pass through: produces very faint shadow or no shadow), or translucent (some light can pass through: shadow may be dim and/or colored). Other sources of light, such as an overhead projector, lamp, light table, or spotlight may be used.

Materials

For Stage I: Exploration

- A place that can be darkened
- A flashlight for every pair of children (If children are very young, having their own flashlights might work better.)
- An overhead projector (optional)
- Screen, white cardboard, or blank wall where children can project shadows
- For every pair of children, a bag with a sample of opaque, transparent, and translucent materials. Include materials that offer the greatest variety among the following:
- Opaque materials: pieces of wood, small toys, fringed cloth, grass, leaves, twigs, foil paper, shapes cut from construction paper or cardboard. Scissors, forks, wide-toothed combs, doilies and holed spatulas also offer possibilities for interesting shadows.
- Transparent and translucent materials: gauze, net, thin nylon, colored and colorless acetate or cellophane, tracing paper, different-sized marbles

For Stage II: Assessment

- A place that is not too bright
- A flashlight
- Two pieces of construction paper, one white, one black
- A crumpled piece of aluminum foil
- One half of an egg carton (preferably the Styrofoam kind)
- Two toy figures, one slightly bigger than the other
- A plastic fork
- Five worksheets (pages 237–241).
- A set of 2" × 2" squares, one of each the following materials: black construction paper; colored construction paper; a piece of clear acetate or cellophane and one the same color as the construction paper; a piece of tissue paper the same color as the acetate/cellophane and colored construction paper. (Before conducting the assessment, color Square C on Worksheet 4 the same color. Color Square B a light gray.)

(Continued)

(Continued)

Procedure

Stage I: Exploration

1. In a large, medium, or small group, introduce the children to thinking about shadows. As in all good teaching, find a way to introduce this topic so that it builds in some natural way off of a child's comment, observation, a question, or an idea raised in a storybook. Ask children questions such as: **"What do you know about shadows?" "How are they made?" "What do we need to make a shadow?"** Show children a flashlight or an overhead projector (the latter works better) and an object such as a block. Ask them, **"How can we make a shadow with this block?"** At some point, guide the children to seeing that an object cannot have a shadow if it is not in front of a light source.

2. Perhaps follow this introductory conversation by reading the poem "My Shadow," by Robert Louis Stevenson or the book by Ron and Nancy Goor, *Shadows Here, There and Everywhere*. Ask, **"What makes shadows move in all these different ways?! "**

3. Give every pair of children a flashlight and a bag with a collection of items similar to the ones listed under Materials. Invite children to use different kinds of objects, including body parts, to produce shadows.

4. Encourage children to explore how the size of the shadow changes by moving the object that is producing it.

5. Ask children to find out if there are some objects that make almost no shadow and others that can produce a color shadow.

6. Challenge the children to make the shadows of two objects touch while the objects do not.

7. As you work with the group, expose children to, and encourage their use of, key vocabulary, such as *dark shadows, light shadows, sharp shadows, fuzzy shadows, color shadows*.

Stage II: Assessment

Depending on the age of the children, you might decide to do this immediately after the exploration or the next day.

1. Invite a child or two to a table or quiet place in the classroom. Have flashlight and bag of materials available for child to use as needed.

2. Briefly remind them what they were doing during the shadow exploration. Then ask them the following questions:
   a. **"What do you need to make a shadow?"** Note their answer on the recording sheet.
   b. Use the pictures on Worksheet 1 to ask the child, **"Where would you put the flashlight if you wanted to make the shadow . . .**
      i. **small?"**
      ii. **big?"**
   c. Use Worksheet 2 and two small plastic figures (such as the ones in Lego sets) to demonstrate how the two figures produce two independent shadows; then place Worksheet 3 in front of the child and ask, **"Where would you put the two figures so they would make only one shadow?"** (If child's answer does not show understanding of the fact that the object must block the path of light to make a shadow, stop assessment here.)
   d. Show the child six small squares (see Materials, #8), and with Worksheet 4 in front of the child, ask, **"Which one of these do you think made . . .**
      i. **shadow A?"**
      ii. **shadow B?"**
      iii. **shadow C?"**
   e. Give child a plastic fork, two pieces of construction paper (one black and one white), a crumpled piece of aluminum foil, and the bumpy side of an opened egg carton. Use Worksheet 5 to ask, **"On which surface would I make my shadow if I wanted it to look like . . .**
      i. **this picture?"**
      ii. **this picture?"**
      iii. **this picture?"**
      iv. **this picture?"**

Exploring Shadows and Light—Worksheet 1

Where would you put the flashlight to make this big shadow?

Where would you put the flashlight to make this small shadow?

Exploring Shadows and Light—Worksheet 2

We have 2 figures that make 2 different shadows.

Exploring Shadows and Light—Worksheet 3

Where would you put the two figures so they would make one shadow?

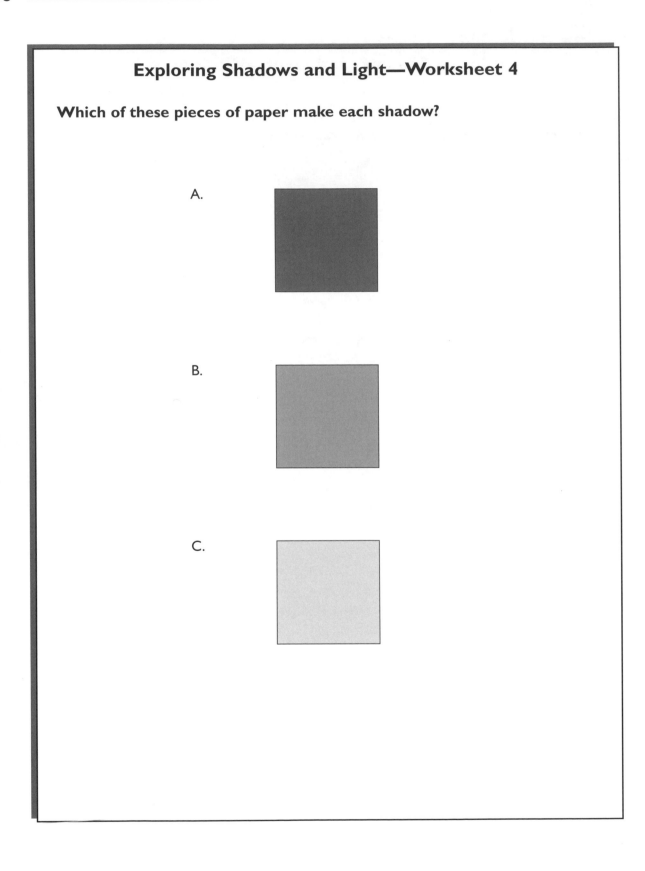

Exploring Shadows and Light—Worksheet 4

Which of these pieces of paper make each shadow?

A.

B.

C.

Exploring Shadows and Light—Worksheet 5

On which surface would I make my shadow if I want it to look like . . .

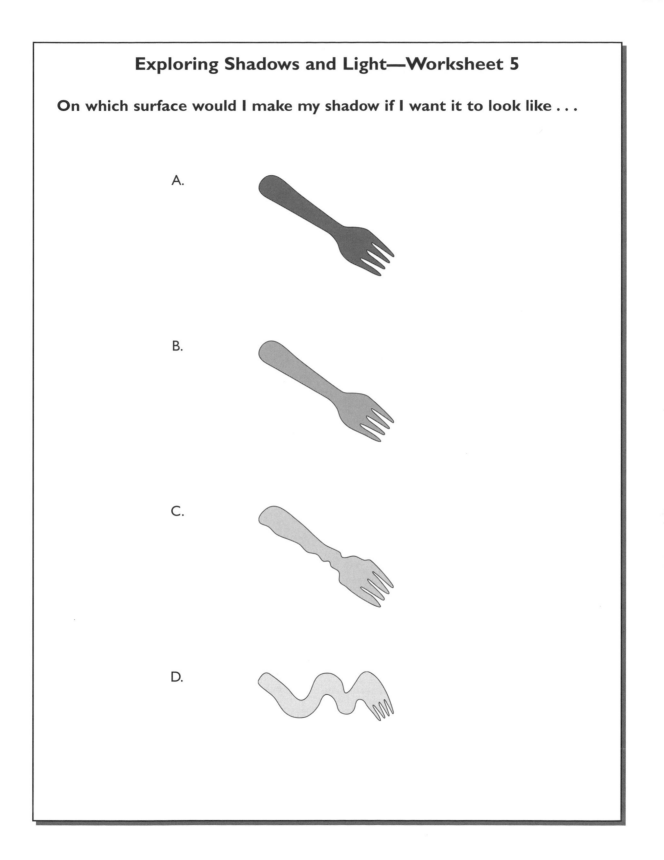

A.

B.

C.

D.

Exploring Shadows and Light

Recording Sheet

Child's name _____ Assess date _____ Assessor _____ Rubric level _____

For each worksheet, check the child's actions that apply:

What do you need to make a shadow?

☐ an object

☐ an object blocking the light

☐ a light

Worksheet #1: How can you make this shadow big?

☐ manipulate object

☐ manipulate light

Worksheet #2: How can you make this shadow little?

☐ manipulate object

☐ manipulate light

Worksheet #3: Where would you put these two objects so they would make only one shadow?

Child's answers/actions

☐ indicate awareness of need to change position of objects and/or light

☐ do NOT indicate awareness of need to change position of objects and/or light

Worksheet #4: Which of these do you think would make . . .

Shadow A? Child chooses

☐ opaque square

☐ translucent square

☐ transparent square

Shadow B? Child chooses

☐ opaque square

☐ translucent square

☐ transparent square

Shadow C? Child chooses

☐ opaque square

☐ translucent square

☐ transparent square

> Use this section to describe what the child does and to make notes about the child's experience during exploration.
>
> **(Stage I: Exploration)**
>
> ☐ Random
>
> ☐ Focused

> Use this section to describe what the child does with the flashlight, if anything, during the assessment.
>
> **(Stage II: Experimentation)**

Worksheet #5: Where would I make my shadow if I wanted it to look like . . .

Shadow A?	Shadow B?	Shadow C?	Shadow D?
Child chooses	Child chooses	Child chooses	Child chooses
☐ white paper	☐ white paper	☐ white paper	☐ white paper
☐ black paper	☐ black paper	☐ black paper	☐ black paper
☐ crumpled foil	☐ crumpled foil	☐ crumpled foil	☐ crumpled foil
☐ egg carton	☐ egg carton	☐ egg carton	☐ egg carton

Exploring Shadows and Light   Evaluative Working Approach Rubric

Circle the number that best describes the child's evaluative working approach in this activity.

Child's Name:

_____

Initial Engagement: How does the child initially respond to the activity?

Hesitant _____ **Eager**

1	2	3	4	5
very hesitant or unwilling to begin activity		becomes involved on his or her own		eager to begin activity

Focus, Attention: How on task is the child throughout the activity?

Distractable _____ **Attentive**

1	2	3	4	5
very easily distracted by other children, events, or materials		attentive some of the time		sustained, absorbed attention to activity

Goal Orientation: How clear is the child working toward the activity's goal?

Personal goal _____ **Activity goal**

1	2	3	4	5
works on personal goal rather than activity goal		child's work vacillates between personal goal and activity goal		works efficiently toward activity goal

Planfulness: How organized is the child in working toward task completion?

Haphazard _____ **Organized**

1	2	3	4	5
random or impulsive; no evidence of organization of materials or approach		organized some of the time		well-organized, methodical in approach or with materials

Resourcefulness: What does the child do when stuck?

Helpless _____ **Resourceful**

1	2	3	4	5
does not ask for help; unable to use help when offered		moves forward a step when help is given		seeks help and makes good use of it to figure out challenges

Cooperation (for group activities): How does the child work with peers to accomplish task?

Difficulty working with others _____ **Helpful to others**

1	2	3	4	5
has difficulty sharing materials or attention, taking turns, supporting the efforts of others		gets along with other children		helps other children with activity, materials, or as a mediator; models ideas for others

Activities: Sciences

Exploring Shadows and Light   Descriptive Working Approach Rubric

Circle the number that best describes the child's descriptive working approach in this activity.

Child's Name:
_____

Chattiness: How much of the child's talk is unrelated to the activity?

Very quiet _____ **Very chatty**

I	2	3	4	5

little conversation and self-talk throughout the activity   talks from time to time   constantly talks about unrelated topics

Pace of Work: What is the child's pace of work?

Slow _____ **Fast**

I	2	3	4	5

slow to start and carry out the activity   moderate pace throughout the activity   quick start and quick finish

Social Referencing: How often does the child check with teachers or peers?

Little interaction _____ **Constant checking**

I	2	3	4	5

focuses on own work   attention to others' work and checks with others about own work occasionally   frequently asks teacher or peer if own work is on track

Playfulness: How animated, lively, or happy is the child during the activity?

Serious _____ **Playful**

I	2	3	4	5

mood/demeanor is serious and cheerless   Business-like with activity   cheerful and sense of humor related to activity

Exploring Shadows and Light · Performance Rubric

Level	Name	Performance Indicators
0	No activity	• Child declines to participate.
1	Unfocused exploration	• Child's exploration focuses more on play than on investigating any of the possibilities offered by the flashlight and materials.
2	Focused exploration	• Child's exploration appears more focused. There is evidence that the child is using some questions to guide inquiry. The child explores changes in size and uses flashlight and materials with some sense of purpose (for example, the child becomes intrigued by the nature of shadows produced by objects that have spaces where the light can go through, like a plastic fork or a doily).
3	Focused exploration and awareness of two basic elements	• Child meets criteria for Level 2 and in answer to the first question mentions **two** of the elements needed to make a shadow-object and source of light.
4	Size of shadow	• Child meets criteria for Level 3 and is aware that manipulating the object and/or the source of light will change the size of the shadow.
5	Object blocking light	• Child meets criteria for Level 4, and answers question on Worksheet 3 reveals that child is aware that object must be blocking light to produce a shadow.
6	Beginning awareness of role of object properties	• Child meets criteria for Level 5 and can correctly answer **one** of the questions on Worksheet 4.
7	Sophisticated awareness of properties of objects	• Child meets criteria for Level 5 and answers **at least two** of the three questions on Worksheet 4.
8	Basic awareness of role of reflection surface	• Child meets criteria for Level 7 and correctly answers **one** of the questions on Worksheet 5.
9	Sophisticated awareness of role of reflection surface	• Child meets criteria for Level 7 and correctly answers **two** of the questions on Worksheet 5.
10	Expert	• Child meets crieria for Level 7 and correctly answers **all** of the questions on Worksheet 5.

Activities: Sciences

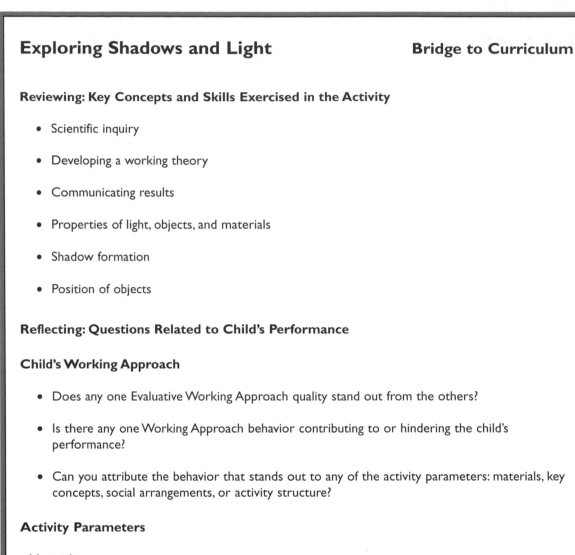

Exploring Shadows and Light　　　　　　　　Bridge to Curriculum

Reviewing: Key Concepts and Skills Exercised in the Activity

- Scientific inquiry

- Developing a working theory

- Communicating results

- Properties of light, objects, and materials

- Shadow formation

- Position of objects

Reflecting: Questions Related to Child's Performance

Child's Working Approach

- Does any one Evaluative Working Approach quality stand out from the others?

- Is there any one Working Approach behavior contributing to or hindering the child's performance?

- Can you attribute the behavior that stands out to any of the activity parameters: materials, key concepts, social arrangements, or activity structure?

Activity Parameters

Materials

- Is the child distracted by the materials available during the exploration stage?

- Are some of these materials not familiar to the child?

Social Arrangements

- Is the child overwhelmed by the noise and bustle of the large group exploration?

Activity Structure

- Is the child intimidated by the open-ended nature of the Exploration Stage?

- Do the more directive questions of Stage II appear to put off the student?

- Does the child benefit from, and respond well to, focused questioning?

Child's Performance

Rubric Levels 1–4	• Can the child use questions to focus exploration (for example, what happens to the shadow when I move the flashlight?)?
	• Can the child generate hypotheses about the role played by light in shadow formation using information from his or her observations?
	• Is the child capable of answering questions about shadows using information from his or her observations?
	• Does the child understand that the power of the light source influences the quality of shadows (that is, dimmer light usually generates paler, less sharp shadows)?
	• Does the child understand that the position of the light relative to the object impacts the size of shadows?
Rubric Levels 5–7	• Does the child understand that an object must be blocking the light in order to produce a shadow?
	• Does the child understand that opaque objects, capable of totally blocking light, generally produce darker, more solid shadows?
	• Does the child understand that translucent objects, which let some light pass, generally produce lighter, and sometimes colored, shadows?
	• Does the child understand that transparent objects, which let most of the light pass, produce a very faint shadow or no shadow at all?
Rubric Levels 8–10	• Does the child understand that a white (or light colored) reflection surface produces more solid, darker shadows?
	• Does the child understand that the texture of the reflection surface impacts the shape and quality of shadows?

Planning: Linking the Assessment Result to Curriculum Ideas

The study of shadows and light is a wonderful focus for study in early childhood classrooms because most children have noticed their shadow at some point in time and have made shadows with objects and their body. Children can readily experiment with the phenomena of shadows with the use of minimal materials. Their own bodies, a few stable objects in the school yard, the sun, and some measuring tools like yardsticks or rulers are all that is needed to launch an extended study of who and what has a shadow, where shadows come from, how and why they change in size, and whether shadows have a color. When you are preparing to study shadows, make note of anything children say about shadows, and use their comments to open up discussion and introduce this area of inquiry.

Questions and experimentation. Children are usually curious about shadows. Teachers can capitalize on this curiosity by providing multiple opportunities for students to ask questions and generate explanations for the interplay between the properties of objects and light, and the resulting characteristics in shadows. To do so, make available different kind of objects, and ask children to predict which will produce a shadow. Provide objects that come in different sizes (for example, unit blocks or different sizes of toy dinosaurs), and later, those made from different materials (that is, solid pattern blocks and transparent pattern blocks). Plan to have a light source that children can manipulate, such as a flashlight and/or overhead projector. Raise questions with the children regarding how the different properties of the material (size, color, shape) affect the shadow they make. Allow children to work in pairs or small groups. Structure the discussions to require children to make predictions followed by trying out an idea, recording what happens, and then reporting to the class what they found. This process provides children with three opportunities to articulate their thinking: initial discussion, drawing or writing their findings, and discussing their efforts with the larger group.

(Continued)

Activities: Sciences

(Continued)

Children's learning can be extended in a "Find out" center where children can post questions. As the teacher, listen closely to the children's conversations and articulate for the class the questions that you hear them raising. What happens to our shadow when . . . ? Can shadows move? How do shadows change? Can you make your shadow touch something if you are not? Is your shadow always attached to you?

What follows are some additional activities that will generate opportunities for questioning and experimentation.

- Early on a sunny morning, take children outdoors, point out the position of the sun in reference to them, and have them put their backs to the sun. Ask them to trace each other's shadows. Use chalk or tape to mark their initials or name on the place where they were standing. Come back at noon, point out where the sun is (over their heads), and have them trace their shadows again as they stand on the same spot as before. Elicit and record their comments and observations. Return later in the afternoon and repeat the process. You might also want to measure their shadows in the early morning, at noon, and in the early afternoon, and compare/contrast their findings. Any part of these experiences will provide abundant material for discussions, drawing, and writing!

- Use an easel or a similar surface to attach different kinds of materials (for example, white, black, gray, yellow, and red construction paper; aluminium foil, smooth and crumpled; dark carpet sample; velveteen fabric or bath towel). With a flashlight, project a shadow on the different surfaces. Encourage the children to predict the kind of shadow that will be reflected on the different surfaces.

- On a sunny day, take a shadow walk and have children make shadows on trees, playground equipment, benches, stairs. Have children draw or write about their shadows as reflected in different places. During group disucssions, present drawings and discuss their findings. Again, it is important to make explicit the connections they see as to what they discovered and how they did it.

Throughout these experiences, give children the chance to generate questions and hypotheses about the different variables that impact shadow formation: quality and position of light, properties of objects, and characteristics of reflection surface.

Establishing connections. Most young children bring to the classroom experiences of noticing shadows. It is important to tap into this previous knowledge and encourage children to make connections between what they already know and what they are learning from current explorations and experimentation. To do this, it can be helpful to record children's predictions and hypotheses before they engage in any activities with shadows. Revisit these predictions and hypotheses after the children have been studying shadows for a while, and help children notice what is changing in their thinking. This can be a very satisfying experience if the teacher is a good listener and does not judge the children's logic but rather shows a keen interest in what they think.

Encourage your children to document their observations and experimentations through drawings or writing, perhaps in a journal. Allow time at the end of the week to discuss children's findings, comparing and contrasting conclusions. Make connections across what the children found out, how they came to their findings, and the new ideas or insights they have come to.

Communicating results and using the vocabulary of science. Some of the best times of the school day ought to be the discussions: with a partner, small groups, and large group class meetings. Discussions are an opportunity to make visible the train of thought that individuals are developing. Children's thinking benefits from talking about their findings, discussing them with others, and being exposed to the vocabulary of science. In setting up discussions, be mindful to:

- Expose children to science vocabulary. Use words like *properties, transparent, translucent,* and *reflection,* being sure to provide concrete explanations and examples to illustrate their meaning every time you use them.

- Invite parents and other adults to the classroom and have students talk to them about some of the things they have been studying. Interested and interesting conversational partners help sharpen children's thinking and reasoning.

Assembling a Nature Display   Procedure

Subject Area	Key Concepts and Skills
• Natural science	• Scientific inquiry
Social Arrangements	• Developing a working theory
	• Communicating results
• *Recommended:* small group, large group	• Environments and organisms
	• Relationships between structure and function
	• Properties of objects and materials

Activity and Goal

Children are invited to classify a variety of objects from nature. The best way to do this activity is to take children on a nature walk and have them collect objects such as rocks, shells, leaves, acorns, and sticks. If this is not feasible, you can request children bring nature items from home.

Materials

- A bag to hold all collected samples
- Broad-tipped markers
- Construction paper
- Disposable camera

Advance Preparation

A week or two ahead:

1. Visit your nature walk destination to check that it is safe and children do not run the risk of encountering unsafe objects. Make sure that the area has varied nature samples in sufficient quantity.

2. If you request that children bring items from home, give enough time in advance for them to gather a diverse collection of objects.

3. Whether you decide to go on a nature walk or ask children to bring items from home, you must also be involved in the collection of nature items to ensure that there will be enough for everyone.

A few days before and again on the day of the nature walk:

1. Discuss with the children what they will encounter in the place they will visit and what kind of samples they might like to put in their collection bags. Emphasize the fact that they will put all items collected into one common area to share with everyone, and that after the class has built a good collection, each child will design and make their own display.

2. Before embarking on this activity, discuss with the children which things are okay to pick up: pebbles, insect remains, bird feathers, acorns, grass, bark that is off the trees, sticks, leaves, and flowers that have fallen off. Items must fit inside the bag. Emphasize the importance of not taking leaves off trees, picking flowers, or otherwise disturbing the environment.

Make sure the collection of nature items includes objects such as:

Shells
Leaves
Grass (various types)
Rocks
Pebbles
Animal skin

Activities: Sciences

(Continued)

Feathers
Insects
Pinecones
Acorns
Seeds
Beans
Dried flowers
Berries
Bark
Small sticks
Twigs
Pine needles
Fur

Procedure

For younger children (ages three to five)

1. Take children to a nearby park, green area, or nature center to collect nature samples, or have children bring nature items from home.

2. Make sure children understand that whatever is collected or brought from home will become part of a class collection available for everyone's use.

3. Small groups work best for this activity. With preschoolers who need monitoring and assistance during the whole process, it is probably best to work with three or four children at a time.

4. Before asking three- and four-year-olds to do this activity, it is important to model some classification schemes.

    A. Put various types of items such as pebbles, acorns, and pinecones on a plate or tray. Talk about how the objects are different and how they are similar. Discuss the meaning of the words *organize* and *classify* by saying to the children, "I want to classify these materials. That means I want to put objects together that are similar, that are alike in some way."

    B. Have each child pick an item and place it on a piece of paper in the center of the table.

    C. Ask one child at a time to group the items and explain how he or she did it. Use and explain the terms *organize* and *classify* in the context of arranging items so that children will learn their meaning.

    D. Repeat this process with each child until everyone has had a turn; continue emphasizing how the same objects can be grouped in different ways.

    E. Arrange the objects yourself, and ask children to guess how the items are organized.

5. Give each child a sample of at least seven different kinds of materials. Take special care to provide a variety of objects in order to promote cross-categorization. For example, make sure they have only one or two of each type of object. This will increase the likelihood that children will search for commonalities in order to make a category, rather than put together a group of leaves because they have so many.

6. Tell the children that each of them is going to create a small display using items from the class collection. Instruct them that their display must include at least **two different categories**. Explain that they can use markers or masking tape to create "boundaries" between different items on their display paper.

7. Allow children to work independently, but pay close attention to the conversations of children as they work. Remain available for consultation, encouragement, and help.

8. Once the child is finished, use the recording sheet to write a brief explanation of the display. Be sure to encourage students to state the rationale they used to organize their display (for example, "I see you have put this little group of leaves apart from the others. Why did you place them that way?").

9. Take a picture of the child's work.

10. Put materials back in the classroom collection. This will guarantee a stable pool of materials that can be used again in the future.

For older children

1. Take children to a nearby park, green area, or nature center to collect nature samples, or have children bring nature items from home.

2. Make sure children understand that whatever is collected or brought from home will become part of a class collection available for everyone's use.

3. Have children choose one item from the collection and bring it to a group meeting. Discuss the concept of categorization, stressing that it is a way to group things that are somehow alike. Have children briefly show the item they chose from the collection; choose a couple of categories and walk children through the process of deciding which objects correspond to which categories. For example, if some children have leaves, flowers, seeds, or berries, they could be grouped as things that come from trees. Repeat this process several times, making sure that the examples illustrate the way different objects can be grouped into more than one category.

4. Have students, in small groups, go through the class collection. Encourage children to observe and comment on the different items.

5. The next day or soon after, have students work in small groups to create a nature display.

6. It is important to provide a wide variety of materials to encourage richer classification schemes. Make sure you make available at least **seven** different types of items. The materials should be displayed and organized in a way that is not overwhelming. Having trays, baskets, or boxes to organize the materials can be very helpful.

7. Tell the children that each one of them will create a small display from the collection. Instruct them that their display must include **at least two categories**. Explain that they can use markers or masking tape to create "boundaries" between different items in their display.

8. Allow children to work independently, but pay close attention to the conversations of children as they work. Remain available for consultation, encouragement, and help.

9. Once the child is finished, use the recording sheet to write a brief explanation of the display. Be sure to encourage students to state the rationale they used to organize their display (for example, "I see you have put this little group of leaves apart from the others. Why did you do that?").

10. Take a picture of the child's work.

11. Put materials back in the classroom collection. This will guarantee a stable pool of materials that can be used again in the future.

Activities: Sciences

Assembling a Nature Display

Recording Sheet

Child's name _____ Assess date _____ Assessor_____ Rubric level _____

Note Grouping Principle Below

☐ **Simple attributes (check those used)**

   ☐ Color

   ☐ Size

   ☐ Shape

   ☐ Other _____

☐ **Basic, very broad categories (list)**

   _____

   _____

☐ **Environment (knowledge of habitats)**

☐ **Structure/Function**

☐ **Complex categories (at least two of the following)**

   ☐ Broad basic

   ☐ Environment

   ☐ Structure/function

☐ **Interrelationship between categories**

   _____

   _____

Assembling a Nature Display

Evaluative Working Approach Rubric

Circle the number that best describes the child's evaluative working approach in this activity.

Child's Name:
_____

Initial Engagement: How does the child initially respond to the activity?

Hesitant _____ **Eager**

1	2	3	4	5
very hesitant or unwilling to begin activity		becomes involved on his or her own		eager to begin activity

Focus, Attention: How on task is the child throughout the activity?

Distractable _____ **Attentive**

1	2	3	4	5
very easily distracted by other children, events, or materials		attentive some of the time		sustained, absorbed attention to activity

Goal Orientation: How clear is the child working toward the activity's goal?

Personal goal _____ **Activity goal**

1	2	3	4	5
works on personal goal rather than activity goal		child's work vacillates between personal goal and activity goal		works efficiently toward activity goal

Planfulness: How organized is the child in working toward task completion?

Haphazard _____ **Organized**

1	2	3	4	5
random or impulsive; no evidence of organization of materials or approach		organized some of the time		well-organized, methodical in approach or with materials

Resourcefulness: What does the child do when stuck?

Helpless _____ **Resourceful**

1	2	3	4	5
does not ask for help; unable to use help when offered		moves forward a step when help is given		seeks help and makes good use of it to figure out challenges

Cooperation (for group activities): How does the child work with peers to accomplish task?

Difficulty working with others _____ **Helpful to others**

1	2	3	4	5
has difficulty sharing materials or attention, taking turns, supporting the efforts of others		gets along with other children		helps other children with activity, materials, or as a mediator; models ideas for others

Activities: Sciences

Assembling a Nature Display   Descriptive Working Approach Rubric

Circle the number that best describes the child's descriptive working approach in this activity.

Child's Name:

_____

Chattiness: How much of the child's talk is unrelated to the activity?

Very quiet _____ **Very chatty**

1	2	3	4	5
little conversation and self-talk throughout the activity		talks from time to time		constantly talks about unrelated topics

Pace of Work: What is the child's pace of work?

Slow _____ **Fast**

1	2	3	4	5
slow to start and carry out the activity		moderate pace throughout the activity		quick start and quick finish

Social Referencing: How often does the child check with teachers or peers?

Little interaction _____ **Constant checking**

1	2	3	4	5
focuses on own work		attention to others' work and checks with others about own work occasionally		frequently asks teacher or peer if own work is on track

Playfulness: How animated, lively, or happy is the child during the activity?

Serious _____ **Playful**

1	2	3	4	5
mood/demeanor is serious and cheerless		Business-like with activity		cheerful and sense of humor related to activity

Assembling a Nature Display   Performance Rubric

Level	Name	Performance Indicators
0	No participation	• Child declines to participate in activity.
1	No display	• Child comes to table and engages with materials but does not produce a display.
2	Display without categories	• Although display may be aesthetically pleasing, items are not organized according to a classification scheme.
3	One attribute	• At least one of the categories in the display is organized according to one physical attribute (for example, size, shape, or color).
4	Two attributes	• At least one of the categories in the display is organized according to two physical attributes (for example, size and shape or size and color).
5	Three attributes	• At least one of the categories in the display is organized according to three physical attributes (for example, size, shape, and color).
6	Basic categories	• At least one of the categories in the display is organized according to general, more encompassing categories that reflect greater flexibility of the classification criteria used (for example, feather, insect wing, and piece of fur belong to animals; leaf, twig, and piece of bark as parts of a tree; different kinds of seeds are placed together because they all are capable of sprouting a new plant).
7	Environment	• At least one of the categories in the display reflects knowledge of environments/habitats (for example, smooth pebbles are separated from rougher rocks because they look as if they might have been in water; leaves, twigs, and blades of grass are classified as necessary for building a nest; pinecone, insect, and feather are together because they can all be found in a forest; berries, seeds, and insects are organized as things a bird can eat).
8	Structure/function	• At least one of the categories in the display is organized according to structure or characteristics that support function of items displayed (for example, feather, dandelion seed, and dry leaf are together because they are all light enough to be carried by the wind; a worm, a rock, and a pinecone are together because they lack limbs).
9	Complex categories	• Display is organized according to at least two of the criteria of Levels 6–8.
10	Inter-relatedness	• Display is organized in two or more categories that, in turn, are related to each other (for example, berries, seeds, and flowers are classified as parts of plants; bee, feather, and piece of fur are classified as part of animal world; **and** child establishes that the berries, seeds, and flowers can be considered sources of food for the animals).

Activities: Sciences

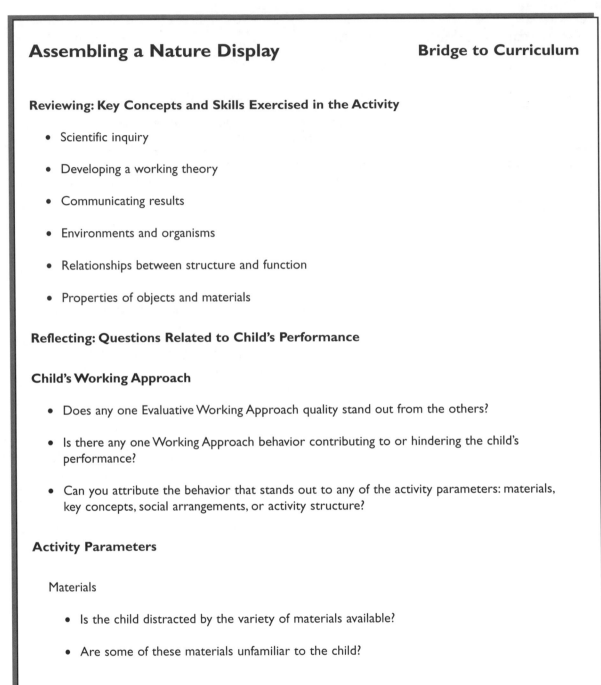

Assembling a Nature Display

Bridge to Curriculum

Reviewing: Key Concepts and Skills Exercised in the Activity

- Scientific inquiry

- Developing a working theory

- Communicating results

- Environments and organisms

- Relationships between structure and function

- Properties of objects and materials

Reflecting: Questions Related to Child's Performance

Child's Working Approach

- Does any one Evaluative Working Approach quality stand out from the others?

- Is there any one Working Approach behavior contributing to or hindering the child's performance?

- Can you attribute the behavior that stands out to any of the activity parameters: materials, key concepts, social arrangements, or activity structure?

Activity Parameters

Materials

- Is the child distracted by the variety of materials available?

- Are some of these materials unfamiliar to the child?

Social Arrangements

- Would the child benefit from working alone and without interruption?

Activity Structure

- Is the child put off by the nature of the categorization task?

Child's Performance

Rubric Levels 1–2	• Does the child understand the meaning of the terms *sorting, grouping,* and *classifying*? • Can the child generate hypotheses about the items available and their properties and characteristics using information from his or her observations? • Is the child using his or her observations of the materials available to generate questions that can help the child choose a classification criterion? • Does the child primarily focus on the aesthetics of objects/display?
Rubric Levels 3–5	• Does the child rely exclusively on the external properties of objects (color, shape, size, texture) to classify/organize materials? • Is the child capable of identifying different parts in organisms?
Rubric Level 6	• Can the child use broader generalization criteria (animals, plants, living things) that go beyond the external attributes of materials to define groupings?
Rubric Levels 7–10	• Is the child aware of the relationship between organisms and habitats/environments? • Can the child use his or her knowledge about the environment or habitat to generate categories that go beyond external characteristics? • Is the child aware of relationships between structure and function? • Can the child use his or her knowledge about relationships between structure and function to generate categories that go beyond external characteristics? • Is the child able to categorize using two or more of the more general criteria (environment/habitat, structure, and function)? • Can the child establish relationships between two or more complex criteria?

Planning: Linking the Assessment Result to Curriculum Ideas

We know that children are naturally inclined to sort and categorize the objects and items they routinely find in their daily lives. Teachers can help develop this ability by designing activities that engage children in utilizing increasingly complex and sophisticated classification criteria. Comparing and contrasting the similarities and differences of objects can be an excellent way of getting children to consciously exercise different classification schema.

Questions and experimentations. Classroom routines and materials are rich with opportunities to engage children in asking questions that will lead to experimenting with different classification criteria. Capitalize on these opportunities by having a plentiful supply of nature items to use in the art area—for example, small pebbles, sticks, acorns, shells. Allow children to feel and explore them or use them in art projects focusing on their aesthetic value.

For a large group meeting, put some objects commonly found in the classroom inside sealed boxes. Ask children to guess what is in the boxes judging by characteristics such as size, weight, and sound. Generate questions they can ask themselves to guide their exploration.

(Continued)

(Continued)

Have available in the classroom a variety of materials that can be used for sorting/classifying: beads, buttons, bottle caps, acorns, pebbles, rocks. Engage children in classifying different objects, and use the terms *sort, group, classify,* and *category* often. Explicitly talk about the criteria you use to decide what to put into each group or category.

Generate and post questions about different topics. For example, you might set up a "Find out" center or board, where you post a question meant to generate some classifying and categorization. The questions can be your own, or better still, the children's. Adjust the type of question to the time of the year, or a topic of study, and be sure to include questions that promote the use of simple as well as more complex and inter-related criteria. Use open-ended questions such as: **"What is the same about butterflies and ladybugs?" "What is the same about birds and trees?" "What is different about rectangles and squares and triangles?"**

Establishing connections. Expand the complexity of children's classifications by revisiting categories and helping students find new ways to organize how these objects can be sorted. For example, if the children grouped buttons by color or size, encourage them to combine these two criteria; a third time you might prompt the children to classify them by color, size, and number of holes in the middle. Make sure that each criterion is explicitly discussed.

Young children enjoy playing "What's my category?" in small or large groups. In this game, you ask a few children to stand up in front of the group. Beforehand, you have chosen one attribute that these few children all have in common (for example, wearing a piece of red clothing). The rest of the group has to guess what category you have used to select this particular group of children. This game can also be called "Going fishing" where the group has to figure out what kind of fish the teacher has "caught" in her net, that is, the group in the middle of the circle. Children can then take turns "catching" particular kinds of fish. Begin by using very simple and obvious categorization criteria, such as length of hair, color of dress, type of shoes. Move on to use more than one attribute (for example, black, Velcro shoes) and then to categorization dependent on other criteria, like who has a younger sister. Once a category has been guessed, go through the process involved in figuring it out. Did they discard a few possibilities before they came to the right one; how did they do that? Help children notice the role observation and inference played in their decisions.

Communicating results. Planning opportunities for children to talk about their classification criteria, discuss them with others, and be exposed to the vocabulary of science is as important as providing students opportunities to generate questions and test their hypotheses. Children will readily come to use words like *properties, sort, group, category,* and *classify* when you include these terms in your conversations with them and when you provide concrete explanations and examples to illustrate their meaning.

Using photos or children's drawings, particularly in a journal format, is one of the best ways to help children notice and document changes in different phenomena over time, such as a pumpkin decomposing; hatching chicks or butterflies; changes occurring in an ant farm or in a tree outside your window. Children can talk about about what is happening, and this will prompt them to find similarities and differences among the various processes.

Activities: Sciences

Building a Model Car   Procedure

Subject Area	Key Concepts and Skills
• Mechanical science	• Scientific inquiry
Social Arrangements	• Developing a working theory
• *Recommended:* small group, large group	• Communicating results
	• Makeup of objects
	• Properties of objects and materials
	• Relationship between structure and function
	• Part–whole relationships
	• Position of objects

Activity and Goal

Children make model cars using a variety of recycled materials.

Advance Preparation

1. Before conducting this activity, you will need to amass plentiful materials so that everyone will have enough to choose from. Some classrooms build many different art projects around the use of such materials and will have a steady supply. Others will want to gather materials just for this project. Children can contribute materials from home. If you collect materials over time, you may need a place to store some of them.

2. Depending on the age and skill level of the children, you may need to pre-cut strips of tape or prepare glue containers.

Note to teacher

- The variety of materials available to children and the way these materials are organized have significant impact on what children construct. For optimal results:
  - ○ Make a wide variety of materials available.
  - ○ Organize them in ways that facilitate their use.
  - ○ Provide plenty of working space.

Materials

- You will want to anticipate materials that children can use for each of the following:

Body	Details
• Different sizes of cardboard tubing	• Buttons
• Cardboard or plastic boxes and containers of different sizes	• String

(Continued)

(Continued)

Wheels and Axles

- Thread spools

- Jar lids with precut holes

- Cutout (round) pieces of cardboard

- Corks

- Pipe cleaners

- Drinking straws

- Brass fasteners

General

- Scotch or masking tape

- Glue sticks, paste

- Scissors

- Markers

- Pencils

- Camera

- Paper clips

1. One way to introduce the activity is by singing "The Wheels on the Bus." Then ask children if they have taken a ride in a car. Ask them about the parts of the car they remember. If possible, take children outside to view a real car and discuss what they see. Imagine with them how it might work, how wheels roll. Finally, you might read a story such as *Mr. Gumpy's Motor Car Ride* by John Burningham and invite children to notice details about this car. Have them name as many different parts of a car as they can. Ask them about the function of each part of the car that they mention and add some they have not brought up. Discuss how each part of the car serves a purpose.

2. Next, introduce students to the materials, and encourage them to try to make their car roll.

3. Clearly indicate that the materials are to be used to build a car; again invite them to think about the different parts they want to include in their car.

4. Encourage children to work as long as possible and permit them to continue over two days if necessary.

5. Younger children will need some assistance with this activity; older children will probably work more independently. Limit intervention to giving help with materials, such as holding pieces together while child tapes them. If children ask, "How can I make the wheels turn?" respond by putting the question back to them, **"How could you do it?" "What ideas do you have?" "What ideas do other children have?" "See what you can figure out given the materials we have." "What else might we need to make them turn?"** Continue to observe for the children's ideas about getting the car to work.

6. After the cars are finished, test (with your students) whether they are able to roll by using a wooden board or cardboard as a ramp.

7. Photograph each child's product.

Building a Model Car

Recording Sheet

Child's name _____ Assess date _____ Assessor_____ Rubric level _____

Use this section to describe/sketch child's completed model car (or attach a photo) and to make notes about the child's experience during the activity.

What aspects of vehicles does the child focus on?

What is the child's interest in whether or not the car rolls?

Child's dexterity and ability to manage materials (check one):

☐ Has considerable difficulty managing materials

☐ Has no particular difficulty managing materials

☐ Very skilled at managing materials

Activities: Sciences

Building a Model Car

Evaluative Working Approach Rubric

Circle the number that best describes the child's evaluative working approach in this activity.

Child's Name:
_____

Initial Engagement: How does the child initially respond to the activity?

Hesitant _____ **Eager**

1	2	3	4	5
very hesitant or unwilling to begin activity		becomes involved on his or her own		eager to begin activity

Focus, Attention: How on task is the child throughout the activity?

Distractable _____ **Attentive**

1	2	3	4	5
very easily distracted by other children, events, or materials		attentive some of the time		sustained, absorbed attention to activity

Goal Orientation: How clear is the child working toward the activity's goal?

Personal goal _____ **Activity goal**

1	2	3	4	5
works on personal goal rather than activity goal		child's work vacillates between personal goal and activity goal		works efficiently toward activity goal

Planfulness: How organized is the child in working toward task completion?

Haphazard _____ **Organized**

1	2	3	4	5
random or impulsive; no evidence of organization of materials or approach		organized some of the time		well-organized, methodical in approach or with materials

Resourcefulness: What does the child do when stuck?

Helpless _____ **Resourceful**

1	2	3	4	5
does not ask for help; unable to use help when offered		moves forward a step when help is given		seeks help and makes good use of it to figure out challenges

Cooperation (for group activities): How does the child work with peers to accomplish task?

Difficulty working with others _____ **Helpful to others**

1	2	3	4	5
has difficulty sharing materials or attention, taking turns, supporting the efforts of others		gets along with other children		helps other children with activity, materials, or as a mediator; models ideas for others

Building a Model Car   **Descriptive Working Approach Rubric**

Circle the number that best describes the child's descriptive   Child's Name:
working approach in this activity.   _____

Chattiness: How much of the child's talk is unrelated to the activity?

Very quiet _____ **Very chatty**

1	2	3	4	5

little conversation and self-   talks from time to time   constantly talks about
talk throughout the activity   unrelated topics

Pace of Work: What is the child's pace of work?

Slow _____ **Fast**

1	2	3	4	5

slow to start and   moderate pace throughout   quick start and quick finish
carry out the activity   the activity

Social Referencing: How often does the child check with teachers or peers?

Little interaction _____ **Constant checking**

1	2	3	4	5

focuses on own work   attention to others' work and   frequently asks teacher
                                  checks with others about   or peer if own work is
                                  own work occasionally   on track

Playfulness: How animated, lively, or happy is the child during the activity?

Serious _____ **Playful**

1	2	3	4	5

mood/demeanor is   Business-like with activity   cheerful and sense of
serious and cheerless   humor related to activity

Activities: Sciences

Building a Model Car
Performance Rubric

Level	Name	Performance Indicators
0	No participation	• Child declines to participate in the activity.
1	Exploring materials	• Child explores properties of glue, tape, or other materials. Nothing joined together or constructed, **OR** • Child uses objects such as an egg carton as a "house" for plastic animals. Materials are not joined together or constructed.
2	Joining materials	• Child focuses on joining several objects together without concern for an end product. There is no name for outcome. Primary interest seems to be practicing gluing and/or taping techniques.
3	Beginning ideas for a car	• Construction has a vague resemblance to a car; little or no detail, <u>unable</u> to roll

4	Simple car	• Construction resembles a car and has **two** of the following (or similar) details:
		  ○ Wheels
		  ○ Headlights
		  ○ Steering wheel
		  ○ Doors
		  ○ Seats
		  ○ Dashboard
		  ○ **and** is <u>unable</u> to roll

5	Simple car with details	• Construction resembles a car and has **three** of the details listed in Level 4 (or similar), and • Car is <u>unable</u> to roll **or** child constructs a simple rolling object without attention to car body.
6	Simple car with details and interest in wheels rolling	• Construction resembles a car and has **four** of the details listed in Level 4 (or similar), **and** • **Car** is <u>unable</u> to roll. Child is concerned about the issue of wheels rolling.
7	Complex car unable to roll	• Construction resembles a car and has **five** of the details listed in Level 4 (or similar), **and** • Some of these parts show some proportional size relationship, **but** • Car is <u>unable</u> to roll.
8	Complex car able to roll	• Construction resembles a car and **has five or more** of the details listed in Level 4 (or similar), **and** • Some of the parts show some proportional size relationship, **and** • **C**ar is <u>able</u> to roll.
9	Complex car with "working" parts	• Meets Level 8 criteria **and** some of the car parts are functional (for example, doors or trunk open; antenna goes up and down).
10	Complex car rolling evenly	• Meets Level 9 criteria **and** car is able to roll evenly.

Activities: Sciences

Building a Model Car

Bridge to Curriculum

Reviewing: Key Concepts and Skills Exercised in the Activity

- Scientific inquiry

- Developing a working theory

- Communicating results

- Makeup of objects

- Properties of objects and materials

- Relationship between structure and function

- Part–whole relationships

- Position of objects

Reflecting: Questions Related to Child's Performance

Child's Working Approach

- Does any one Evaluative Working Approach quality stand out from the others?

- Is there any one Working Approach behavior contributing to or hindering the child's performance?

- Can you attribute the behavior that stands out to any of the activity parameters: materials, key concepts, social arrangements, or activity structure?

Activity Parameters

Materials

- Is the child distracted by the variety of materials available?

- Are some of these materials not familiar to the child?

- Are the materials available to allow the child to incorporate different parts into his or her model car?

Social Arrangements

- Would the child benefit from working alone and without interruption?

Activity Structure

- Is the child put off by the specific goal of this task?

(Continued)

(Continued)

Child's Performance

Rubric Levels 1–3	• Is the child only interested in exploring the materials? • Is the child having difficulties with cutting, taping, or gluing? • Is there evidence that the child is capable of holding a mental image of a car that includes its major parts (tires, body)? • Is the child capable of using observation of the different materials to answer questions related to the task of building a model car? • Can the child generate hypotheses about how different materials work or function? • Can the child test these hypotheses?
Rubric Levels 4–5	• Is there evidence that the child is capable of holding a mental image of a car that also includes minor parts or details (steering wheels, headlights, seats)? • Does the child have the motor skills needed to translate his mental image of a car to the model?
Rubric Levels 6–10	• Is the child able to attain some kind of proportion between the different parts? • Can the child use the available materials to make "functional" parts in the model car? • Are there materials that allow the child to build an axle?

Planning: Linking the Assessment Result to Curriculum Ideas

Children are naturally drawn to use materials in novel ways. Early childhood classrooms are fertile ground to engage children in the exploration of the properties of materials and how these attributes determine the function and utility of objects. Given that development in the early childhood years is very physical in nature, classrooms will want to provide materials in each discipline—math, science, and the arts—that provide opportunities to study how things work and to experiment with using them.

Questions and experimentations. Since children's curiosity is the foundation for learning in science, learning and teaching begin with children's explorations. These explorations are followed by teachers' observations and questions to provoke and sustain further experimentation and questioning on the part of the child. Questions and experimentation are processes for the child and the teacher in dialogue with one another. To nurture such activity, you will want to have a plentiful supply and a variety of recycled materials to use in the art/science area. Encourage children to use them for exploring and building different things using scissors, glue, and tape. Encourage children to use the recycled materials to build toys and objects to be used in different areas of the room and for different purposes: props for the sociodramatic or block area, a maze for the pet hamster. Point out how properties of materials influence what they can build.

During the opening days and weeks of school, have children bring to school—and then help sort and organize—a wide variety of recycled materials to be housed in the art/science area. Support children in using explicit categorization criteria, including possible uses of materials. Create a space to keep boxes of different sizes and shapes (square, rectangular, round, and cylindrical) to be used for building toy objects or structures.

Establishing connections. Guide children to notice simple machines in their daily lives and to wonder about how they work. To stimulate their thinking, make use of construction-building toys, such as Mobilos, Duplos, K'nex, Flexiblocks, Legos, and Tinkertoys. Encourage children to "copy" different items, such as toy car or truck, using different building blocks (Legos, K'nex, etc.). Have them talk about their designs as well as invent their own.

When possible, include a carpentry center in your room where children can experiment with wood and tools. Have different kinds of wood in different sizes: white pine (soft), yellow pine or spruce (moderately soft), and oak are good choices. Include hammers, sandpaper, and at least three types of nails, screws and screwdrivers. This can encourage children to make connections and inferences about the properties of materials.

For younger children, the water table is an excellent place to encourage learning about materials and their properties. New objects such as sieves, funnels, spoons, and measuring cups will generate questions to guide children's further experimentation.

Communicating results and using the vocabulary of science. Children can be encouraged to draw plans for building objects using different materials. Have an exhibit where they show their original plan and the finished product. Have children talk about the plans that guided their constructions. You will find that the opportunity to talk about how tools and machines work will provide some children enormous incentive to participate and will motivate others to become engrossed in physical science activities.

Activities: Sciences

Activities

Performing Arts

WHAT WE KNOW

Movement is a child's first language; from the moment of birth, infants are exploring and learning about themselves in space and in the caregiving environment around them through movement of their arms, legs, and body. A baby's first forms of communication are physical. They find their rhythm and equilibrium in the give and take of physical caregiving: holding, positioning, sounds, and the ongoing pace of what hopefully become routines. The use of words—spoken language—is the newcomer to the repertoire of communicative resources that young children are mastering from roughly age two on.

The performing arts offer an opportunity to find creative expressions for the rhythms and beats that organize our common experiences. Including movement and music in early childhood classrooms is one of the most important ingredients to establishing a group life. Music and movement invite young children to bring their total self—intellectual, physical, and emotional—to the process of learning. As children make music, they explore pitch, tone, and rhythm. As children move and sing, they grow aware of and become more disciplined about force, motion, momentum, and time using their voice and body muscles. They learn to respond to others in myriad unique ways. As with all performing arts, exploration provides new opportunities for children to exhibit and improve skills as well as develop their creativity in areas such as dexterity, coordination, critical thinking, listening, and expressiveness, awareness of number and pattern, and distinctions between types of sounds.

Language, culture, and community are central influences to the performing arts experiences in the classroom. Classroom activities involving singing songs, as well as listening to, dancing to, and playing along with music provide powerful ways to bring the richness of diverse cultural backgrounds into school. Music exists in divergent forms in every culture, and in each, it is used for a variety of purposes: some of them are religious, some signal special occasions, and some have significant meaning for families. Songs and dances commemorate special occasions and holidays. They tell stories; they cheer us up and support our inclination to play; they comfort us when we are mourning. By incorporating music evocative of children's "other lives" in school, teachers help them make new connections to the curriculum. Some children reveal skills and talents teachers and peers may have been unaware of, and thus these children share more of themselves with others in school.

WHAT BRIDGING PROVIDES

Bridging's performing arts activities provide children with different opportunities to demonstrate strengths that are rooted in music. Acting Out a Story (in the language arts and literacy area) is a performing arts activity as well. Because it is integrally connected to story dictation and language development, we include the activity in that section of assessment. As with the other assessment activities, performing arts activities only have meaning to the extent that children have weekly if not daily experience with these art forms in their classroom. Their development, as noted in a rubric score, is directly connected with experience on an ongoing basis in the classroom.

Together, the performing arts activities provide a window into the music and movement interests and talents many young children bring with them to school. For young children up through age eight, early musical proclivities cannot only provide an important foundation for later musical education but also function as a support for and a path to children's understanding of key concepts involving rhythm and pattern in math and reading. The beat and patterning of word sounds are key to decoding words, as is the recognition of principles of patterning central in mathematical thinking.

WHY THESE THREE ACTIVITIES

The three Bridging performing arts activities are Moving to Music, Playing an Instrument, and Singing a Song. These activities provide opportunities for children to make music with their voice, hands (using an instrument), and bodies. In Moving to Music, children use their whole body—a salient medium for young children—to indicate what they can hear, analyze, and represent. Teachers may find this opportunity to perform creatively in a comfortable medium gives children a chance to demonstrate rhythmic strengths that can be connected to other classroom activities. In Playing an Instrument, children coordinate and control a series of actions, including watching for direction, listening, and manipulating an instrument. In this task, children who can integrate these actions find ease in participating with the class as a large group making music. In Singing a Song, children have the opportunity to give expression to their favorite rhythms and beats using their voice. Teachers can observe many important skills, such as the ability to memorize words, understand and convey word meaning, carry a tune, and keep a beat.

Activities: Performing Arts

Relationship Between Standards and Bridging Activities in Performing Arts Area

Standards for Performing Arts	Bridging Activities		
	Moving to Music	Playing an Instrument	Singing a Song
Dance and Movement			
• Meaning in Movement	√		
• Variation in Movement	√		
• Listening and Moving	√		
• Types of Movements	√		
• Qualities of Movement	√		
• Levels of Movement	√		
• Structure in Movement	√		
• Coordination of Movement With Others		√	
• Ideas in Movement	√		
Music			
• Playing With		√	
• Choosing How to Play		√	
• Listening and Playing		√	
• Variety of Instruments		√	
• Musical Qualities	√	√	√
• Listening and Moving	√		
• Voice Control			√
• Communicating With Songs			√
• Types of Songs			√
• Making Music With Others		√	
• Improvising vs. Planning		√	
• Describing Music			
• Musical Tastes			
• Ideas in Music	√	√	√

Standards listed here are a combination of those defined by the National Standards for Art Education (available at http://artsedge.kennedy-center.org/teach/standards.cfm) and the Illinois State Board of Education (available at http://www.isbe.state.il.us/ils/).

Definition of Performing Arts Standards

Dance and Movement

- **Meaning in Movement** Movement/dance can create and communicate meaning.

- **Variation in Movement** Variations in types of movement can represent varying ideas and feelings.

- **Listening and Moving** Movement that responds to and augments the meanings presented by music requires listening while moving.

- **Types of Movements** Movement consists of both nonlocomotor/axial movements (such as bend, twist, stretch, swing) and locomotor movements (such as walk, run, hop, jump, skip) that move the entire body through space.

- **Qualities of Movement** Movements can vary in type, speed, direction, and shape.

- **Levels of Movement** The body can create visual shapes at low, middle, and high levels.

- **Structure in Movement** Movement/dance can incorporate both patterns that repeat, and an overall structure with beginning, middle, and end.

- **Coordination of Movement With Others** Movement/dance with others requires close attention and interaction between partners.

- **Ideas in Movement** Movement/dance can be used to represent ideas from other disciplines, such as visual arts, literature, or science.

Music

- **Playing With** A musical instrument can be played along with other musical instruments in such a way as to augment the music or create new music.

- **Choosing How to Play** Playing an instrument requires making choices about timing, volume, and mood as well as executing some technical control over the instrument.

- **Listening and Playing** Playing an instrument in a way that augments other music requires listening while playing.

- **Variety of Instruments** Each instrument is played in a different way and produces a distinct sound.

- **Musical Qualities** Music has qualities, such as rhythm, pitch, volume, and tone, that are planfully varied to create mood and meaning.

- **Voice Control** Singing requires vocal control of pitch, rhythm, and volume.

- **Communicating With Songs** A song can convey both ideas and feelings.

- **Types of Songs** There are many different genres (for example, expression of feeling, ballad/storytelling, political anthem, spiritual music) and styles (for example, jazz, classical, rap, folk, chant) of songs, and they come from many different cultures.

Activities: Performing Arts

(Continued)

- **Making Music With Others** Both singing and playing instruments can be done in groups, which requires special efforts at coordination, including listening and watching for cues regarding timing, tone, volume, and rhythm.

- **Improvising vs. Planning** Sometimes music is made up, on the spot, without planning, while at other times, it is planned or even written down using specific musical notation.

- **Describing Music** Musical styles can be described in words.

- **Musical Tastes** People usually like particular types of music better than other types, and usually respond more readily to music that is culturally familiar.

- **Ideas in Music** Music can be used to represent ideas from other disciplines, such as visual arts, literature, or science; patterns, as in rhythms and melodic intervals, can be used metaphorically, just as musical style and mood can convey or augment stories and themes.

Moving to Music

Procedure

Subject Area	Key Concepts and Skills
• Performing arts **Social Arrangements** • *Recommended:* small or large group, depending on space available	• Meaning in movement • Variation in movement • Listening and moving • Qualities of movement • Musical qualities • Structure in movement • Types of movement • Levels of movement

Activity and Goal

Children have the opportunity to improvise movement to recorded music.

Materials

- A large, uncluttered area
- Tape or CD player
- Tapes or CDs

Procedure

1. Choose an instrumental piece of music for children to move to. Use the following criteria to select music:
   - No selections that have lyrics.
   - Music that is unfamiliar to the children; this will help them to listen more attentively.
   - A musical piece three to five minutes long, which will provide ample time for movement activity.
   - Select music with some variation in beat, tempo, and/or mood within it; that is, it should have two or more distinct sections that vary from one another (the more such changes, the better).
   - Avoid music that is so complex that you cannot identify a beat or tune.
   - Avoid anything too slow or too fast for children's motor abilities.

Below are suggestions for pieces of music that work well:

Classical	• *The Best of Rossini* (EMI Classics) • Itzhak Perlman, *In the Fiddler's House* • *Claudio Abbado Conducts Mussorgsky* (RCA)
World Music	Mikis Theodorakis and Zulfic Livaneli, *Together*
Jazz	Duke Ellington, *Three Suites*

(Continued)

Activities: Performing Arts

(Continued)

2. Select an area with open floor space so that children in the group can move freely and safely. If floor-length mirrors are available in the space, they can help children focus on their movements. If children will be moving within a regular classroom space that is often used for other purposes, the movement space should be clearly marked. For example, children can be told to "stay on the rug" or a large space can be marked off with masking tape. Keep the space's borders away from large pieces of furniture.

3. Ask children to sit while you introduce the activity. Explain **"Today we will move around the room to music. Before we do, we have to be sure we know how to move together safely. Stand up in the place where you were sitting. Spread out your arms, and if you have to, move away from other children so that your arms will not touch anyone, even if you twist your body around with your arms spread out. That is your movement space. Remember, we have to move without touching other children, and we will all stay in the group movement space."**

4. Have the children sit down in their movement space to be introduced to the music. Say **"People have different ways of moving to music, and different types of music make you move in different ways. Sometimes people even use their bodies to try to tell the story of the music. First you will sit and listen to this music and picture in your mind how you might move to the music I'm going to play. Remember, we are sitting and listening right now, and thinking about how we can move. I will play the music again and then we will move to it."**

5. Have the children listen while you play a little of the first piece. After they've heard about one minute of it, say, **"This is the music you are going to move to. Let's see what the beat is like. That will help you decide how to move. I'm going to keep the beat in my lap— you try it too. Think about how you are going to move the rest of your body to match the sounds you hear."** Tap your thigh with your open palm in time to the music and encourage the children to do the same. Listen to at least one more minute of the music in this way. Turn off the music.

6. Invite the children to get up and be ready to move. Say, **"Now I'll play the music again, only this time I'll play the whole song. This is your time to move to show how the music makes you feel or what it makes you think about. Remember your movement space and our rule of no touching while moving."** Play the music.

7. Do not talk while the children are moving, because talk detracts from the children's listening. You will want to model quiet concentration and observation of others. Carefully observe the movement of the child(ren) you are assessing, using the recording sheet.

8. When the music is over, gather children together to sit, relax, and reflect on the activity. Now is the time to point out notable movements observed: enthusiastic use of whole body, showing mood of music in graceful/fluid ways.

Moving to Music

Recording Sheet

Child's name _____ Assess date _____ Assessor _____ Rubric level _____

Use this section to record observations of child during the activity.

For each area below, check the box that applies.

Participation

☐ Observes other children, but does not move

☐ Moves tentatively, but not to beat

☐ Movement not rhythmic, but enthusiastic

☐ Movement responsive to music, rhythmic at least

Combining Movements

☐ Single movement at a time

☐ Combines movements

Types of Movements

☐ No axial (bending, twisting, stretching), only locomotor or involving arms/legs

☐ Axial movements (bending, twisting, stretching, swaying hips)

Response to Music Change

☐ Does not respond to marked changes in music with changes in movement

☐ Alters speed, size, type, mood of movement or facial expression in response to changes in music

Use of Visual Levels

☐ Movements tend to cluster in one area all the time or are scattered across the body simultaneously

☐ Movement demonstrates child's pointed attempt to create visual shapes at low, middle, and high levels

Patterns of Movement

☐ Movement demonstrates motifs that repeat throughout the piece

☐ Child demonstrates the use of a pattern of movement or shows interest in repeating movements with distinct variations

Moving to Music

Evaluative Working Approach Rubric

Circle the number that best describes the child's evaluative working approach in this activity.

Child's Name:
_____

Initial Engagement: How does the child initially respond to the activity?

Hesitant _____ **Eager**

1	2	3	4	5
very hesitant or unwilling to begin activity		becomes involved on his or her own		eager to begin activity

Focus, Attention: How on task is the child throughout the activity?

Distractable _____ **Attentive**

1	2	3	4	5
very easily distracted by other children, events, or materials		attentive some of the time		sustained, absorbed attention to activity

Goal Orientation: How clear is the child working toward the activity's goal?

Personal goal _____ **Activity goal**

1	2	3	4	5
works on personal goal rather than activity goal		child's work vacillates between personal goal and activity goal		works efficiently toward activity goal

Planfulness: How organized is the child in working toward task completion?

Haphazard _____ **Organized**

1	2	3	4	5
random or impulsive; no evidence of organization of materials or approach		organized some of the time		well-organized, methodical in approach or with materials

Resourcefulness: What does the child do when stuck?

Helpless _____ **Resourceful**

1	2	3	4	5
does not ask for help; unable to use help when offered		moves forward a step when help is given		seeks help and makes good use of it to figure out challenges

Cooperation (for group activities): How does the child work with peers to accomplish task?

Difficulty working with others _____ **Helpful to others**

1	2	3	4	5
has difficulty sharing materials or attention, taking turns, supporting the efforts of others		gets along with other children		helps other children with activity, materials, or as a mediator; models ideas for others

Moving to Music

Evaluative Working Approach Rubric

Circle the number that best describes the child's evaluative working approach in this activity.

Child's Name:

_____

Chattiness: How much of the child's talk is unrelated to the activity?

Very quiet				**Very chatty**
1	2	3	4	5
little conversation and self-talk throughout the activity		talks from time to time		constantly talks about unrelated topics

Pace of Work: What is the child's pace of work?

Slow				**Fast**
1	2	3	4	5
slow to start and carry out the activity		moderate pace throughout the activity		quick start and quick finish

Social Referencing: How often does the child check with teachers or peers?

Little interaction				**Constant checking**
1	2	3	4	5
focuses on own work		attention to others' work and checks with others about own work occasionally		frequently asks teacher or peer if own work is on track

Playfulness: How animated, lively, or happy is the child during the activity?

Serious				**Playful**
1	2	3	4	5
mood/demeanor is serious and cheerless		business-like with activity		cheerful and sense of humor related to activity

Activities: Performing Arts

Activities: Performing Arts

Moving to Music

Performance Rubric

Level	Name	Performance Indicators
0	No participation	• Child declines to participate in the activity.
1	No movement	• Child watches others but does not move.
2	Tentative movement	• Child moves around, but is hesitant and shows little evidence of responding to the music's beat.
3	Enthusiastic movement	• Child shows no evidence of responding to music's beat but is enthusiastic (for example, jumping up and down).
4	Responds to beat repetitive single movement	• Child's movement shows ability to respond to music's beat some of the time. Does not use hands and feet at same time. Might only sway upper body, nod head, clap, or tap foot; there is a tendency to repeat a single movement over and over.
5	Responds to beat— no axial movements	• Child's movement shows ability to respond to music's beat some of the time. Uses more than single repetitive movement, but large muscle movements tend to be locomotor, that is, moves the body across the floor, such as marching, jumping, skipping, and there is an absence of axial movements, including bending, twisting, stretching, swaying hips.
6	No axial movement, response to music change	• There are still no axial movements (bending, stretching, twisting, swaying hips), but child uses more than a single repetitive movement and can respond to changes in beat or mood of music by changing at least **one** aspect of movement: ○ fast/slow movements ○ large/small movements (for example, small/large steps, small/large arm gestures) ○ kind of movement (for example, twirling, stamping, etc.) ○ facial expressions mirror mood of music ○ movements mirror mood of music (calm, mysterious, energetic)
7	Axial movement	• Child responds to beat using axial movements, such as bending, stretching, twisting, swaying hips; demonstrates understanding of movement being possible in a single location on the floor.
8	Axial movement and response to music change	• Child responds to beat using axial movements, such as bending, stretching, twisting, swaying hips; demonstrates understanding of movement being possible in a single location on the floor and can respond to changes in beat or mood of music by changing at least **one** aspect of movement listed at Level 6.
9	Use of visual levels	• Child's movement is at Level 8 **and** child's movement pointedly creates visual shapes at low, middle, and high levels.
10	Expert	• Child's movement is at Level 9 **and also** shows evidence of at least one of the following: ○ Repeating motifs ○ Pattern and variations

Moving to Music

Bridge to Curriculum

Reviewing: Key Concepts and Skills Exercised in the Activity

- Meaning in movement
- Variation in movement
- Listening and moving
- Qualities of movement
- Musical qualities
- Structure in movement
- Types of movement
- Levels of movement

Reflecting: Questions Related to Child's Performance

Child's Working Approach

- Does any one Evaluative Working Approach behavior stand out from the others?
- Is there any one Working Approach behavior contributing to or hindering the child's performance?
- Can you attribute the behavior that stands out to any of the activity parameters: materials, key concepts, social arrangements, or activity structure?

Activity Parameters

Materials

- Was there a distinct enough or simple enough beat for the child to identify it and move with it?
- Were the changes in beat or mood dramatic enough for the child to notice or hear them?
- Was the music too culturally unfamiliar for the child?

Social Arrangements

- Was there enough room for the child to move around without running into another child?
- Were there too many children present, so that the child felt overwhelmed, or too few, so that the child felt self-conscious?

Activity Structure

- Does the creative aspect of this activity help the child to stay involved?
- Does this child need more structure in an activity in order to become readily involved?

(Continued)

Activities: Performing Arts

(Continued)

Child's Performance

Rubric Levels 1–3	• Does the child have experience with music, either listening to it or producing it? • Does the child have prior experience moving to music in school or at family, religious, or cultural events? • Is the child familiar with the concept of a "beat"?
Rubric Levels 4–5	• Can the child control his or her body to produce voluntary movement? • Can the child hear differences within a single piece of music, recognizing that different parts convey different ideas and feelings?
Rubric Levels 6–7	• Does the child benefit from ideas for different ways to move? Will the child benefit from discussion and demonstration of different ways to move? • Does the child demonstrate the ability to match styles of movement with repeating parts of the music? • Does the child understand how to repeat a movement, while varying its details as a form of experimentation and expression? • Does the child have ideas for moving his or her body besides locomotor movement (walking, hopping, or jumping)?
Rubric Levels 8–10	• Can the child describe what he or she is doing while moving? • Does the child see and understand movements made by other children? • Can the child help other children think of movements to make?

Planning: Linking the Assessment Result to Curriculum Ideas

Young children move all the time. This is the most common observation (and at times, complaint!) of early childhood teachers. The challenge for teachers is to harness and give form to what children already want to do. In one sense, a teacher can view the performing arts as "classroom judo," the ancient Japanese art of using force coming at oneself to one's advantage. In what looks like giving in to the oncoming force, judo masters align themselves with the other person's strength and momentum to protect themselves and maintain their own balance. So too can early childhood teachers use the inclination of young children to move by providing them lots of opportunities for disciplined creative movement.

There are several key ideas to making moving to music a successful classroom activity. First is to have movement activities every single day. Just as dramatization ought to be a daily part of the experience of enacting stories and poems children are hearing and reading, so too should conscious deliberate moving to music be a part of young children's day. Pick a time of day when you know children are likely to be getting a bit restless—perhaps after a time when they have been sitting and listening to a story, participating in group activities, or having completed writing, drawing, or math work. As you construct your daily schedule, consider the rhythm of movement that the children will have, and particularly if there is no recess for the children, be sure to plan for physical movement to ground their ability to stay focused and cooperative with group life in school.

A second key idea to making this activity successful is to remember that the teacher needs to teach the children how to move in school. Safety first! Yes, the children know how to move but they do not know how to do so in the confined spaces of classrooms with lots of physical constraints such as tables, chairs and curricular materials around. The teacher must be clear, detailed, and explicit about the boundaries and expectations for moving in the classsroom. Teachers need to give reminders of the physical space that is open, that is within the boundaries you will allow for this activity. You need to make the physical space readily apparent. Perhaps the space is an open rug area for group meetings; perhaps it is an area of the classsroom where there are no desks and chairs. Perhaps you have a floor space that is bordered by a painted line or lines you make with colored masking tape. Make sure that children can readily tell whether they are in or outside of the allowed space for movement.

Children need to become conscious of their personal space inside of this designated space for the class to move. A necessary ground rule, as in dramatization activities, is no touching of anyone else's body—ever. Never! This rule must be absolutely clear to the children. They will have heard this undoubtedly many times, but for this activity, you will actually teach them how to move without bumping into anyone else's body or space!

A good way to teach this skill is to have children stand in the designated space for movement with arms extended being sure that the tips of their fingers do not touch anyone else's fingers. Then have children rotate in a 360-degree circle being sure that they are not touching anyone behind or in front of them. This is the first step. You will want to remind children always that this is the home position—standing with arms outstretched touching nobody.

While standing rooted in this space, invite children to see how many different ways they can move their bodies without moving their feet. Their feet must have deep roots, or strong glue, that keep them stationary in their space. Give children a few minutes to warm up and show each other what they can do. As they discover satisfying movements, give children a chance to copy each other—all do the same movements one after another. Encourage them to imitate, borrow, and extend each other's ideas!

Have the children sit down in their space, being sure that they keep their space around them. Have children hold up their hands and be sure that all their fingers can move in all different directions. Then introduce the first piece music that they will move to. Ask children to listen to the music and give form to what they hear using their fingers and hands only. Practice moving to music with fingers and hands only!

On the following day, begin the moving to music time by having children find a place in the movement area where they do not touch anyone. Have them check their space by moving in a circle, hands outstretched, being sure they touch no one. Then invite the children to pretend that they are a baby chick inside of an eggshell. Have them feel the walls of the eggshell from the inside sensing an imaginary bubble around them that is delicate. Tell them they must not bump others or else the shell will break. Have children spend several minutes moving inside of their eggshell and feeling its shell wall. When they have done this, put on music and have children move to music around the room while inside of their eggshell.

On each successive day, you will want to review the steps you have practiced so far about moving inside their eggshell. The goal of today's lesson will be to have the children make their first moves about the room (no music yet) inside of their eggshells, getting used to seeing others without bumping into them. When the children are in their spaces and inside of their eggshells, have everyone practice moving three steps and then stop. Count to three out loud as they take each step and then, using a musical instrument that you play to signal, announce: "Stop!" Have the children check their eggshells—are any broken?! Have them try five more steps and then stop.

At the beginning of the school year, this kind of detailed practice will be essential to getting the children conscious of this familiar activity (moving about) in a new setting (school classroom). It also may be important to return to these introductory activities after a weekend, and after a school holiday, when attempting to help the children remember and regain their skills for moving in careful ways in the classroom.

When you are confident that children have the feel for moving inside of their eggshell, introduce music, preferably the same music you used for the finger and hand movements earlier in the week, something with a definable beat but not fast paced. You will want to give the class plenty of practice.

Activities: Performing Arts

(Continued)

(Continued)

With these routines in place for checking safety and activity procedures, you are ready to explore the many dimensions of potential that this activity holds for young children and their development. In the opening months of school, you will want to focus on developing the activity's procedures and exposing children to a wide variety of music. Each dimension of the activity—location and procedures, the music, and the movement—is discussed further to help you plan the paths for supporting the children's growth that will emerge from the initial establishment of the activity routines.

Location. Space for learning in all areas of the curriculum is an important factor in an activity's success. Often teachers have to be resourceful in arranging the available classroom space to serve multiple functions. Since movement during the school day is so vital to children's well-being, you may want to experiment with moving in more than one location. On some days, you may have the gym available to you, a theater space, or even an outdoor space in a courtyard. Take advantage of such opportunities to talk explicitly with the children about the need to carry the class rules and routines with them as they experiment with new locations. As a teacher, you may want to have the class divide into two or three smaller groups to do movement activities while you get the feel for how it will work in a particular space.

Music. Over time, you will want to introduce different styles of Western music (classical, jazz, folk, and country) and then the huge variety of world music available. In the beginning, you will want to make use of music that has a distinct beat and dramatic changes in beat and/or mood that will provide opportunities for children to change the way they move. Also over time, you will want to vary the cultural roots of the music, being sure to draw on music reflecting the cultural heritage of children in the class.

Make tapes or CDs and headphones available to children who want to listen to music by themselves during activity choice time in your classroom. Some children may find this an important time to further their appreciation of the music and find time to turn inward during the school day.

Movement. Children's experiences with movement will progress through several stages as they gain exposure to, experience with, and practice in moving to music. In the beginning, teachers of children at all grade levels will want to guide children in becoming conscious of every different body part and how it can move: hands only, feet, arms, ears, toes, knees, arms and feet together, only fingers. Notice the interesting different variations children come up with as you slowly and consciously help them think about each movement. Practice making large and small movements with each body part. Practice making sharp and smooth movements. Have children find as many ways as they can to move their bodies without moving their feet, such as twisting, stretching, and bending. Have children watch each other and discuss how such movements make them feel.

Next, and perhaps a day or two later, you will want to introduce movement to music. It is great to begin with listening to three to four minutes of music and finding the beat in your lap: moving hands in rhythm to the music. Find music that is good for marching, jumping, shaking, waving. After listening while sitting and moving hands (and no touching), have children stand and move about the room doing one motion: skipping, marching, hopping . . . to the beat.

As you play different selections of music over time, discuss as a group changes within a song from one part to another. Ask children about volume, instrumentation, rhythm, and general mood changes. Notice repeating patterns. When you listen to a new piece of music, discuss with the group what kinds of movements might "go with" what you've heard. Give children a chance to demonstrate their ideas.

In time, introduce ballet and opera music that has an explicit accompanying story (for example, *Peter and the Wolf, The Nutcracker*) and have children use movement to help tell the story. Try making up movements to go with other stories, like *The Three Little Pigs* or *The Three Billy Goats Gruff*. At this stage, children are coming to use their bodies not only for physical pleasure but for symbolic and communicative purposes also.

Playing an Instrument

Procedure

Subject Area	Key Concepts and Skills
• Performing arts	• Playing along with
Social Arrangements	• Listening and playing
• *Recommended:* small or large group, depending on number of instruments available	• Choosing how to play
	• Variety of instruments
	• Musical qualities

Activity and Goal

A group of children explore rhythm instruments and create an instrumental accompaniment to recorded music.

Materials

- Tapes or CDs
- Tape player or CD player
- Rhythm instruments: These can be "homemade" (like drums made with oatmeal boxes, shakers made from containers with dried beans inside, rhythm sticks) or they can be purchased. Provide instruments that sound lovely and provide a variety of sounds. Some possibilities include drums, tambourines, rhythm sticks, and xylophones. Small maracas called "chickitas" are inexpensive and make an interesting sound.

Procedure

This assessment can be conducted as a one- or two-day activity. The first step provides the opportunity to handle the instruments and explore their musical possibilities; everyone needs the chance to try a variety of instruments. The second step (which can be conducted the same day or one day later) provides an opportunity for guided, directed playing of the instruments and provides the assessment opportunity.

Step 1

1. Choose an instrumental piece of music for children to play with. Use the following list to select music:
   - Avoid selections that have lyrics.
   - The music should be unfamiliar to the children; this will help them to listen more attentively.
   - The music should be 3 to 5 minutes long to provide ample movement time.
   - The music must have some variation in beat, tempo, and/or mood within it; that is, it should have two or more distinct sections that vary from one another (the more such changes, the better).
   - Avoid music that is so complex that you cannot identify a beat or tune.
   - Avoid anything too slow or too fast for children's motor abilities.

Activities: Performing Arts

(Continued)

(Continued)

Below are suggestions for pieces that work well:

Classical	• *The Best of Rossini* (EMI Classics) • Itzhak Perlman, *In the Fiddler's House* • *Claudio Abbado Conducts Mussorgsky* (RCA)
World Music	Mikis Theodorakis and Zulfic Livaneli, *Together*
Jazz	Duke Ellington, *Three* Suites

2. Select a group of children. Group size will depend on how many instruments are available. You will want to have more instruments than there are children so that each child can have a choice between at least two instruments without creating conflict among children.

3. Introduce the activity by asking the children to sit down together. Say, **"Today we will experiment with making music using instruments."** Distribute instruments in some equitable manner, and tell the children that they will pass their instruments to the person next to them every time you raise your hand. This creates a structure for children to try out several instruments during this activity session.

4. Give children time to experiment with their instruments without recorded music. Ask them to play soft/loud, fast/slow. Ask them all to play together, then ask two children at a time to play a duet. Remind them that playing together requires listening while playing.

Step 2

1. Introduce a piece of instrumental music. Begin this part while no one has instruments in hand, but while the group is sitting and listening. Say, **"Now we're going to play our instruments along with some recorded music. I'm going to play a bit of the music so you get an idea of what it's like. Let's listen together."** Play a couple minutes of the piece, using your open palm to keep the beat in your lap. Encourage the children to keep the beat the same way.

2. Stop the music and say, **"Let's listen and see if we can hear when the music changes in some way."** Encourage children to keep the beat with their hand. Play music for two or three minutes more. Then stop, rewind the tape, and prepare to start the music from the beginning again. Ask, **"Did anyone hear the music change?"**

3. Say **"Sometimes we'll all play together, and then we'll each have a turn playing alone, or solo. I'll tell everyone to stop like this (demonstrate gesture), and then I'll point to the soloist who gets to play alone until I say we can all play together again. Let's practice all watching me so we can take turns while we clap to the music."** Play the music and practice directing children in taking turns. Do not expect everybody to get the directions the first time.

4. Pass out the instruments, letting children choose an instrument they like, if possible. Say, **"Listen closely to the music while you play, and try to make your instrument make sounds that go with the music. Remember to watch me to see whose turn it is to do a solo."**

5. Start the piece again and invite the children to play along. Let everyone play together for several minutes before highlighting soloists. Let each soloist play through more than one section of the music (verse and chorus, for example) so you can see them respond to the music's changes. Play the piece more than once if necessary to give everybody a turn.

Playing an Instrument

Recording Sheet

Child's name _____ Assess date _____ Assessor _____ Rubric level _____

Use this section to record observations of child during the activity.

For each area below, check the boxes that apply.

Participation

- ☐ Observes other children, but does not play instrument
- ☐ Plays instrument, but does not pause when directed
- ☐ Plays instrument, but will not play alone
- ☐ Plays instrument, pauses when directed, plays alone

Playing style

- ☐ Plays tentatively
- ☐ Plays enthusiastically

Response to music

- ☐ Playing is not responsive to music
- ☐ Playing is occasionally responsive to music
- ☐ Playing is generally responsive to music

Response to changes in music

- ☐ No changes
- ☐ Fast playing/slow playing
- ☐ Loud playing/soft playing
- ☐ Accenting particular beats
- ☐ Smaller/larger playing movements
- ☐ Alternating which beats are played

Patterning

- ☐ No patterning apparent
- ☐ Repeating motifs
- ☐ Patterns and variations

Activities: Performing Arts

Playing an Instrument
Evaluative Working Approach Rubric

Circle the number that best describes the child's evaluative working approach in this activity.

Child's Name:
_____

Initial Engagement: How does the child initially respond to the activity?

Hesitant _____ **Eager**

1	2	3	4	5
very hesitant or unwilling to begin activity		becomes involved on his or her own		eager to begin activity

Focus, Attention: How on task is the child throughout the activity?

Distractable _____ **Attentive**

1	2	3	4	5
very easily distracted by other children, events, or materials		attentive some of the time		sustained, absorbed attention to activity

Goal Orientation: How clear is the child working toward the activity's goal?

Personal goal _____ **Activity goal**

1	2	3	4	5
works on personal goal rather than activity goal		child's work vacillates between personal goal and activity goal		works efficiently toward activity goal

Planfulness: How organized is the child in working toward task completion?

Haphazard _____ **Organized**

1	2	3	4	5
random or impulsive; no evidence of organization of materials or approach		organized some of the time		well-organized, methodical in approach or with materials

Resourcefulness: What does the child do when stuck?

Helpless _____ **Resourceful**

1	2	3	4	5
does not ask for help; unable to use help when offered		moves forward a step when help is given		seeks help and makes good use of it to figure out challenges

Cooperation (for group activities): How does the child work with peers to accomplish task?

Difficulty working with others _____ **Helpful to others**

1	2	3	4	5
has difficulty sharing materials or attention, taking turns, supporting the efforts of others		gets along with other children		helps other children with activity, materials, or as a mediator; models ideas for others

Playing an Instrument   Descriptive Working Approach Rubric

Circle the number that best describes the child's descriptive working approach in this activity.

Child's Name:
_____

Chattiness: How much of the child's talk is unrelated to the activity?

Very quiet _____ **Very chatty**

I	2	3	4	5
little conversation and self-talk throughout the activity		talks from time to time		constantly talks about unrelated topics

Pace of Work: What is the child's pace of work?

Slow _____ **Fast**

I	2	3	4	5
slow to start and carry out the activity		moderate pace throughout the activity		quick start and quick finish

Social Referencing: How often does the child check with teachers or peers?

Little interaction _____ **Constant checking**

I	2	3	4	5
focuses on own work		attention to others' work and checks with others about own work occasionally		frequently asks teacher or peer if own work is on track

Playfulness: How animated, lively, or happy is the child during the activity?

Serious _____ **Playful**

I	2	3	4	5
mood/demeanor is serious and cheerless		business-like with activity		cheerful and sense of humor related to activity

Activities: Performing Arts

Playing an Instrument   Performance Rubric

Level	Name	Performance Indicators
0	No participation	• Child declines to participate in the activity.
1	No sound	• Child may listen, observe, or hum, but does not play instrument.
2	Does not stop on cue	• Child does not stop playing when it's someone else's solo.
3	Plays only with others	• Child plays when others are playing, but does not play a solo.
4	Tentative sounds	• Child plays during solo and is tentatively experimenting with the instrument, but its sound is not responsive to the music. May have novel ways to use the instrument but not in rhythm with the music.
5	Eager experiments	• Child experiments with the instrument enthusiastically along with the music but not in response to or in reference to the music.
6	Responsive playing **some** of the time	• Child's playing shows an occasional ability to respond to the music (for example, plays in time with the beat of the music for a measure or so; plays softly in the soft parts for several beats).
7	Responsive playing **most** of the time	• Child's playing shows ability to respond to the music **most** of the time (for example, generally plays in time with the beat of the music, plays softly in the soft parts).
8	Accurate accompaniment to changes in beat or mood of music— **one dimension**	• Child can respond to changes in beat or mood of music by changing **one** aspect of playing: ○ Fast/slow tempo ○ Loud/soft playing ○ Accenting particular beats ○ Smaller/larger playing movements ○ Alternating which beats are played
9	Accurate accompaniment to changes in beat or mood of music— **two or more dimensions**	• Child can respond to changes in beat or mood of music by changing **more than one** aspect of playing as described for Level 8.
10	Expert	• Child's playing is at Level 9 **and also** shows evidence of at least one of the following: ○ Repeating motifs ○ Pattern and variations

Playing an Instrument

Bridge to Curriculum

Reviewing: Key Concepts and Skills Exercised in the Activity

- Playing along with
- Listening and playing
- Choosing how to play
- Variety of instruments
- Musical qualities

Reflecting: Questions Related to Child's Performance

Child's Working Approach

- Does any one Evaluative Working Approach behavior stand out from the others?
- Is there any one Working Approach behavior contributing to or hindering the child's performance?
- Can you attribute the behavior that stands out to any of the activity parameters: materials, key concepts, social arrangements, or activity structure?

Activity Parameters

Materials

- Was there a distinct enough or simple enough beat for the child to identify it and play with it?
- Were the changes in beat or mood dramatic enough for the child to notice and hear them?
- Was the music too culturally unfamiliar to the child?
- Were there enough instruments available so that the child could pick one he or she felt comfortable with?

Social Arrangements

- Were there too many children present, so that the child felt overwhelmed, or too few, so the child felt self-conscious?

Activity Structure

- Does the creative aspect of this activity help the child to stay involved?
- Does this child need more structure in an activity in order to be successful?
- Does the child enjoy this opportunity to perform alone?
- Does this child need more support from others in an activity in order to demonstrate strengths?

(Continued)

(Continued)

Child's Performance

Rubric Levels 1–3	• Has the child had experiences with music, either listening to it or producing it? • Is the child familiar with the concept of a "beat"? • Has the child ever used an "instrument" before?
Rubric Levels 4–5	• Is the child aware that a single piece of music has different parts that convey different ideas and feelings? • Is the child able to control the instrument to produce sound? • Does the child need assistance identifying when changes in the music occur?
Rubric Levels 6–7	• Does the child need ideas for different ways to make sound with the instrument? • Using an instrument, can the child produce sounds to repeating parts of the music? • Does the child understand how to repeat a sound using an instrument, but vary its details as a form of experimentation and expression?
Rubric Levels 8–10	• Can the child describe what he or she is doing while playing? • Can the child help other children think of ways to play their instrument?

Planning: Linking the Assessment Result to Curriculum Ideas

Playing instruments allows children the opportunity to make music with objects in the environment, to creatively explore sound as a medium of expression. For this activity, children benefit from experiences listening to sounds and then creating them. As with movement, listening and then making sounds are experiences children have every day of their lives. They hear the phzzz of a bottle of soda just opened, they hear rain falling on windows and roofs, they hear the rumble of trains and other vehicles, they hear horns, they hear the sounds of pots and pans in the kitchen. They have probably noticed sound patterns that are pleasing and fun to re-create. As a starting point for this activity, teachers can invite children to listen for sounds that are pleasing and ones the group can re-create. Listening for sounds, noticing them, and talking about what we hear is the starting point for musical experiences.

Next, teachers will consciously want to expose children to different kinds of music within group experiences, and experiment with making music along with recorded musicians. Be sure to use music with a distinct beat in the beginning, music with dramatic changes in beat and/or mood. Over the course of a week, musical selections ought to reflect music from a variety of cultures. While listening to music as a group, notice and describe changes within a song from one part to another. Notice volume, instrumentation, rhythm, and general mood changes. Notice repeating patterns.

For an introduction to instruments, begin by having children use their body as an instrument to accompany music the group listens to: clapping, stamping their feet, snapping fingers, tapping their arm. It can be useful in the beginning if children all play the same instrument as the group brainstorms different ways of making sounds. Have all children clap: loud, soft, in different beats. Teachers can then introduce children making simple instruments, using rhythm sticks, kitchen spoons, or making simple maracas with beans inside a lidded container. With these experiences, children become accustomed to finding the beat in a piece of music and experimenting with sounds that expand and extend the score with new sounds.

Listen to a piece of music and then discuss as a group what kinds of sounds might "go with" what you've heard. Give children a chance to demonstrate their ideas. Children can then take turns leading the group playing an instrument in a specific way. Children can form "duets" or "trios" in which they all play at the same time. Over time, children can create their own orchestras with a collection of instruments that accompany recorded music, and eventually, they will play on their own. Such "orchestra" activities will greatly expand their musical experiences.

Singing a Song

Procedure

Subject Area	Key Concepts and Skills
• Performing arts	• Voice control
Social Arrangements	• Communicating with songs
• *Recommended:* small group (8–12)	• Parts of a song
• *Viable:* large group	• Musical qualities

Activity and Goal

Children sing a song they know.

Materials

• Plastic microphone, or an object (such as a thick pencil) to represent a microphone

Advance Preparation

• A day or two before the activity, tell the class that you will soon have a song-sharing time, and you would like them to be thinking of a song they know to sing. Perhaps they would like to talk about it with their families. Present this as a low-key, enjoyable activity.

Procedure

1. Gather a group of children. Introduce the activity by saying, "Today we will sing songs together and individually. Let's start by singing some favorite songs together. Which one will we begin with?" If no one in the group offers a song, suggest one that you know is familiar, perhaps a favorite among the children, and one that is easy for young children to sing. The purpose of singing together is to help the children warm up with this activity.

2. Say, **"Now you each get a chance to sing your own song, and when it is your turn, you can use the microphone if you like."** Have the children think quietly for a minute or two to think of a song. Then have the children pass the microphone around the circle taking a turn to sing a song when they hold the microphone. Encourage children to sing their own favorite song. It is not a problem, however, if several children sing the same song.

3. Since it may be difficult for some children to sing in front of a group, prepare to be patient, reassuring, and encouraging. Let them know that it's okay if they can't remember all the words or if they feel nervous at first. Remind them that even famous singers feel a little nervous when they perform; it helps them focus and concentrate better.

Singing a Song

Recording Sheet

Child's name _____ Assess date _____ Assessor _____ Rubric level _____

Use this section to record observations of child during the activity.

Participation (check one)

☐ Observes other children, but does not sing at all

☐ Sings only with others, not alone

☐ Sings solo, but it cannot be heard/understood

☐ Sings solo, but with no tune or rhythm

Enthusiasm

☐ Tenative performance

☐ Eager, enthusiastic performance

Tunefulness

☐ Sometimes

☐ Most of the time

Rhythm

☐ Sometimes

☐ Most of the time

Artistic elements (check all that apply)

☐ Volume and tone match mood of lyrics

☐ Changes pitch or rhythm easily and smoothly

☐ Corrects a mistake in words, tune, or rhythm

☐ Integrates facial expression or gestures

☐ Enjoys music's potential for communication and entertaining

Singing a Song — Evaluative Working Approach Rubric

Circle the number that best describes the child's evaluative working approach in this activity.

Child's Name: _____

Initial Engagement: How does the child initially respond to the activity?

Hesitant _____ **Eager**

1	2	3	4	5
very hesitant or unwilling to begin activity		becomes involved on his or her own		eager to begin activity

Focus, Attention: How on task is the child throughout the activity?

Distractable _____ **Attentive**

1	2	3	4	5
very easily distracted by other children, events, or materials		attentive some of the time		sustained, absorbed attention to activity

Goal Orientation: How clear is the child working toward the activity's goal?

Personal goal _____ **Activity goal**

1	2	3	4	5
works on personal goal rather than activity goal		child's work vacillates between personal goal and activity goal		works efficiently toward activity goal

Planfulness: How organized is the child in working toward task completion?

Haphazard _____ **Organized**

1	2	3	4	5
random or impulsive; no evidence of organization of materials or approach		organized some of the time		well-organized, methodical in approach or with materials

Resourcefulness: What does the child do when stuck?

Helpless _____ **Resourceful**

1	2	3	4	5
does not ask for help; unable to use help when offered		moves forward a step when help is given		seeks help and makes good use of it to figure out challenges

Cooperation (for group activities): How does the child work with peers to accomplish task?

Difficulty working with others _____ **Helpful to others**

1	2	3	4	5
has difficulty sharing materials or attention, taking turns, supporting the efforts of others		gets along with other children		helps other children with activity, materials, or as a mediator; models ideas for others

Activities: Performing Arts

Activities: Performing Arts

Singing a Song   Descriptive Working Approach Rubric

Circle the number that best describes the child's descriptive working approach in this activity.

Child's Name:
_____

Chattiness: How much of the child's talk is unrelated to the activity?

Very quiet _____ **Very chatty**

1	2	3	4	5
little conversation and self-talk throughout the activity		talks from time to time		constantly talks about unrelated topics

Pace of Work: What is the child's pace of work?

Slow _____ **Fast**

1	2	3	4	5
slow to start and carry out the activity		moderate pace throughout the activity		quick start and quick finish

Social Referencing: How often does the child check with teachers or peers?

Little interaction _____ **Constant checking**

1	2	3	4	5
focuses on own work		attention to others' work and checks with others about own work occasionally		frequently asks teacher or peer if own work is on track

Playfulness: How animated, lively, or happy is the child during the activity?

Serious _____ **Playful**

1	2	3	4	5
mood/demeanor is serious and cheerless		business-like with activity		cheerful and sense of humor related to activity

Singing a Song   Performance Rubric

Level	Name	Performance Indicators
0	Child does not participate	• Child declines to participate in activity.
1	No participation	• Child may sing with the group but does not sing alone.
2	Can't be heard or understood	• Child's singing is either too quiet or too garbled to be understood.
3	Attempts to sing	• Child's singing is more like saying a few lyrics to a song; you cannot detect the tune or rhythm.
4	Eager singing attempt	• Child's eager singing attempt includes recitation of song verse or two but little tune or rhythm, mostly monotone.
5	Tune **or** rhythm *some* of the time	• You can recognize either the tune **or** the rhythm *some* of the time. For example, you can clap to the beat **or** hum along *during parts* of the song.
6	Tune **or** rhythm *all* the time	• You can recognize either the tune **or** the rhythm *all* the time. For example, you can clap to the beat or hum along *throughout* the song.
7	Tune **and** rhythm at least *sometimes*	• You can recognize both the tune **and** the rhythm at least *some* of the time. For example, you can clap and hum along during some parts.
8	Tune, rhythm, and **one** artistic element	• Child's singing is at Level 7 and shows **one** of the following: ○ Volume and tone match mood of lyrics (for example, soft and gentle for lullaby) ○ Can change pitch and/or rhythm easily and smoothly ○ Corrects a mistake in words, tune, or rhythm ○ Integrates facial expression or gestures with words of the song ○ Enjoys music's potential for communicating and entertaining
9	Tune, rhythm, and **two** artistic elements	• Child's singing is at Level 7 and shows **two** of the artistic elements listed at Level 8.
10	Tune, rhythm, and **three** artistic elements	• Child's singing is at Level 7 and shows **three or more** of the artistic elements listed at Level 8.

Activities: Performing Arts

Singing a Song   Bridge to Curriculum

Reviewing: Key Concepts and Skills Exercised in the Activity

- Voice control
- Communicating with songs
- Parts of a song
- Musical qualities

Reflecting: Questions Related to Child's Performance

Child's Working Approach

- Does any one Evaluative Working Approach behavior stand out from the others?
- Is there any one Working Approach behavior contributing to or hindering the child's performance?
- Can you attribute the behavior that stands out to any of the activity parameters: materials, key concepts, social arrangements, or activity structure?

Activity Parameters

Materials

- Did the child pick a song with complicated words or a complex or difficult melody?
- Was the song so simple or so short that it was difficult to see the child's singing strengths?

Social Arrangements

- Were there too many children present, so that the child felt overwhelmed, or too few, so the child felt self-conscious?

Activity Structure

- Does the strong element of personal choice in this activity help the child to stay involved?
- Does the child enjoy this opportunity to perform alone?
- Does this child need more structure in an activity in order to be successful?
- Does this child need more support from others in an activity in order to demonstrate strengths?

Child's Performance

Rubric Levels 1–3	• Will the child benefit from more experiences with songs, either listening to them or producing them? • Does the child know any songs by heart? • Can the child repeat a short string of words back to you?
Rubric Levels 4–6	• Can the child repeat a short series of notes back to you using "la, la, la"? • Can the child clap on the beat to a simple piece of music, such as "Twinkle, Twinkle, Little Star"? • Can the child control his or her speech or voice so that it is regularly understood?
Rubric Levels 7–10	• Can the child use his or her voice to sing both loud and soft? • Are movements between one vocal pitch and another smooth and fluid, or are they more abrupt and awkward? • Can the child tell you what the song is about and who the child "is" when singing it? • Does the child make eye contact with others while singing? • Does the child's facial expression appear to consciously convey a message to others? • Does the child's body and posture appear physically relaxed? • Does the child use any appropriate gestures to help convey the song's meaning?

Planning: Linking the Assessment Result to Curriculum Ideas

Every early childhood classroom needs to include singing daily. The occurrence of singing is one of the surest ways to bring joy and good will to the group life. You will want to develop a rich repertoire of songs to introduce over the school year that will build the children's familiarity with a variety of musical traditions and styles. The task of collecting songs is parallel to the task of building a rich book collection for the classroom library. Songs will include ones as simple as nursery rhymes, folk songs, and songs that can be sung in rounds or in parts, to longer songs that tell a story. You will want to build a collection of class favorites as well as invite children to bring songs from home for the group to enjoy. Singing a song as an assessment activity only makes sense if there is an environment with regular routines for singing that starts on the first day of school. Children ought to be hearing a new song at least every three to four days.

When singing is a part of the classroom life, children will develop favorites just as they do with story books. You may decide to begin the morning meeting, end the day, or both with the singing of songs. Singing songs might be something you do during cleanup time to keep children focused and working as a group. You might introduce songs that have finger or body motions while you are waiting with a group of children for lunches to arrive. Within a context of music and song, children can be encouraged to sing alone or with partners: duets and trios.

As children develop a repertoire of songs, you can introduce discussions of similarities and differences between songs. Talk about how the "pitch" in a song can move up or down; practice going "up" and "down" by having children "reach up high" when you play or sing a high note and "squat down low" when you play or sing a low note. Which songs are quiet, and what are they about? When a song is happy, how does the singer's voice sound? Lead children in singing the same song in different ways: soft, slow, fast. Discuss how each choice makes the song "feel." Have children discuss a song's meaning, and encourage them to use their body and face to help tell the song's "story." Such animated, lively daily singing will create the context for inviting children to sing their favorite song on a day that you recognize as an assessment day but, in fact, is just another day of fun singing for the children.

References and Recommended Readings

Applebee, A. (1978). *The child's concept of story: Ages two to seventeen.* Chicago: University of Chicago Press.

Baroody, A. J. (2004). The developmental bases for early childhood number and operations standards. In D. H. Clements & J. Sarama (Eds.), *Engaging young children in mathematics* (pp. 173–220). Mahwah, NJ: Lawrence Erlbaum.

Borko, H., & Putnam, R. (1995). Expanding a teacher's knowledge base. A cognitive-psychological perspective on professional development. In T. R. Guskey & M. Huberman (Eds.), *Professional development in education: New paradigm and practices* (pp. 35–65). New York: Teachers College Press.

Bransford, J., Brown, A. L., & Cocking, R. R. (Eds.). (1999). *How people learn: Brain, mind, experience, and school.* Washington, DC: National Academy Press.

Calfee, R., & Hiebert, E. (1991). *Teacher assessment of achievement: Advances in program evaluation.* Greenwich, CT: JAI Press.

Carey, S. (1988). Reorganization of knowledge in the course of acquisition. In S. Strauss (Ed.), *Ontogeny, phylogeny, and historical development* (pp. 1–27). Norwood, NJ: Ablex.

Chen, J. Q. (2004). The Project Spectrum approach to early education. In J. Johnson & J. Roopnarine (Eds.), *Approaches to early childhood education* (4th ed., pp. 251–179). Columbus, OH: Merrill/Prentice Hall.

Chen, J. Q., & Gardner, H. (2005). Assessment based on multiple intelligences theory. In D. P. Flanagan, J. L. Genshaft, & P. L. Harrison (Eds.), *Beyond traditional intellectual assessment: Contemporary and emerging theories, tests, and issues* (2nd ed., pp. 77–102). New York: Guilford Press.

Chen, J. Q., Isberg, E., & Krechevsky, M. (Eds.). (1998). *Project Spectrum: Early learning activities.* New York: Teachers College Press.

Chen, J. Q., Krechevsky, M., & Veins, J. (1998). *Building on children's strengths: The experience of Project Spectrum.* New York: Teachers College Press.

Cole, M. (1996). *Cultural psychology: A once and future discipline.* Cambridge, MA: Harvard University Press.

Cole, M., & Griffin, P. (1986). A sociohistorical approach to remediation. In S. De Castell, A. Luke, & K. Egan (Eds.), *Literacy, society, and schooling* (pp. 110–131). New York: Cambridge University Press.

Cole, M., & Scribner, S. (1974). *Culture and thought: A psychological introduction.* New York: John Wiley.

Darling-Hammond, L., & Baratz-Snowden, J. (Eds.). (2005). *A good teacher in every classroom: Preparing the highly qualified teachers our children deserve.* San Francisco: Jossey-Bass.

Darling-Hammond, L., & Bransford, J. (2005). (Eds.). *Preparing teachers for a changing world: What teachers should learn and be able to do.* San Francisco: Jossey-Bass.

Darling-Hammond, L., & Snyder, J. (1992). Reframing accountability: Creating learner-centered schools. In A. Lieberman (Ed.), *The changing contents of teaching* (91st yearbook of the National Society for the Study of Education). Chicago: University of Chicago Press.

Dehaene, S. (1997). *The number sense: How the mind creates mathematics.* New York: Oxford University Press.

Dunn, R. S., Beaudry, J. S., & Klavas, A. (1989). Survey of research on learning styles. *Educational Leadership, 46*(6), 50–58.

Dunn, R., & DeBello, T. C. (Eds.). (1999). *Improved test scores, attitudes, and behaviors in America's school: Supervisors' success stories.* Westport, CT: Bergin & Garvey.

Eisner, E. W. (1977). On the uses of educational connoisseurship and criticism for evaluating classroom life. *Teachers College Record, 78*(3), 346–358.

Fountas, I. C., & Pinnell, G. S. (1996). *Guided reading: Good first teaching for all children.* Portsmouth, NH: Heinemann.

Gardner, H. (1987a). Beyond the IQ: Education and human development. *Harvard Educational Review, 57,* 187–193.

Gardner, H. (1987b). The theory of multiple intelligences. *Annals of Dyslexia, 37,* 19–35.

Gardner, H. (1991). *The unschooled mind: How children think and how schools should teach.* New York: Basic Books.

Gardner, H. (1993). *Multiple intelligences: The theory in practice.* New York: Basic Books.

Gardner, H. (1999). *Intelligence reframed: Multiple intelligences for the 21st century.* New York: Basic Books.

Gardner, H. (2004). *Frames of mind: The theory of multiple intelligences* (20th anniversary ed.). New York: Basic Books.

Geiser, W. F., Dunn, R., Deckinger, E. L., Denig, S., Sklar, R., & Beasley, M. (2000). Effects of learning style awareness and responsive study strategies on achievement, incidence of study, and attitudes of suburban eighth-grade students. *National Forum of Applied Educational Research, 13*(2), 37–49.

Gelman, R. (1982). Basic numerical abilities. In R. J. Sternberg (Ed.), *Advances in the psychology of human intelligence* (Vol. 1, pp. 181–205). Hillsdale, NJ: Lawrence Erlbaum.

Gelman, R., & Gallistel, C. R. (1978). *The child's understanding of numbers.* Cambridge, MA: Harvard University Press.

Gelman, S. A. (1989). The development of induction within natural kind and artifact categories. *Cognitive Psychology, 20,* 65–95.

Gutierrez, K. D., & Rogoff, B. (2003a). Cultural ways of learning: Individual traits or repertoires of practice. *Educational Researcher, 32*(5), 19–25.

Gutierrez, K. D., & Rogoff, B. (2003b). *Marching to different drummers* (2nd ed.). Alexandria, VA: Association for Supervision and Curriculum Development.

Hanson, J. R. (1989). *Learning model styles: Trends, pitfalls and needed new directions.* Moorestown, NJ: Hanson Silver Strong.

Hoerr, T. (2004). How MI informs teaching at New City School. *Teachers College Record, 106*(1), 40–48.

Illinois State Board of Education. (1997). *Illinois learning standards.* Springfield: Author. Available at http://www.isbe.state.il.us/ils

Kagan, J. (1994). *Galen's prophecy: Temperament in human nature.* New York: Basic Books.

Kagan, S. L., Moore, E., & Bredekamp, S. (1995). *Reconsidering children's early development and learning: Toward common views and vocabulary* (Goal 1 Tech. Planning Group Rep. No. 95-03). Washington, DC: National Education Goals Panel.

Keil, F. C. (1986). The acquisition of natural kinds and artifact terms. In W. Demopoulos & W. A. Marras (Eds.), *Language learning and concept acquisition: Foundational issues.* Norwood, NJ: Ablex.

Krechevsky, M. (1998). *Project Spectrum: Preschool assessment handbook.* New York: Teachers College Press.

Krechevsky, M. (2001). Form, function, and understanding in learning groups: Propositions from the Reggio classrooms. In Project Zero & Reggio Children, *Making learning visible: Children as individual and group learners* (pp. 246–271). Reggio Emilia, Italy: Reggio Children.

Leont'ev, A. N. (1978). *Activity, consciousness, and personality.* Englewood Cliffs, NJ: Prentice Hall.

Leont'ev, A. N. (1981). The problem of activity in psychology. In J. W. Werstch (Ed.), *The concept of activity in Soviet psychology* (pp. 37–71). Armonk, NY: Sharpe.

Lionni, L. (1975). *Pezzetino.* New York: Pantheon.

Masur, A. (2004). *Working approach: A new look at the process of learning.* Unpublished doctoral dissertation, Erikson Institute, Chicago.

McCray, J., Chen, J. Q., & McNamee, G. (2004, April 4). *Assessing diverse cognitive abilities in young children's learning.* Paper presented at the annual meeting of the American Education Research Association, San Diego, CA.

McLane, J. B., & McNamee, G. D. (1990). *Early literacy: The developing child*. Cambridge, MA: Harvard University Press.

McNamee, G. (2000). Child development research in early childhood classrooms. *Human Development, 45*(4–5), 246–251.

McNamee, G., & Chen, J. Q. (2004, August 9). *Assessing diverse cognitive abilities in young children's learning*. Paper presented at the International Congress of the International Association for Cross Cultural Psychology, Xi'an, China.

Meisels, S. J., Bickel, D. D., Nicholson, J., Xue, Y. G., & Atkins-Burnett, S. (2001). Trusting teachers' judgments: A validity study of a curriculum-embedded performance assessment in kindergarten to grade 3. *American Educational Research Journal, 38*(1), 73–95.

Nelson, B., Dunn, R., Griggs, S. A., Primavera, L., Fitzpatrick, M., Bacilious, Z., et al. (1993). Effects of learning style intervention on students' retention and achievement. *Journal of College Student Development, 34*, 364–369.

Piaget, J. (1954). *The construction of reality in the child*. New York: Basic Books.

Piaget, J. (1977). The origins of intelligence in children. In H. Gruber & J. J. Vonche (Eds.), *The essential Piaget* (pp. 215–249). New York: Basic Books.

Piaget, J., & Inhelder, B. (1969). *The psychology of the child*. New York: Basic Books.

Popham, J. (2005). *Classroom assessment: What teachers need to know* (4th ed.). Boston: Allyn & Bacon.

Project Spectrum. (1984). *The monitoring of intellectual propensities in early childhood*. Harvard Project Zero, Cambridge, MA: Author.

Reys, R. E., Suydam, M., & Lindquist, M. M. (1995). *Helping children learn mathematics* (4th ed.). Boston: Allyn & Bacon.

Riding, R. (1997). On the nature of cognitive style. *Educational Psychology, 17*(1–2), 29–49.

Rinaldi, C. (2001). Introduction. In Project Zero & Reggio Children, *Making learning visible: Children as individual and group learners* (pp. 28–31). Reggio Emilia, Italy: Reggio Children.

Rogoff, B. (1998). Cognition as a collaborative process. In D. William, D. Kuhn, & R. S. Siegler (Eds.), *Handbook of child psychology: Vol. 2. Cognition, perception, and language* (5th ed., pp. 679–744). New York: Wiley.

Rogoff, B., & Wertsch, J. (Eds.). (1984). *Children's learning in the "Zone of Proximal Development."* San Francisco: Jossey-Bass.

Shulman, L. (1986). Those who understand: Knowledge growth in teaching. *Educational Researcher, 15*(2), 4–14.

Shulman, L. (1987). Knowledge and teaching: Foundations of the new reform. *Harvard Educational Review, 57*(1), 1–22.

Sophian, C. (2004). A prospective developmental perspective on early mathematics instruction. In D. H. Clements & J. Sarama (Eds.), *Engaging young children in mathematics* (pp. 253–267). Mahwah, NJ: Lawrence Erlbaum.

Storytelling and story acting with Vivian Gussin Paley [Videotape]. (2002). Muncie, IN: Ball State University, Indiana Center on Early Childhood Development. (Available from National Association for the Education of Young Children, 1313 L Street NW, Washington, DC 20005; (800) 424-2460. Available at http://www.naeyc.org)

Sulzby, E. (1985, Summer). Children's emergent reading of favorite storybooks: A developmental study. *Reading Research Quarterly*, pp. 458–481.

Vygotsky, L. (1978). *Mind in society: The development of higher psychological processes*. In M. Cole et al. (Eds.). Cambridge, MA: Harvard University Press.

Zelazo, P. D. (2004). The development of conscious control in childhood. *Trends in Cognitive Sciences, 8*(1), 7–12.

Zelazo, P. D., Muller, U., Frye, D., Argitis, G., Bosevski, J., Chaing, J. K., et al. (2003). The development of executive function on early childhood. *Monographs of the Society for Research in Child Development, 68*(3), vii–137.

Zhang, L. F., & Sternberg, R. J. (2006). *The nature of intellectual styles*. Mahwah, NJ: Lawrence Erlbaum.

LANGUAGE ARTS AND LITERACY

Applebee, A. (1978). *The child's concept of story: Ages two to seventeen.* Chicago: University of Chicago Press.

Clay, M. (1993). *An observation survey of early literacy achievement.* Portsmouth, NH: Heinemann.

Fountas, I. C., & Pinnell, G. S. (1996). *Guided reading: Good first teaching for all children.* Portsmouth, NH: Heinemann.

Illinois State Board of Education. *Illinois learning standards for English language arts.* Available at http://www.isbe.state.il.us/ils/ela/standards.htm

National Council of Teachers of English & International Reading Association. *Standards for the English language arts.* Available at http://www.reading.org/resources/issues/reports/learning_standards.html

Paley, V. G. (1981). *Wally's stories: Conversations in the kindergarten.* Cambridge, MA: Harvard University Press.

Paley, V. G. (1990). *The boy who would be a helicopter: The uses of storytelling in the classroom.* Cambridge, MA: Harvard University Press.

Paley, V. G. (2001). *In Mrs. Tully's room: A child care portrait.* Cambridge, MA: Harvard University Press.

Sulzby, E. (1985, Summer). Children's emergent reading of favorite storybooks: A developmental study. *Reading Research Quarterly,* pp. 458–481.

VISUAL ARTS

Consortium of National Arts Education Associations. *National standards for arts education.* Available at http://artsedge.kennedy-center.org/teach/standards.cfm

Illinois State Board of Education. *Illinois learning standards for fine arts.* Available at http://www.isbe.state.il.us/ils/fine_arts/standards.htm

Kellogg, R. (1969). *Analyzing children's art.* Palo Alto, CA: Mayfield.

Lowenfeld, V., & Lambert Brittain, W. (1964). *Creative and mental growth.* New York: Macmillan.

Smith, N. R. (with Fucigna, C., Kennedy, M., & Lord, L.). (1993). *Experience and art: Teaching children to paint.* New York: Teachers College Press.

MATHEMATICS

Baroody, A. J. (2004). The developmental bases for early childhood number and operations standards. In D. H. Clements & J. Sarama (Eds.), *Engaging young children in mathematics* (pp. 173–220). Mahwah, NJ: Lawrence Erlbaum.

Bjorklund, D. F. (2000). *Children's thinking.* Stamford, CT: Wadsworth.

Carpenter, T. P., Fennema, E., Franke, M. L., Levi, L., & Empson, S. E. (1999). *Children's mathematics: Cognitively guided instruction.* Portsmouth, NH: Heinemann.

Charlesworth, R., & Lind, K. K. (1999). *Math and science for young children.* Albany, NY: Delmar.

Clements, D. H. (2004). Geometric and spatial thinking in early childhood education. In D. H. Clements & J. Sarama (Eds.), *Engaging young children in mathematics* (pp. 267–298). Mahwah, NJ: Lawrence Erlbaum.

Cossen, R. (1993). *Power block ideas for teachers.* Saratoga, CA: Center for Innovation in Education.

Dehaene, S. (1997). *The number sense: How the mind creates mathematics.* New York: Oxford University Press.

Duncan, A. (1996). *What primary teachers should know about math.* London: Hodder & Stoughton.

Fuson, K. (1988*). Children's counting and concepts of number.* New York: Springer-Verlag.

Fuson, K. C., & Hall, J. W. (1983). The acquisition of early number word meanings: A conceptual analysis and review. In H. P. Ginsburg (Ed.), *The development of mathematical thinking* (pp. 50–109). Orlando, FL: Academic Press.

Geary, D. C. (1996). *Children's mathematical development: Research and practical applications.* Washington, DC: American Psychological Association.

Gelman, R., & Gallistel, C. R. (1978). *The child's understanding of number.* Cambridge, MA: Harvard University Press.

Hands on pattern blocks. (1986). New York: Creative Publications.

Illinois State Board of Education. (1997). *Illinois learning standards.* Springfield: Author. Available at http://www.isbe.state.il.us/ils

Kallick, B., & Brewer, R. (1997). *How to assess problem-solving skills in math.* New York: Scholastic Professional Books.

Lang, F. K. (2001, April). What is a "good guess" anyway? Estimation in early childhood. *Teaching Children Mathematics, 7*(8), 462–466.

National Council of Teachers of Mathematics. *Principles and standards for school mathematics.* Available at http://www.nctm.org/standards/standards.htm

Resnick, L. B. (1983). A developmental theory of number understanding. In H. P. Ginsburg (Ed.), *The development of mathematical thinking* (pp. 110–152). Orlando, FL: Academic Press.

Riley, M. S., Greeno, J. G., & Heller, J. I. (1983). Development of children's problem-solving ability in arithmetic. In H. P. Ginsburg (Ed.), *The development of mathematical thinking* (pp. 153–200). Orlando, FL: Academic Press.

Sophian, C. (2004). A prospective developmental perspective on early mathematics instruction. In D. H. Clements & J. Sarama (Eds.), *Engaging young children in mathematics* (pp. 253–267). Mahwah, NJ: Lawrence Erlbaum.

Van De Walle, J. A. (2001). *Elementary and middle school mathematics: Teaching developmentally.* New York: Longman.

SCIENCES

Althouse, R. (1988). *Investigating science with young children.* New York: Teachers College Press.

Aram, R. J., & Bradshaw, B. (2001, October). How do children know what they know? *Science and Children, 39*(2), 28–33.

Chaille, C., & Britain, L. (1997). *The young child as scientist. A constructivist approach to early childhood science education.* New York: Longman.

Charlesworth, R., & Lind, K. K. (1999). *Math and science for young children.* Albany, NY: Delmar.

Gallas, K. (1995). *Talking their way into science: Hearing children's questions and theories, responding with curricula.* New York: Teachers College Press.

Harlan, J. D., & Rivkin, M. S. (2004). *Science experiences for the early childhood years.* Upper Saddle, NJ: Person-Merrill/Prentice Hall.

Hoover, E., & Mercier, S. (1990). *Primarily plants: A plant study for K–3.* Fresno, CA: AIMS Education Foundation.

Kellough, R. P., Carin, A. A., Seefeldt, R., Babour, N., & Saviney, R. J. (1996). *Integrating mathematics and science for kindergarten and primary children.* Newark, NJ: Prentice Hall.

Martin, D. J. (2001). *Constructing early childhood science.* Albany, NY: Delmar Thomson Learning.

National Center for Improving Science Education. (2002). *Concepts* [Nine scientific concepts for science education]. Available at http://www.ed.gov/pubs/parents/Science/Concepts.html

National Science Academy. (1996). *National science education standards.* Washington, DC: National Academy Press. Available at http://books.nap.edu/html/nses/overview.html

Sprung, B. (2001). Science explorations with young children. *Scholastic Early Childhood Today, 15*(6), 40–46.

Taylor, B. (1990). *Fun with simple science: Shadows and reflections.* New York: Warwick Press.

Worth, K., & Grollaman, S. (2003). *Worms, shadows and whirlpools.* Portsmouth, NI I: Heinemann.

PERFORMING ARTS

Andress, B. L., Heimann, H. M., Rinehart, C. A., & Talbert, E. G. (1973). *Music in early childhood.* Reston, VA: Music Educators National Conference.

Feierabend, J. (1990, July/August). Music in early childhood. Design for *Arts in Education, 91*(6), 15–20.

Illinois State Board of Education. *Illinois learning standards for fine arts.* Available at http://www.isbe .state.il.us/ils/fine_arts/standards.htm

Mies, S. G. (1990). *Jumping for joy: Creative movement for young children: Theory and practical application in the classroom.* Presentation at Erikson Institute, Chicago.

National standards for art education. Available on the Kennedy Center ArtsEdge Web site at http://artsedge.kennedy-center.org/teach/standards.cfm

Swanwick, K. (1988). *Mind in education.* London: Routledge.

Facilitator's Guide to Bridging and Teacher Development

Teacher educators play a key role in creating the context for teacher change and growth at both preservice and inservice levels. This guide is developed to help teacher educators engage either preservice or inservice teachers in the Bridging assessment process. Given the range of time frames available to teachers and varying teacher needs, we provide several options for inservice teacher professional development as well as for preservice teacher education courses.

INSERVICE PROFESSIONAL DEVELOPMENT

Table 1 provides an overview of three professional development formats that can be used to introduce Bridging to inservice teachers: half-day, weeklong, and yearlong programs. The three formats share similar goals: learning about *what* Bridging is, *how* to implement Bridging in the classroom, and *why* Bridging is useful in improving teaching and learning. They vary, however, in the scope and depth of the content covered as well as the reflective practice engaged in by participants. In the half-day program, for example, facilitators use Bridging to engage teachers in discussion of the relationship between classroom assessment and effective teaching. The weeklong program is intensive, taking place usually during the summer. In the yearlong program, teacher educators have the opportunity to work with teachers over a period of time to introduce the Bridging assessment process in relation to classroom practice. Having multiple sessions allows time for teachers to try out Bridging assessment activities in a particular curricular area between sessions and then bring problems, challenges, and insights to the group for discussion. Given that the longer format is an extension of the shorter ones, facilitators can always start with the half-day workshop format and extend it to the weeklong or yearlong program when time and resources become available.

Regardless of the format, teacher educators can work with teachers in two ways. In one, they can convene a group of 25 to 30 teachers from different schools in a

Table 1 Bridging Inservice Professional Development Formats

Goals	Learn about what Bridging is, how to implement Bridging in the classroom, and why Bridging is useful in improving classroom teaching and learning.		
Time Available	Half Day (3 hours)	Week (15 hours over 5 days)	Year (30 hours over 10 months)
CPDUs* Offered	3 CPDUs	15 CPDUs or 1semester hour	30 CPDUs or 2 semester hours
Major Topics Covered	• Introduction to Bridging and understanding the relationship between classroom assessment and effective teaching • Learning about content knowledge and diverse learners through using Bridging	• Introduction to Bridging and understanding the relationship between classroom assessment and effective teaching • Gaining familiarity with Bridging's assessment components and activities while implementing a few Bridging activities • Planning to use the Bridging assessment process in the classroom • Understanding the development of children's content knowledge in each curricular area through study of the rubrics	• Becoming familiar with the use and practical applications of Bridging assessment process • Gaining greater understanding of key concepts in five Bridging content areas in relation to learning standards • Connecting assessment results to curriculum planning and instructional practice • Examining one's own practices with colleagues with the goal of gaining greater efficacy as educators

*CPDU = Continuing Professional Development Units

central location for the professional development program. Such an approach invites eager participants and helps teachers extend their network beyond their school walls. Another approach involves teacher educators working with all early childhood teachers in one school as part of the school's ongoing professional development. Because teachers from the same school often share similar concerns and agenda, this professional development arrangement can be more tailored to a group's needs.

To provide quality teacher professional development experiences, facilitators need to prepare, including reading the *Bridging* handbook ahead of time. We also recommend that facilitators videotape children engaging in some of the Bridging assessment activities before leading the professional training. In the yearlong program, participating teachers videotape their own assessment process with children in the classroom; this provides an excellent means for engaging teachers in reflective practice. In the shorter training programs, such as half-day or weeklong time frame, facilitators' preparing videotapes in advance can significantly enhance the quality of the professional development.

When possible, facilitators will want to design the training program to meet requirements for teacher participation in ongoing professional development. One example is to attach the Bridging training to Continuing Professional Development Units (CPDUs) or semester hour credits. Aligning professional development with teachers' desire for new knowledge increases their incentives for participation and engagement. What follows is a detailed outline for each of the three professional development program formats depicted in Table 1, focusing on major topics, content, and related chapters from this book for reading.

Half-Day Professional Development Program

Major Topics

- Understand the relationship between classroom assessment and effective teaching.
- Introduce Bridging: a classroom assessment tool for effective teaching.
- Learn about content knowledge and diverse learners through using Bridging.

Content and Related Reading

- Readings (teachers read ahead of time): *Bridging* handbook: Chapters 1 and 2.

Hour 1

- Introduce the concept of assessment *for* and *of* teaching and learning.
- Familiarize teachers with Bridging, its purposes and distinctive features.

Hour 2

- Introduce the concept and practice of expected and actual performance levels.
- Introduce two Bridging language arts and literacy activities (for example, Reading Books, Dictating Stories) and two visual arts activities (for example, Drawing a Self-Portrait, Pattern Block Pictures).
- Work with teachers to develop expected performance levels for the children in their classrooms and compare the results.

Hour 3

- Engage teachers in discussion about the challenges in establishing the expected performance levels (for example, key concepts and skills in content areas, knowledge about children's development in a particular content area).

- Discuss the importance of teacher knowledge and expertise in establishing children's expected performance levels in the Bridging assessment process.
- Discuss the practice of creating children's learning profiles based on the Bridging assessment results in diverse content areas. Contrast a Bridging learning profile with a standardized test score to consider the range of ways that a learning profile might contribute to effective teaching practices.

Summer Weeklong Professional Development Program

Major Topics

- Understand the relationship between classroom assessment and effective teaching.
- Introduce Bridging: a classroom assessment tool for effective teaching.
- Gain familiarity with Bridging's assessment components and activities.
- Implement some of the Bridging activities with children, as available.
- Plan to use the Bridging assessment process in the classroom.

Content and Related Readings

Day 1

- **Teachers read ahead of time:** *Bridging* handbook: Preface, Chapters 1 and 2, and Language Arts and Literacy section.
- **Focus on the instrument:** Discussion of assessment for teaching and learning with an overview of what Bridging offers and assessment of content of learning (using the material in the Chapters 1 and 2).
- **Focus on Bridging's content:** Language arts and literacy; teachers try out activities before Day 2.

Day 2

- **Teachers read ahead of time:** *Bridging* handbook: Chapters 3 and 7, and Mathematics section. **Focus on the instrument:** Studying the process of learning: evaluative and descriptive working approaches (using the material in Chapter 3) and logistics of conducting the Bridging assessment process (using the material in Chapter 7).
- **Focus on Bridging's content:** Review and discussion of language arts and literacy activities; introduction to mathematics. Teachers try out mathematics activities before Day 3.

Day 3

- **Teachers read ahead of time:** *Bridging* handbook: Chapters 4 and 5, and Visual Arts section.
- **Focus on the instrument:** Introduction to the concept of activity as the unit of analysis in Bridging assessment process. Studying materials and social arrangements for children's learning: teacher-child, child-child, small group, large group (using material in Chapter 5).
- **Focus on Bridging's content:** Review and discussion of mathematics activities; introduction to visual arts. Teachers try out visual arts activities before Day 4.

Day 4

- **Teachers read ahead of time:** *Bridging* handbook: Chapter 6 and Science section.
- **Focus on the instrument:** Using rubrics to trace the development of key concepts and skills in a curricular area and then set expected performance levels, considering various roles of teachers in the Bridging assessment process.
- **Focus on Bridging's content:** Review and discussion of visual arts activities; introduction to science activities. Teachers try out science activities before Day 5.

Day 5

- **Teachers read ahead of time:** *Bridging* handbook: Performing Arts section.
- **Focus on the instrument:** Developing children's learning profiles and using findings to plan curriculum (using the material in Chapter 7) or making plans for using the Bridging assessment in the class in the coming year.
- **Focus on Bridging's content:** Review and discussion of science activities; introduction of performing arts activities. Discussion of connections across the five content areas.

Yearlong Professional Development Program

Major Topics

- Understand the relationship between classroom assessment and effective teaching.
- Become familiar with the use and practical applications of Bridging assessment process.
- Gain greater understanding of key concepts in five Bridging content areas and how these key concepts relate to national and local learning standards.
- Use knowledge gained from the Bridging assessment process to design and implement curricula tailored to the needs of students and responsive to content expectations.
- Examine one's own practices with colleagues with the goal of gaining greater efficacy as educators.

Content and Related Readings

Key Components for Teachers

- Participation in ongoing seminars with professional development facilitator and colleagues to learn about Bridging assessment process.
- Implementation of Bridging activities with children in their classrooms.
- Videotaping of oneself carrying out Bridging activities with children in one's classroom for review and discussion in monthly seminars.
- Presentation of case studies of children and their learning profiles to the seminar, discuss findings and share insights gained through the Bridging assessment process (see Appendix I for Guidelines for Bridging Presentation and Reflective Assessment Report).

- Engaging in reflective practice with colleagues and professional development facilitators, considering one's own strengths and weaknesses in content areas of teaching and understanding children.
- Completion of a reflective paper (3–5 pages) on Bridging assessment and teaching of children in their classroom (see Appendix I for Guidelines for Bridging Presentation and Reflective Assessment Report).

Session 1—Overview of Bridging Assessment Process

- **Teachers read ahead of time:** *Bridging* handbook: Preface, Chapters 1 and 2.
- **Focus on the instrument:** Discussion of assessment for teaching and learning with an overview of what Bridging offers and assessment of content of learning (using the material in the Chapters 1 and 2).
- **Assignments:** Identify two children in the classroom for Bridging assessment. Reading *Bridging* handbook: Chapter 3 and Language Arts and Literacy section.

Session 2—Focusing on Language Arts and Literacy Assessment and Teaching

- **Focus on the instrument:** Review and discussion of the process of learning: evaluative and descriptive working approaches (using the material in Chapter 3).
- **Focus on Bridging's content:** Review and discussion of language arts and literacy activities; work in small groups to study rubrics and determine expected performance levels for particular age groups of children in the language arts and literacy area.
- **Assignments:** Work with the two identified children to carry out all three Bridging assessment activities in the language arts and literacy area. Videotape or photo the activities if possible. Reading *Bridging* handbook: Chapter 7 and Visual Arts section.

Session 3—Focusing on Visual Arts Assessment and Teaching

- **Revisiting the last session:** Reflection on the process of carrying out language arts and literacy activities, considering issues, challenges, and findings.
- **Focus on the instrument:** Review and discussion of logistics of conducting the Bridging assessment process in classrooms (using the material in Chapter 7).
- **Focus on Bridging's content:** Review and discussion of visual arts activities; work in small groups to study rubrics and determine expected performance levels for particular age groups of children in the visual arts area.
- **Assignments:** Work with the two identified children to carry out all three Bridging assessment activities in the visual arts area. Save the children's artwork and photo the pattern block pictures that the children create. Reading *Bridging* handbook: Chapter 5 and Mathematics section.

Session 4—Focusing on Mathematics Assessment and Teaching

- **Revisiting the last session:** Reflection on the process of carrying out visual arts activities, considering issues, challenges, and findings.
- **Focus on the instrument:** Review and discussion of task parameters in Bridging assessment process (using the material in Chapter 5).

- **Focus on Bridging's content:** Review and discussion of mathematics activities; work in small groups to study rubrics and determine expected performance levels for particular age groups of children in the area of mathematics.
- **Assignments:** Work with the two identified children to carry out all three Bridging assessment activities in the mathematics area. Videotape or photograph the activities if possible. Reading *Bridging* handbook: Chapter 4 and Sciences section.

Session 5—Focusing on Sciences Assessment and Teaching

- **Revisiting the last session:** Reflection on the process of carrying out mathematics activities, considering issues, challenges, and findings.
- **Focus on the instrument:** Review and discussion of activity as the unit of analysis in Bridging assessment process (using the material in Chapter 4).
- **Focus on Bridging's content:** Review and discussion of science activities; work in small groups to study rubrics and determine expected performance levels for particular age groups of children in the science area.
- **Assignments:** Work with the two identified children to carry out all three Bridging assessment activities in the science area. Photograph the activity and save the children's work samples. Reading *Bridging* handbook: Chapter 6 and Performing Arts section.

Session 6—Focusing on Performing Arts Assessment and Teaching

- **Revisiting the last session:** Reflection on the process of carrying out science activities, considering issues, challenges, and findings.
- **Focus on the instrument:** Review and discussion of teachers' role in Bridging assessment process (using the material in Chapter 6).
- **Focus on Bridging's content:** Review and discussion of performing arts activities; work in small groups to study rubrics and determine expected performance levels for particular age groups of children in the performing arts area.
- **Assignments:** Work with the two identified children to carry out all three Bridging assessment activities in the performing arts area. Videotape or photograph the activities if possible. Re-reading *Bridging* handbook: Chapters 2 and 3.

Session 7—Creating Children's Learning Profile

- **Revisiting the last session:** Reflection on the process of carrying out performing arts activities, considering issues, challenges, and findings.
- **Focus on the instrument:** Work in small groups to complete the summary sheet and chart learning profile for each child (using the materials in Chapter 7). Compare the expected performance levels with the child's actual performance level. Discuss the reasons for difference between the two levels.
- **Assignment:** Prepare the presentation.

Sessions 8 and 9—Bridging Assessment Process Presentation

- **Individual presentation:** Each participant gives a 15- to 20-minute presentation on the two target children for the Bridging assessment process. The presenters use the five questions outlined in the Appendix I to guide their presentation. Each presentation is followed by a 5-minute discussion period.

- **General discussion:** Participants will engage in a broader discussion upon the completion of all of the presentations for the day. The general discussion, led by the facilitator, focuses on the connections between the assessment findings and effective teaching and learning.

Session 10—Bridging Classroom Assessment to Teaching and Learning

- **Assessment reflection:** Work in small groups to reflect on the entire Bridging assessment process. What have we learned about our children? What have we learned about ourselves as teachers? What we have learned about the content areas through the assessment process? How does this assessment process inform us about effective teaching and learning?
- **From assessment to curriculum and instruction:** Use knowledge gained from assessment with the Bridging assessment process to design and implement curricula tailored to the needs of students and responsive to content expectations. Examine one's own practices with colleagues with the goal of gaining greater efficacy in supporting young children's learning.

PROFESSIONAL STUDIES FOR PRESERVICE TEACHER CANDIDATES

Table 2 presents three sample courses that integrate Bridging into early childhood teacher education programs: Assessment for Teachers, Preschool Curriculum, and Student Teaching Seminar. While the three courses make use of Bridging content, each one focuses on unique aspects in preparing teacher candidates for a career in classroom teaching. Assessment for Teachers focuses on the procedures of administering and scoring the Bridging assessment activities as well as how to construct and analyze children's learning profiles. Preschool Curriculum emphasizes content knowledge, engaging teacher candidates in a curriculum analysis of key concepts and skills in diverse curriculum areas for three- to five-year-olds. There are additional curriculum courses in teacher education programs addressing the content areas through the primary grades. In Student Teaching Seminar, the emphasis of Bridging is its effective use and practical applications in different contexts, with different curricular approaches used in schools, mandated assessments, and with varied student populations across different student teaching sites.

In Erikson Institute's Teacher Education Program, teacher candidates learn and implement Bridging in all three courses mentioned above. Of great advantage to such an approach is students' sense of mastery and the opportunity for them to apply the theory to practice. The in-depth understanding of Bridging equips teacher candidates with the fundamentals to effective teaching—the integration of knowledge in child development, with content areas and teaching methods. Bridging is a flexible system; teacher educators can cover part or all of its content in any one of the courses listed in Table 2, as well as other teaching methods courses in the areas of early reading, mathematics, or arts integration. There is no one right way to introduce Bridging to teachers.

It is important to point out that Bridging presents only part of the curriculum regardless of the courses used to introduce its content. The following discussion summarizes how we present Bridging information in Assessment for Teachers, Preschool Curriculum, and Student Teaching Seminar. As will be seen, each course includes Bridging for teaching and student assignment, but it also covers many other topics relevant to the content areas of the coursework.

Table 2   Bridging Preservice Coursework Samples

Course Title	Assessment for Teachers	Preschool Curriculum	Student Teaching Seminar
Credits Offered	2 or 3 semester hours	2 or 3 semester hours	3 or 6 semester hours
Shared Content	• Understanding of the conceptual framework of Bridging • Study of key concepts and skills in five Bridging content areas • Administration and scoring of assessment activities • Interpretation of results • Use of results to inform curriculum planning and instructional practice		
Different Foci	• Understanding the differences between assessment *for* and *of* learning • Gaining familiarity with Bridging's assessment components and activities • Learning about procedures to administer and score the assessment activities • Constructing and analyzing children's learning profiles	• Understanding the relationship between classroom assessment and effective teaching • Becoming familiar with Bridging's assessment components and activities • Offering curriculum analysis through regular classroom activities • Gaining greater understanding of key concepts and skills in five Bridging content areas in relation to learning standards	• Understanding the relationship between theory and practice • Becoming familiar with the use and practical applications of the Bridging assessment process • Offering a window to gain in-depth understanding of individual children in regular classroom environment • Integrating processes of assessment, curriculum, and instruction • Participating in a community of learners

Assessment for Teachers

Appendix II provides the Assessment for Teachers course description and objectives, overview of course topics, and the one course assignment that uses Bridging. As indicated in the overview of course topics, teacher candidates develop classroom assessment knowledge and skills, including how to assess the classroom environment, conduct developmental screenings, give readiness tests, administer standardized tests, assess second language learners, and analyze children's homework assignments.

Bridging is introduced to students as an example of classroom or performance-based assessment. Compared to many other existing performance-based assessment instruments, Bridging presents a powerful conceptual framework, a defined approach to classroom assessment, and a structured way to use classroom activities to hone teacher candidates' observational skills.

One of the three assignments for Assessment for Teachers is to ask teacher candidates to create learning profiles for two children based on the Bridging assessment results (see Appendix I). In teams of two, teacher candidates work together to plan the assessment procedure, conduct the assessment activities, analyze the data, and present the results to the class. The assignment also requires teacher candidates to conduct a teacher interview and a reflective conversation with the children. In this process, teacher candidates acquire working knowledge of how to assess children using Bridging alongside the understanding of its conceptual framework and significance to teaching and learning. In addition, teacher candidates improve their interview as well as observational skills in a collaborative setting.

Preschool Curriculum

Appendix III provides an overview for the Preschool Curriculum course, including its objectives, course topics, and an assignment using Bridging. The course introduces teacher candidates to a range of curricular approaches and models, such as Montessori, Reggio Emilia, Waldorf, Direct Instruction, Creative Curriculum, and High Scope, to name a few. Teacher candidates in the Preschool Curriculum course concentrate on the understanding of key concepts and skills and their development in the five Bridging content areas in relation to local and national learning goals and standards. For many teacher candidates, standards appear to be rather abstract and not so easy to put into action. Bridging provides a means to operationalize the standards through regular curricular activities at typical teaching moments in a range of curricular approaches.

As in the Assessment for Teachers course, teacher candidates in Preschool Curriculum conduct an assignment using Bridging (see Appendix II). They are grouped in teams of two to assess two children with Bridging activities, but the assessment takes place in the context of different curricular approaches covered in the course. Teacher candidates study content areas and engage in curriculum analysis, with regard to both key concepts and skills manifested in children's performances with Bridging activities and learning performance–based assessment procedures with young children.

Student Teaching Seminar

This course is designed to accompany the student teaching internship in an early childhood classroom (PreK–3; see Appendix IV). The primary purposes of the seminar are to facilitate the integration of theory and knowledge with classroom teaching and to engage student teachers in reflecting on their use of deliberate teaching practices. In the field of teacher education, student teaching is too often an irregular experience that does not ensure occasions to encounter certain kinds of teaching problems or to develop and practice particular teaching skills. As a result, the power of "learning about practice in practice" is significantly diminished. Bridging helps focus student teachers' thinking and action, creating weekly deliberate opportunities for inquiry. It also provides a shared framework and a common language for student teachers to discuss classroom experiences. This kind of deliberate practice—purposefully and critically rehearsing certain kinds of skills, concepts, and performances—is particularly important to the development of teacher expertise.

Student teachers complete the Time 1 assessment process before beginning full-time classroom teaching. They use the assessment results to generate a learning profile for each target child. Following the assessment of target children in the fall, student teachers use selected Bridging activities ongoing with groups of children in their classroom throughout the remainder of the year. Such activities include children reading books, dictating and acting out stories, moving to music, singing songs daily, and carrying out the number sense activities.

In weekly seminar sessions, student teachers discuss processes and outcomes of using Bridging activities for assessment and curriculum development. Specifically, student teachers analyze children's learning profiles to consider each child's strengths and discuss areas requiring more attention. They also practice applying what they have learned about individual children to the development of curriculum and instruction. This often leads to further discussion of the rubrics.

Table 3   Sample Questions for Student Teachers Using the Bridging Process

- Does your target child perform at a higher level in some content areas than in others?
- Does the variability in performance levels point to a pattern in the child's strengths and vulnerabilities?
- What factors seem to facilitate or impede the child's performance?
- How would you describe the child's approach to learning? Is the child's approach to learning similar across activities?
- If not, what factors might affect the child's approach to learning?
- How will you translate the assessment results into lesson plans and curricular activities?

The seminar is led by a teacher education faculty member. To encourage critical thinking and reflection, the seminar leader challenges student teachers with a set of questions throughout the year (see Table 3). Toward the end of the student teaching period, each student writes a reflection paper. The paper synthesizes their experience using Bridging to learn about individual children, to advance their content knowledge in different curricular areas, and to plan curriculum and instruction.

BUILDING A COMMUNITY OF LEARNERS

For both inservice teacher professional development and preservice student teaching seminar experience, we emphasize the importance of spending time together with colleagues or peers during the Bridging assessment process. To maximize its effectiveness as a tool for teacher development, Bridging must be used within a community of learners. *Bridging* is not a scripted text with standard answers; rather, it provides teachers with a tool to engage in reflective practice with colleagues.

Teacher educators are critical in helping build a community of learners. The inservice teacher meetings or weekly student teaching seminars are not simply a time for reporting on activities they have implemented or assessment findings on their children. They are working sessions for all participants actively involved in the process of analyzing what they know about curricular content, children and their development, and methods of teaching. Teacher educators inevitably convey knowledge through meetings or seminar sessions, but equally important is the role of their facilitating teachers thinking deeply about their children's performance and how to connect the assessment findings to opportunity for teaching and learning. By providing such leadership, teacher educators open the way for more challenging, exciting, and rewarding professional learning and development opportunities.

In the community of learners, teachers learn from and with each other as well as from the teacher educators. The learning is a collaborative process with each participant's expertise contributing to advances in the group's understanding of teaching and learning. All teachers are engaged in inquiry. Knowledge is constructed in the group and ideas are generated and evaluated. The group as a whole analyzes problems and thinks through strategies for moving toward resolution.

Appendix I

Guidelines for Bridging Presentation and Reflective Assessment Report

REQUIREMENTS

Participants in our Bridging seminar will make a 15- to 20-minute presentation on two children in their classroom in Spring semester and write up the findings from their presentation into a 3- to 5-page typed summary report.

GOALS

The goal of the presentation is to provide you with the opportunity to discuss your findings and thoughts with colleagues who share your vested interest in children's learning and growth. You will benefit from the insights your colleagues bring to your thinking about children you are working with.

The goal of the reflective assessment report is for you to synthesize and articulate your thoughts based on the Bridging assessment process and findings. It also gives you the opportunity to integrate your colleagues' insights into your summary.

FORMAT FOR PRESENTATION

Participants will make a 15- to 20-minute presentation on two children identified for the Bridging assessment process. This will be followed by a short discussion period. Participants will engage in a broader discussion upon the completion of all of the presentations for the day. The general discussion, led by the facilitator, will focus on the connections between the assessment findings and effective teaching and learning.

PROCEDURE FOR PREPARING FOR PRESENTATION

Complete the profiles of the target children, including their performance rubric scores and working approaches. Use the children's work samples, such as photos, artwork, and videotapes, to assist in your presentation. As always, use your observations and ongoing knowledge about each child to help you think about what you learned from observing the child during the Bridging assessment process.

PRESENTATION GUIDELINES

Each presentation will have five parts:

1. **Initial questions, concerns about a child:** In the fall, you were asked to focus your assessment on two children that were challenging to you for any reason. What were the initial issues, questions, concerns that prompted your closer focus on these children?

2. **Bridging assessment process:** Which activities did you carry out with the two children, and what were your findings on their activity performance and working approach?

3. **What you learned:** What patterns, surprises, and insights did you come to from assessing these two children? How do the children's work on Bridging activities compare to other classroom tasks the children engage in? How different is it between the child's expected performance level and his or her actual performance level? What does this difference reveal to you?

4. **Curriculum planning for these children and the rest of the class:** In what ways have you and can you adapt your curriculum to meet the needs of these children and the rest of the class in your ongoing program? How can you bridge the identified strengths of the children to the areas requiring attention and intervention?

5. **Remaining questions:** What are you still wondering about with these children? Do you have any questions about how to build bridges to improve these children's school learning and performance?

REFLECTIVE ASSESSMENT REPORT GUIDELINES

Use the five sets of questions for presentation to guide your written report. Include a copy of recording sheets and samples of children's work where relevant. The report is limited to five double-spaced pages and is due at the last seminar session.

Appendix II

Assessment for Teachers—Course Overview and Assignment

COURSE DESCRIPTION AND OBJECTIVES

This course examines the construct and practice of assessment for PreK–3 classroom teachers. In this course, teacher candidates are expected to:

1. Understand critical issues regarding assessment and accountability in schools, paying attention to why assessment is necessary, who the various assessment audiences are, what kind of assessment information is useful for each audience, and the time frame appropriate for such assessment information;

2. Acquire a working knowledge of such basic measurement concepts as reliability, validity, norm- and criterion-referenced, and standardization;

3. Become familiar with a variety of assessment methods currently used to evaluate teaching and learning in classrooms, including classroom-based observation, screening tests, achievement tests, learning diagnostic instruments, and curriculum-embedded and performance-based assessments;

4. Develop skills in assessing specific curriculum content areas, such as the development of early literacy and mathematics, as well as acquire a repertoire of effective assessment strategies that can be used to continuously monitor children's progress in all areas of learning and development;

5. Increase understanding of family, school, community/culture, second language learning, and disability as significant assessment issues;

6. Examine and critique different assessment tools and strategies in light of their sensitivity to individual differences and sociocultural contexts; and

7. Learn to use assessment results to inform the process of planning for daily classroom teaching and learning. This might include integrating information obtained through various assessment sources to describe the development of individual children, making decisions about how to support children's continuous learning and development, and planning curriculum and monitoring instructional approaches appropriate to students' learning needs.

Overview of Course Topics	
Week	Topic
1	Introduction and overview
2	Basic measurement and testing concepts
3	Observation of classroom environment
4	Developmental screening and school readiness
5	School achievement and high-stakes testing
6	Assessing the content of children's learning
7	Assessing the process of children's learning
8	Assessing culturally and linguistically diverse students
9	Unit of analysis in child assessment
10	Assessing language and early reading skills
11	Assessing early mathematical thinking and skills
12	Assessing early scientific concepts and skills
13	Assessing children's visual arts and performing arts abilities
14	Creating children's learning profiles
15	Linking classroom assessment to teaching and learning

COURSE ASSIGNMENT USING BRIDGING: CREATING AND ANALYZING CHILD'S LEARNING PROFILE (ONE OF THREE COURSE ASSIGNMENTS)

General Description

- In teams of two, you will assess two children (PreK–3) in the same classroom using at least five activities of the following 12 Bridging assessment activities (see chart below). Based on the assessment result, you will create a learning profile for each child and present the results to the class. Partners in each team are required to work together—planning the assessment procedure, conducting the assessment activities, analyzing the data, and presenting the results. Partners will receive the same grade for this assignment. The class will work together to create a rubric for peer evaluation.

Area	Activity
Language Arts and Literacy	1. Reading a Book 2. Dictating a Story 3. Acting Out a Story

Area	Activity
Mathematics	4. Exploring Number Concepts 5. Solving Pattern Block Puzzles 6. Creating Pattern Block Pinwheels
Sciences	7. Exploring Shadows and Light 8. Building a Model Car
Visual Arts	9. Drawing a Self-Portrait 10. Making Pattern Block Pictures
Performing Arts	11. Moving to Music 12. Singing a Song

Assessment Procedures

- *Preparation:* Identify a teacher, describe the project to that teacher, and gain the teacher's consent for you to work with two children in the classroom. With the teacher's help, identify two children for your study.
- *Teacher Interview:* Conduct a brief interview with the teacher to get background information on each child. Questions for the teacher might include:
  - School Adjustment—separation anxiety, coping strategies, response to routines and transition, time on tasks, and attitude toward school and learning;
  - Social/Emotional Development—relationship with peers and adults, friendship, self-esteem, self-control, and any concerns;
  - Academic Functioning—mastery of tasks, language development, attention to work, capacity for play with others and/or objects, curiosity, level of academic achievement, special interests and/or talents, and particular concerns.

- *Classroom Observation:* Observe the children's academic skills and behavior in the context of regular classroom activities. Consider the overall assessment objectives when planning the observation. Use an open-ended, narrative recording method and pay attention to verbal as well as nonverbal behavior (for example, body language). You can be either a participant observer or passive observer.
- *Conducting the Assessment:* Get acquainted with the children so that you are no longer a complete stranger to them. Please note if at any time the child does not want to participate in any assessment activity, you must honor the child's wish and not press him or her to do so. Please follow the protocol closely, take photos whenever necessary, and document the sequence of the activities being conducted. Many Bridging activities can be carried out in small groups (see chart below). In such cases, you only record the behavior and performance of the two children for your study.

Area	Activity		Possible Social Structure	Documentation
	Performance Rubric	*Working Approach*		
Language and Literacy	1. Reading a Book 2. Dictating a Story 3. Acting Out a Story		Individual Individual/Dyad Small or Large Group	Recording sheet Recording sheet Recording sheet

(Continued)

(Continued)

Area	Activity		Possible Social Structure	Documentation
	Performance Rubric	Working Approach		
Mathematics	4. Exploring Number Concepts 5. Solving Pattern Block Puzzles 6. Creating Pattern Block Pinwheels		Individual Individual/Dyad/Small group Individual/Dyad/Small group	Recording sheet Recording sheet Photo Recording sheet Photo
Sciences	7. Exploring Shadows and Light 8. Building a Model Car		Individual/Dyad/Small group Individual/Dyad/Small group	Recording sheet Recording sheet Photo
Visual Arts	9. Drawing a Self-Portrait 10. Making Pattern Block Pictures		Individual/Dyad/Small group Individual/Dyad/Small group	Recording sheet Work samples Recording sheet Photo
Performing Arts	11. Moving to Music 12. Singing a Song		Dyad/Small group Individual/Dyad/Small group	Recording sheet Photo Recording sheet Photo

- *Scoring:* Independently score both children's performances, including rubric on performance and working approaches, on the same day the activity is carried out. Compare the scores with your partner and if differences appear, discuss them to come to a consensus.
- *Child's Opinion:* At the end of the assessment process, present photos of all assessment activities to each child (you need to prepare these photos while conducting the activities). First ask the child to name each picture/activity; remind the child if he or she has trouble recognizing any, and then ask the following questions:

  1. "Which activity is your favorite? Why?"
  2. "Which activity do you think you did the best on? How do you know?"
  3. "Which activity do you think you did the worst on? How do you know?"
  4. "Which activity is the easiest for you? Why?"
  5. "Which activity is the hardest for you? Why?"

- *Creating the Child's Profile and Sharing the Profile With Teacher:* Complete the summary sheet for each child and graph each child's learning profile. Discuss the assessment results of both children with the classroom teacher and ask for the teacher's comments. Compile all of the information for the class presentation.

Preparing the Presentation

- *Basic Information:* Include the children's name, age, gender, and educational history based on the information gained from the teacher interview and classroom observation. Briefly describe the classroom setting, such as the physical arrangement, classroom routines, curriculum and instructional practice, and social interaction patterns among children and between children and teachers.

- *Reporting Assessment Results*: Report the assessment results, focusing on each child's strengths, vulnerabilities, and working approaches. Describe the child's verbal and nonverbal behavior during the assessment process. Compare the assessment results with interview and observational data as well as the child's own judgment. Use photos and child's work samples to aid your presentation.

- *Analyzing Assessment Profiles*: Compare/contrast the assessment profiles of the two children and look for patterns. For example, how are the children's performances affected by various factors such as area (for example, language versus math), structure of the activity (for example, structured versus open-ended), type of materials used (for example, pattern blocks versus paper and pencil in the visual arts area), emphasis on the key concepts (for example, spatial and part–whole relationship versus number concepts in the mathematics area), social structure (for example, one-on-one versus small group), and working approach (for example, impulsive versus goal-oriented). How do these factors interact to facilitate or impede the children's performance? Do some working approaches appear to facilitate while others hinder the children's learning?

- *From Assessment to Teaching:* Recommend strategies and approaches to working with the children based on assessment results; consider the classroom context and be realistic when making the recommendations. Explain why you think these alternative approaches may have a positive impact on the children.

Appendix III

Preschool Curriculum—Course Overview

COURSE DESCRIPTION

This course examines the history of, and current research base for, quality education programs for preschool and kindergarten children of diverse cultural, economic, and developmental backgrounds. The course explores how teachers of three- to five-year-old children can promote the development of knowledge and skills of thinking and symbolic representation in literacy, mathematics, science, social studies, physical growth, and the fine arts. The course examines the dynamics of teachers and children in a variety of teaching and learning formats. The course addresses the questions: How do educators promote the intellectual potential of children using a range of strategies without turning early childhood classrooms into academic boot camps? How do teachers integrate learning activities such as dramatic play, group problem solving, observation, direct instruction, and Socratic discussions into a curriculum for children three to five years of age?

COURSE OBJECTIVES

1. Develop an understanding of, and become knowledgeable about, appropriate learning outcomes for the intellectual and academic development of children three to five years of age in the areas of math, science, literacy, social studies, physical growth, and the fine arts.

2. Recognize how the state and national standards can be met through a variety of curricular approaches in preschool and kindergarten classrooms.

3. Know about and understand the function of, and place for, various pedagogical approaches such as dramatic play, practicing of skills, process-oriented learning through projects, and direct instruction.

4. Become familiar with and able to critique current preschool and kindergarten programs for their strengths and weaknesses in relation to philosophy, environmental design, curriculum content, program schedule and routines, and their vision for the role of teachers and their strategies for working with a wide range of children in the learning process.

5. Develop a frame of reference for assessing programs and children: What constitutes a quality preschool, kindergarten, and primary classroom? How can a vision of quality take into account the diversity of programs available with different philosophies and curricula, the wide diversity among populations of children to be served, and the diversity among professionals interpreting and implementing their visions of best practice with three- to five-year-olds? How do quality programs assess the development of children as to whether or not they are reaching identified early learning outcomes?

6. Understand the basis of establishing a preschool and kindergarten program where diversity among children and their families is respected, valued, and nurtured. Understand how to create a classroom environment and curriculum that promotes tolerance, inclusion, democracy, and social justice.

7. Understand the principles for effective classroom management that promote positive supportive relationships among children, that provides a structure for conflict resolution, and that promotes self-control, motivation, and self-esteem for each child and the group as a whole.

Overview of Course Topics	
Week	*Topic*
1	Historical context for curriculum planning for early childhood education
2 & 3	Goals for language arts and literacy development in early childhood education
4 & 5	Goals for mathematics and science in early childhood education
6	Goals for visual and performing arts in early childhood education
7 & 8	Curriculum planning for special needs children in early childhood education
9	Classroom management in early childhood classrooms
10	Promoting tolerance and respect for diversity in early childhood classrooms
11	European contributions to early childhood curriculum: Montessori, Waldorf, Reggio Emilia
12	Play curriculum and therapeutic curriculum in early childhood classrooms
13	Constructivist/Piagetian approaches to early childhood education
14	Direct instruction in preschool and kindergarten
15	Profiles of children learning in early childhood settings—presentations

Appendix IV

Student Teaching Seminar— Overview and Assignment

COURSE DESCRIPTION

This course is designed to accompany the student teaching internship in an early childhood classroom (PreK–3). The weekly seminar sessions support teacher candidates with integrating theory and practice, refining methods of teaching, deepening their understanding of how to work effectively with children and families from diverse backgrounds, reflecting on all aspects of professional teaching practice, and developing further goals for professional development.

COURSE OBJECTIVES

Teacher candidates will:

1. Develop a rationale for teaching (philosophy of education).

2. Design and implement a grade-level curriculum for children that affirms and respects their home language and culture and the learning needs of all children in the class.

3. Further develop skills in observing and interacting with young children in classroom settings in order to both recognize the most effective strategies for different children and evaluate their progress.

4. Learn to use technology resources effectively to support the development of children's understanding of ideas in all curricular areas.

5. Complete yearlong assessment of two children in all curricular areas including recommendations for their needs in the coming new school year.

6. Develop skills for reflection and self-awareness on the teacher's role in creating a classroom environment and community context conducive to learning.

7. Develop appropriate and effective group management skills.

COURSE ASSIGNMENT

During the year of student teaching, you are required to complete the assessment of at least two children using Bridging assessment activities. The faculty seminar leader will oversee the completion and evaluation of this assignment. To carry out this assignment you will:

1. Pick two children in your classroom who are different from you in culture, language background, and/or special needs circumstances. You will carry out each Bridging assessment activity with both children in the context of working with them individually, in a small group, and/or in a large group.

2. You will choose two activities in each of the five Bridging content areas and assess children twice, fall and spring. In order for the information gathered on children to be useful, it is important to carry out all assessment activities with each child within a two- to three-week period. The documentation of the children's performance on each activity needs to be done on the same day the assessment was carried out.

3. For the two children you assess in detail, you will need to hand in a copy of the following at the end of the year as part of your student teaching portfolio:
   o Children's Bridging Summary Sheet
   o A copy of all recording sheets for all of the Bridging activities
   o Photos or copies of children's work on activities as appropriate (for example, copy of dictated story, photo of building of a model car)

4. You will complete a reflection paper (8–10 pages, double spaced) summarizing your observations and insights about each child you assessed using the questions in the *Bridging* handbook to guide your discussion. This paper will include the following:
   o An introduction describing the two children and the context for assessment
   o A summary of Time 1 assessments with your insights from that time as to what kind of learning experiences you thought these two children would benefit from
   o Description of Time 2 assessments with a summary of the two children's performance, comparison of them to Time 1, and your summary of what you learned about the two children and what is likely to make a difference in their learning in the coming year

Index

CORWIN PRESS

The Corwin Press logo—a raven striding across an open book—represents the union of courage and learning. Corwin Press is committed to improving education for all learners by publishing books and other professional development resources for those serving the field of PreK–12 education. By providing practical, hands-on materials, Corwin Press continues to carry out the promise of its motto: **"Helping Educators Do Their Work Better."**